MARC LLEWELLYN is an award-winning travel writer for Australian and international newspapers and magazines. He has travelled most of his life, and is the president of the Australian Society of Travel Writers.

Finding Nino

Marc Llewellyn

For you....
Marc Llewellyn

HarperCollins*Publishers*

HarperCollins_Publishers_

First published in Australia in 2008
by HarperCollins*Publishers* Australia Pty Limited
ABN 36 009 913 517
www.harpercollins.com.au

HarperCollins_Publishers_
25 Ryde Road, Pymble, Sydney, NSW 2073, Australia
31 View Road, Glenfield, Auckland 10, New Zealand
1–A, Hamilton House, Connaught Place, New Delhi – 110 001, India
77–85 Fulham Palace Road, London, W6 8JB, United Kingdom
2 Bloor Street East, 20th floor, Toronto, Ontario M4W 1A8, Canada
10 East 53rd Street, New York NY 10022, USA

National Library of Australia Cataloguing-in-Publication data:

Author: Llewellyn, Marc.
Title: Finding Nino/author, Marc Llewellyn
Publisher: Pymble, N.S.W.: HarperCollins, 2008.
ISBN: 978 0 7322 8743 6 (pbk.)
Subjects: Llewellyn, Marc – Travel – Italy – Lipari Island.
Fishers – Italy – Lipari Island.
Parenthood – Italy – Lipari Island.
Lipari Island (Italy) – Social life and customs.
Lipari Island (Italy) – Description and travel.
Dewey Number: 914.581104

Cover image: label for 'Vesuvius Brand Tomato', courtesy of History San Jose
    (www.historysanjose.org/research/library)
Cover and internal design by Natalie Winter
Typeset in 12/17.5 pt Sabon by Kirby Jones
Printed and bound in Australia by Griffin Press
70gsm Bulky Book Ivory used by HarperCollins*Publishers* is a natural, recyclable product made
from wood grown in sustainable forests. The manufacturing processes conform to the
environmental regulations in the country of origin, Finland.

5 4 3 2 1   08 09 10 11

Thence we went on to the Aeoli island where lives Aeolus son of Hippotas, dear to the immortal gods. It is an island that floats (as it were) upon the sea, iron bound with a wall that girds it ... Jove had made him captain over the winds, and he could stir or still each one of them according to his own pleasure.

From Homer's *Odyssey*

ITALY

Aeolian Islands ★

SICILY

Stromboli

Mediterranean Sea

Panarea

Salina

Filicudi

Lipari

Alicudi

Tyrrhenian Sea

Vulcano

Sicily

Finding Nino

Prologue

I have no watch, but I have plenty of time to feel the grapes, cool and luxurious beneath my feet, the skins and flesh slipping between my toes.

A fisherman dances beside me, raising his knees to his chest, his arms held out like wings. Women and children clap their hands and Nino hangs over the side, pushing fruit in front of us with a well-worn brush. The juice gushes through a drain hole in the crushing vat, into an open pipe, and then onwards through a cane-mesh sieve. It settles in a depression in the floor: a red frothy slick, ready to be scooped up in buckets and poured into demijohns.

Our stomping has attracted two faces, spying on us through a gap between the green flaking doors. One asks in broken Italian if he can take a picture.

'Of course,' Nino bellows, waving the tourists closer. 'Do you want to join in?' But they are shy, and hover around the doorway, fidgeting with their cameras. Their reluctance to become part of it all makes me understand how far I've come. I'm stained brown by the sun and my shins are purple with grape juice. These interlopers have no way of knowing I'm a foreigner, like them. They've captured me on film. A local. Crushing grapes. By foot. How authentic!

It's funny how someone can look as though they belong when they don't.

One

There's a time when men's strongest
need is for the winds.

Pindar

'I could never live like you,' said Orlando the fisherman. 'In a city there's too much … confusion.'

He was in his late twenties and had been over to Sicily and as far as Rome. 'Those cars, the people, those smells and all those buildings, and everyone rushing around. Why are they going so fast? It looks like they're trying to escape from something.'

'I know what you mean,' I said absentmindedly, before crunching through the crispy shell of a shrimp he'd caught that morning. It was one of a batch he'd fried in olive oil and sprinkled with sea salt. It was surprisingly sweet. The undercarriage of bright blue eggs tasted strangely milky.

'Why don't you live on Lipari, then?' he said, referring to the island we'd washed up on just recently, off the north coast of Sicily. It's the largest outcrop of the Aeolian Islands, known in English as the Islands of the Winds.

Our wives exchanged glances. Orlando was studying me, but I was silent. I was startled by his question. We were on holiday. His suggestion was the kind of throwaway challenge to reality I might have come up with after a few drinks. But Orlando was perfectly sober.

'Well, we couldn't survive,' I spluttered at last, almost spraying the table with half-chewed shrimp legs. 'I mean, where would we live? What would we eat? We'd have to get jobs ...'

'*Gamberetti,*' he said, pointing to the pile of glistening crustaceans in front of us, 'and fish and octopus. You can eat pasta like us. You can work like us. A fisherman. We could pay you in seafood. You could live here. I don't know, maybe we can find you a home.'

'And what about me?' Rohan, my wife, put in. 'What am I supposed to do?'

'You can be an Italian *mamma* and have babies,' said Justine archly.

Rohan laughed. It was the furthest thing from her mind.

Justine was the daughter of a friend of ours. She was just twenty-two. Three years earlier she had been living in an Australian country town of little repute: the kind of place where girls get pregnant in their teens, and where brighter prospects are few. Her mother's boyfriend had travelled the world, and on his insistence the couple took Justine on a holiday to Italy in a last-ditch attempt to show her there was more to life than early pregnancy and menial work. One night, in a bar in Rome, Justine spotted Orlando. Apart from a couple of fleeting trips over to Sicily, it was the only time he'd left his island. It was a brief holiday. He was travelling with one of his brothers.

Orlando was dark and handsome, and he shot Justine a look that only Italians can, with eyes as ripe and dark as olives. When he knew he had caught her attention he winked so slowly it buckled her knees.

They couldn't speak each other's languages, but they both knew it was love at first sight, and Justine felt compelled to follow her fisherman back to Lipari — which was just as well, because we wouldn't have been eating shrimp as tasty as these if she hadn't.

We were to sleep on a sofa bed in their kitchen that night, but I was far too unsettled to rest. So after a while I shook Rohan awake and asked the question I'd been desperate to voice for hours.

'Would you live here too?' I asked.

'What?'

She pulled out an earplug.

'We could, couldn't we? I mean, it's a good opportunity, knowing these people and everything ...'

'Just go back to *sleep*!'

'I wasn't asleep.'

'*I* was!'

But I'm not good at resting when I have an idea scurrying around in my mind.

The alleyways in the fishermen's quarter were still and hot that night. The sheets stuck to my body like plastic. A motor scooter clattered past, the noise amplified by the thin corridor of buildings that snaked down to the fishing boats in the harbour. A woman cried out. A door slammed. More scooters zoomed by. A cat yowled. A dog barked unstoppably …

And so the night went on, until I felt a hand firmly shake my shoulder.

It was four in the morning and Orlando was leaving for work on his fishing boat. 'So what do you think?' he whispered, before blowing on his coffee. 'What I said before; I'm serious. I'll help you.'

'Thanks. I'll think about it,' I said, vague and groggy.

I felt Rohan stirring beside me.

'What did he want?' she asked drowsily, as she fumbled with her earplug again.

I told her.

'Look, it's a nice dream,' she said. 'Orlando must know people like us can't just leave everything behind to live in a place like this.'

It was midsummer on Lipari and the island's alleyways were strung with sheets and undergarments. Red geraniums broke up the walls. A bell tolled faintly in the distance. Lethargy called out. The place smelled of olive oil and anchovies.

To escape the heat we borrowed Orlando's motor scooter and headed up to the hills, on a road that coiled beside an arm of the Mediterranean called the Tyrrhenian Sea.

Ten minutes of driving later we reached a village and spotted a turn-off, a cratered pathway that led past clusters of simple rock dwellings, prettied with pink bougainvillea.

We rode on through shimmering olive groves and neat lines of vines, until we eventually pulled over beside an old wall of boulders. We had packed shiny black olives, rinsed salted anchovies, sheep's-milk cheese and some local wine: a golden, syrupy *Malvasia*.

We sat there for a long time, wrapped in drowsiness and a peculiar feeling of contentment — that rare sensation that comes with a full stomach and mild intoxication on a warm sunny day. We were living in the moment, and wanted it to last forever.

But, however attuned we are to a point in time, it's our nature to move away from it. So we pushed on, more slowly now, through a stark, glaring landscape of wheat grass, sliced by a sickle of ocean. My eyes rested for a second or two on each green-backed ruin lizard basking on the boundary walls of neglected fields, and on caper plants cart-wheeling from cracks between the dry stone. The air was infused with the crushed-daisy tang of wormwood. Cicadas drummed from eucalyptus trees. There were few people. I saw only a woman walking towards an unfamiliar shop, a dot of a man, way below, setting off to sea in his tiny fishing boat, and a child making her way home to a house I'd never see inside. But I wondered what their lives were like, and how they saw things, and what it would be like to be them, living here, going home somewhere close.

The holiday ended, as they always do, and before we knew it we were absorbed into our old Sydney lives again, with their usual stresses and money issues, and a relationship worn thin by commitments.

I was working as a journalist: a word whore, caught up in a grind of corporate work in an office and part-time freelancing. All so I could clutter my life up with stuff that made things seem a little more bearable.

As for Rohan, she was working as a researcher in an office block. It was stressful, and she was shocked by the amount of time she spent on trains and buses each year. She'd added up the hours. It amounted to three whole weeks.

And for what? However hard we both worked we always seemed to be just staying afloat, both financially and emotionally. We passed each other without slowing, barely talking, rarely eating together. We knew something was missing, something was wrong, but we couldn't quite put our fingers on how to make things better. And all along the clock was ticking away and our lives were leaking time like a paddlewheel.

Then, one morning, I woke to the alarm. It was Wednesday, halfway through the working week. I was lying there, still tired from the previous day of toil, not wanting to get up. I pressed the snooze button: ten minutes extra to try and rescue that luxurious dream state that comes with waking up slowly. Then came the buzzer again, and with it a profound realisation: I didn't want this life any more.

For as long as I remembered I'd been forced out of sleep. I got up at a certain time, caught the train at a certain time, worked largely for the benefit of someone else, then struggled home with my fellow bondservants on a joyless commuter train. My evenings were usually spent ironing clothes, eating in front of the television, and falling asleep on the couch. Weekends saw me battling with traffic, meeting friends I barely had time to know, and pushing a trolley through a supermarket. And then it was back to work again.

So I called in sick. But I was at a loss for something to do with myself. I turned on the television, but it had no answers. I thought of ringing a friend, but realised he was at work, and wouldn't be home for hours. I wandered around the house, ate breakfast, had a bath, and finally began trawling my bookcase. I had a few false starts with some good-life-abroad books; a ratty *Tropical Fish Hobbyist* magazine; a work exhorting the health benefits of drinking your own urine (something I was regrettably yet to test through personal experience); a guide to the trees of Europe; German in one month; Russian in three months; Welsh in five years.

My next foray revealed a sliver of a volume by Seneca, the ancient Roman philosopher. It was one of those books that I'd bought from a second-hand bookshop, years ago, in a misguided attempt to impress a girlfriend with my stupendous learning. If I remember correctly, both it and I were abandoned soon afterwards.

I rubbed away the dust on the volume that called out to me. I opened it at no particular page, and read:

And so there is no reason for you to think that any man has lived long because he has grey hairs or wrinkles; he has not lived long — he has existed long. For what if you should think that that man had had a long voyage who had been caught by a fierce storm as soon as he left harbour, and, swept hither and thither by a succession of winds that raged from different quarters, had been driven in a circle around the same course? Not much voyaging did he have, but much tossing about.

I sat bolt upright. That was it! I wasn't living. I was just a tosser. I wasn't going anywhere.

I needed a drink, so I applied myself to a glass of wine and retired to a deck chair with the rest of the bottle. And I began to daydream.

I soon saw myself waking up each morning, naturally, without an alarm, and thinking: 'What am I going to do today?'

It was the most delicious of thoughts, and from there I was drawn towards a perfumed landscape of herbs and cypresses, olive trees, sea salt and summer dust. I had visions of long lingering meals beneath the stars with people who didn't have to rush away. I imagined time to talk and read, and to make love … and to finally be myself, living in my own time, instead of someone else's.

Then Orlando's suggestion raised its head, just when I'd thought I'd buried it along with the rest of the impractical ideas that have a habit of popping up in life. I knew there might be work involved, and early rises too, if I went fishing for shrimp. But I'm not one to let reality get in the way of a romantic idea.

'What if we did leave our old lives behind?' I pondered.

Of course, there were plenty of major reasons why it could be a bad idea. As well as my work and the house and the dog, there was my wife and *her* job. These were hurdles no one could possibly vault on a whim and a bottle of sauvignon blanc.

Years ago, though, I'd cleared almost as many hurdles on a very similar sort of whim. I'd left Britain for Australia to escape the recession of the 1980s. I'd found a job and a country I thought I loved far more than the one I was born in. But, as time passed, I felt myself suffering from a vague sense of displacement. I was yearning for the old country, yet when I returned for occasional visits, it wasn't too long before I was missing Australia again. I was torn between two places, and neither on its own could satisfy me. Perhaps Italy was the place to give me what I wanted? It had the sunshine I loved, and the depth of European culture I craved.

But I needed more convincing, so I turned once more to the book at hand. I read:

> *Most wretched is the condition of those who labour at engrossments that are not even their own, who regulate their sleep by that of another, their walk by the pace of another, who are under orders in case of the freest things in the world — loving and hating. If these wish to know how short their life is, let them reflect how small a part of it is their own.*

These words haven't altered a jot in relevance in almost two thousand years. Certainly, Seneca was managing to persuade me that I should live more slowly and more meaningfully. I'd definitely take great pleasure in saying goodbye to bosses and bills and letters of demand. I yearned to empty my wallet of video shop memberships, useless receipts, discount coupons, and all those supermarket loyalty cards I'd been mysteriously collecting.

Still, it came as a jolt when the phone rang that very afternoon. It was Justine, calling from the Islands of the Winds. She'd found a house for us to live in, she told me, up in the hills, overlooking the sea. We could stay for as long as we liked ... if we were interested. She was a kind-hearted soul, but she did have an ulterior motive, she confessed. It would be good to have friends nearby, people who were more like her, with whom she could speak English. It would ease the isolation she was feeling. She often felt she was the odd one out in a tight community. Besides, her mother might come over from Australia and stay for a few weeks, so she could use the house too. Her mother would spend all day with her in town, she explained, but because the house in the hills had two bedrooms, and Justine's little fisherman's cottage in town was so cramped, then it would work out well if her mother had somewhere else to stay at night.

It sounded perfect, but it also felt like an incredible coincidence that she'd rung when I was open to something like this, and I told her so.

'Perhaps it's fate,' she said.

'Maybe it is.'

I told her we'd give it some serious thought and, with that, what could have easily remained a lazy, wine-soaked dream, had suddenly turned into a genuine opportunity to cast ourselves adrift.

Even before the call from Justine, Rohan had been coming around to the idea. As her thirtieth birthday drew near, she began to fear that her long-held hope to live abroad for a while would never eventuate. The lures of private health cover, life insurance and superannuation were calling like sirens. She'd rather avoid being shipwrecked by them though, at least for the time being, especially when there was the sniff of adventure in the air.

The finances looked like they might work, too. A few years earlier we'd bought a small, one-bedroom apartment. A tenant was helping to pay off the mortgage while we continued to live in a crumbling rented house with a threadbare garden. We had a dog, so it was a better option. We planned to sell the apartment, and though we wouldn't be rich by a long shot, at least we wouldn't have a mortgage to worry about for a while.

It was this broth of events that finally led to the phone call to Lipari, to say we were coming.

We hadn't counted on Rohan getting pregnant. We certainly weren't trying for a baby. In fact, we'd survived so many pregnancy scares over our eight years together that in the end we'd abandoned our attempts at contraception. We presumed that one of us was infertile. It was a source of regret, but our lives were too busy to dwell on it. And now Rohan was holding up a plastic lollypop stick with two crimson stripes on it.

'What does it mean?' I asked.

She showed me a diagram on the brochure that came with the kit she'd bought just in case this one wasn't a scare.

'I think it means we're having a baby.'

I kissed and hugged her. She didn't respond, but kept shaking her head, a stunned look on her face.

But I couldn't stop smiling, and soon neither could she.

Until reality stepped in.

As the days progressed we began torturing ourselves about the future. We weren't cut out to make good parents, we reasoned. We were selfish. We liked our freedom too much. Our lives would change forever. We'd lose all our friends. We'd neglect our dog. We couldn't go to Italy.

The skies only began to clear when we saw the ultrasound pictures. There it was: a foetus the size of a broad bean, with a beating heart and fingers and toes. It was sitting up, with a hand held high, ordering a stiff drink like its dad on a long-haul plane trip. The bean was kicking and nodding, and we could see its eyes, looking out, maybe trying to reassure us.

'So what's wrong?' I asked Rohan one dark evening as I wiped a finger through a tear on her cheek.

'I'm terrified.'

'Of what? Giving birth?'

'No, not really.'

'The pregnancy?'

'Partly, I think. I mean, I'm worried that I might do something that causes a miscarriage, and worried that I'm getting worried and that might be bad for the baby. But it's more than that …'

'Well, what?'

'Look, I know that our lives will never be the same again, and I'm not too worried about that. I'm looking forward to a new phase in a way. But there are thoughts that … frighten me.'

'Like what?' I pushed again.

'Like when I think about those middle-class mums with their designer baby clothes and matching nappy bags.'

I laughed.

'No, I'm serious. I'm scared that if I stay here I'll just become like them: a mother in the suburbs doing whatever they do with their spanking new prams and lactation consultants. I'm just not ready for it.'

She paused, then lowered her voice, as if worried about being caught saying something she might later regret.

'Perhaps we *should* go to Italy — after the baby's born. I'll have a year's maternity leave and I might as well spend it there. I'd just be looking after the baby anyway. Neither of us really has family here that can help. I mean, imagine my father babysitting a newborn. At least on Lipari I'd know Justine.'

She had a point. My parents lived in England, in different towns since their divorce. Rohan's parents were separated too. Her mother lived in Germany with her new husband, while her dad just wasn't the type to take a newborn off our hands, despite living just down the road.

'And another thing,' Rohan put in. 'You'd be able to spend a lot of time with the baby. I'd like that. Not many fathers get the chance.'

We celebrated that evening with a fortuitous spaghetti, while Tetley, our riotous German Shorthaired Pointer, licked his chops in anticipation. Of course, we'd have to pack him up in a crate and take him with us too.

Our baby arrived in November, at five in the afternoon, after a gruelling four-day labour. The contractions started on a Tuesday and continued, with spasms of pain coming and going at odd intervals, sometimes lasting up to six minutes at a time. By Thursday evening the midwife was concerned and called us into the hospital. An examination revealed that the baby was facing the wrong way, with its back towards Rohan's spine. Finally, after many more hours, the doctor decided on a caesarean. But the baby turned in the womb at the very last moment, and made a forceful entrance into the world, hand first, announcing trouble.

'You've got a little boy,' the midwife called, holding him up with his cord still attached.

It was the most momentous thing Rohan had ever done, and the most impressive thing I'd ever seen. It had drawn on all of her resources of energy and emotion — and mine — and had been the most naked, most raw experience of our lives.

A few moments later he was in his mother's arms, resting on her chest, making snuffling noises, staring into her eyes, bonding already. And I stood there, stroking Rohan's hair, in awe and in tears as we waited for the cord to stop pulsating before it was cut.

Louis was heavier than we'd expected, more solid, and he was warm and slippery. His eyes looked like mine. I recognised my nose too, and my eyebrows. When I got to pick him up I cried like a child over the one in my arms. It all made sense. A hole I'd had in myself for years had just been filled. Everything until that moment — all my successes, embarrassments, failures, and all my relationships apart from those with my wife and child — were now insignificant. I was a beginner again, and so was Rohan. We knew we had so much to learn, and not just about nipple shields and sucking blisters either. It was a daunting prospect, but exciting too. And Italy seemed just the place to embark on our new lives together.

Two

I know what I am fleeing from,
but not what I am in search of.

MICHEL EYQUEM DE MONTAIGNE

It's funny how preconceptions of a place can end up so drastically wrong. A Mediterranean island in February has little in common with all those glossy pictures you find in holiday brochures. Winters are bitterly cold, for a start, and the Aeolian Islands aren't called the Islands of the Winds for no reason.

But here we are, rolling out of the car hold of an inter-island ferry from Sicily late one dark evening, in a car bought in Germany after a visit to Rohan's mother.

Three-month-old Louis is strapped in a car seat, and excreting prodigiously from various orifices. The dog needed no time in quarantine on his arrival in Europe, and is whining behind his grate in the back. I can see herring gulls huddled along the causeway, shadowy salt-crumbled buildings with filigree balconies, and cars with steaming exhausts.

I wind down the window to suck in the atmosphere and a gust of cold air rushes in. I hear the giant metal buoys clanging tonelessly as they knock against the jetty walls with the swell, and shouts of recognition carrying on the wind. Then I react to Rohan's incredulous glare. I remember the baby — it's far too cold for him — and I wind the window up again as fast as I can.

'There she is! Over there …'

Rohan has spotted Justine, standing under a streetlamp in a heavy coat, her four-year-old son holding her hand, her hair blowing wildly.

We pull up at one of the parking spaces that line the dock and clamber out. I call her name. Justine rushes over. She hugs us both, and as we free little Louis the air is immediately awash with questions.

When you live on an island the arrival of newcomers is an intoxicating experience. The rest of the world seems so remote, and visitors bring more than just themselves: they're a connection with lands far away. Through them, you can cast a line across the sea and pull in something exotic. Today the exotic is our baby buggy. It's got three wheels instead of the usual four, and pneumatic tyres.

'It turns so easily,' Justine squeals. 'You don't see them like this on the island. Mine manoeuvres like a tank.'

She looks at us again and I can almost see her mind flitting across the sea to a mythical land of ingenious technology, a place so far away, a culture she can barely contemplate because she's been away from it for so long. But it's a fleeting glimpse, and her attention soon returns to the present as she feels the cold wind bite. She points towards a café shedding its light over a chilled stretch of paving stones that will become, in time, a summer courtyard.

'Orlando's waiting inside,' she bubbles, then skips off like a moth, towing her son behind her.

We follow her down a short flight of steps, past a pile of old wooden fruit boxes, and enter a world of hissing coffee machines and icing sugar.

We find Orlando standing at the bar with their youngest child beside him. The fisherman shakes our hands, unfurls a slow boyish smile, and orders drinks without asking. Soon there appears a round of tiny cups full of deep brown coffee as thick as honey, each with a sheen of oil on its surface.

'*Espresso ristretto*,' Orlando says, as he raises his cup.

The aromatic compounds rush into my nostrils, and I follow Orlando's lead as he drinks it down in a single embracing mouthful. And with that gulp of bitter coffee I know I am in Italy again.

'We can't stay long,' Orlando says as soon as our tales of the journey south from Germany have been told.

'It's getting late,' Justine confirms, 'and you all look tired.'

After we leave the café, Justine wanders off through the cobbled streets with their children and Orlando drives ahead of us on his motor scooter towards the hills. Soon our headlamps are picking out red geraniums on high rock walls, then sweeping across the cliffs and over a dark wedge of sea. Up and up we go on the coiling back of this snaking road until, at last, we turn into a narrow laneway. Our route is edged with more rock walls now, and the ground is broken with potholes. A little further and the laneway narrows even more, and we are forced to stop and fold back the wing mirrors.

A string of whitewashed dwellings appears, followed by some tumbledown farmhouses. Around a corner I catch sight of a small white house, its feature-wall lit by a single bare bulb. It's square, and flat-roofed, with tiny windows, in the typical island style.

Orlando slows and pulls over. He unlocks the front door, and reaches inside for a switch. A fluorescent light flickers and goes on. He waves me forward. 'You have to go first,' he says. 'You're the head of the family.'

Louis is sleeping in his car seat. The dog is whining, and Rohan decides to put on his lead and let him out to stretch his legs.

I walk over to the doorway, and look inside. I see a set of marble steps leading straight down to a washbasin. There's another door at the bottom of the stairs, off to the right. I put my foot on the first step and take my time going down, relishing the discovery ahead of me, knowing that it will never seem quite like this again. At the bottom I push open the second door, half-expecting a rustic interior to reveal itself, dusty with time. Instead I discover a large, bone-clean room, sparsely furnished, with wooden chairs tucked neatly under a table in its centre. I spot a simple cushioned bench to my left and a cooker to my right. The floor and walls are plastered in sparkling white tiles.

It's unthinkable to walk across such a pristine surface with shoes I'd just tramped the muddy laneway in, so I stoop to untie my laces. I'm barely through taking one shoe off when I'm hit hard by something heavy, going at speed. Somehow Tetley has managed to slip his collar, and is bundling into the kitchen. But, in his haste to explore, he's miscalculated the effect of spinning claws on freshly-scrubbed tiles. With legs flailing wildly he skates from one end of the kitchen to the other. I wince as he slams snout-first into the far wall.

It might have been the result of the long journey, or the fright of suddenly finding himself hurtling forward with no traction, but whatever the reason, the result is a stream of liquefied dung, stretching the length of the room.

As the sight sinks in, and the smell begins to percolate, Orlando turns on his heels, frantically searching his pockets for cigarettes.

Rohan brushes past him on the stairs, Louis on her shoulder. 'Oh no,' she says grimly when she discovers the reason that our fisherman friend is starting up his motor scooter. 'Do we even have a bucket and mop?'

Justine had known from the start that finding a house for us to stay in for the long run would be difficult, but she confessed after we arrived that it had been even harder than she'd imagined. It wasn't that there were no houses to rent: there were plenty. It was just that the islanders were used to adjusting their rates to take advantage of the tourist runs. Long weekends in Germany meant a rush of visitors and an upward adjustment in charges. Island festivals caused rental spikes too, and around Easter rates tripled. Then in August, when millions of Italians fled the cities for the coast, places rented out for ten times as much as the off-peak rate.

In theory, several people were willing to let us stay for longer than the usual one or two weeks, as long as we were prepared to renegotiate the rent every weekend, and would be willing to vacate almost at once if they got a better offer. All this and Justine hadn't even mentioned the dog.

Needless to say, when she did there followed a period of awkward silence. Popular wisdom suggested there were three types of canine: the ill-tempered lap dog that would shred the furniture given half the chance, the cunning, opportunistic hunting hound that would slip its chains and retrieve their chickens by the throat or, worst of all, the rabid street dog, willing to decapitate their entire family. Whichever demented animal she was touting, it certainly wasn't welcome.

Then, just as Justine was about to give up, word came through from Arturo, Orlando's eldest brother. His wife's family lived in a house in the hills, and had a small building opposite that they sometimes rented out. It was in a tiny hamlet of peasant farmers. The building in question had two bedrooms and incredible views of the sea. There was just one hitch. The dog.

Although they were a farming family, they didn't like the idea of an animal they knew nothing about. As it was they already had to put up with the neighbourhood dogs, which barked all night. The presence of another dog might set them off all the more.

With characteristic charm, Justine went to work on them. Tetley was a tiny thing, she lied sweetly, hovering a hand around her ankle. He's named after a type of teabag. He's hardly worth bothering about. As far as she knew he slept all day. He never barked. All in all, you'd barely even notice the sweet little puppy was there …

Finally, after sworn promises that we would keep the dog locked up in one of their barns, they decided to take a chance on us.

And so we find ourselves here, on the first evening of our shared adventure, swabbing down the kitchen in the glow of a fluorescent light, with a bucket of disinfectant between us.

I drift out of sleep into astonishing darkness, uncertain of the time and vaguely aware of the translucent rims of two secretive portholes high up on the walls of our basement bedroom. I stumble out of bed, cold and groggy, after a night of tossed blankets and the hungry wails of our child.

'Turn the light on,' Rohan says under her breath. 'It must be morning by now.'

'I think it is. How did you sleep?'

She ignores me. It's a stupid question. We have a baby.

I get up, switch on a light, stand on a stool, and pull back the porthole flaps above Louis' cot. Daylight surges in, and I find myself surveying the concrete surface of the laneway we'd driven down the night before. The other small window has intimate views of a parking space.

It will emerge that the only wall in our bedroom that lacks an opening is the one that has the potential for expansive views of the sea. But glass is more expensive than concrete, and it lets in more heat in the hot months of summer. If you can't have sea views then something just as spiritually uplifting will do — like the shrine fashioned out of an alcove in the seaward wall. Here I find a foot-high figurine of Jesus wrapped in a chipped plaster-cast toga. Someone has snapped an arm off, and glued it back on again so that it's thrust outwards in an open-palmed salute. A fluffy koala key-ring dangles from his wrist.

Beside this irreverent idol is a fractured Joseph, dressed in flaking purple robes. At his feet is a crouching, hatchet-faced infant: a baby Saviour, who appears to be levitating over an invisible potty. His right arm has been amputated and lost. His left hand is grasping the stem of a bunch of white silk flowers, each one larger than his face.

Behind this curious trinity is another Messiah, this one a harrowed and emaciated character, losing streams of plastic blood. He's nailed to a cross, or rather a wooden clothes peg split in half and tacked into position with a drawing pin.

Just as intriguing are the contents of a formal glass-fronted cabinet on the far wall. It's filled with genial plastic angels, glass cats, ballerinas in pink tutus, a squirrel family and their toadstool house, and furry miniature animal toys. We guess they are *bombonieri*, which Italians give people in gratitude for turning up to their wedding, or their child's christening, or some other major event in their lives. It's rumoured that a proficient Italian mother can nail a disruptive child on the head with one of these at twenty paces.

Thankfully, the air in the kitchen has cleared since last night, so we have no qualms about rummaging through the cupboards. We find almost all the utensils and pans we will need. A side door reveals a shower and toilet.

Upstairs we discover another room, with a lumpy bed and an empty wardrobe. As part of the deal we need to keep it clear for Justine's mother, who may arrive at any time. At the far end, a set of patio doors opens on to an extensive terrace, which we guess is the roof of our kitchen. If we turn our backs to the laneway we look across the nearby roof of a neighbouring house, set back from ours and further downhill. We have a perfect view of a steep driveway and a courtyard edged by what looks like a large garage or shed. Stretching between the house and this building is a washing line. It's billowing with bed sheets, pyjamas and voluminous underwear. It's a sunny winter's day, perfect for drying.

Just to our left is a mulberry tree, and pottering around this are a few chickens, some just scruffy fledglings. Others roam a series of half-hearted terraces, planted with plum and apricot trees, which fall away to a country roadway, a squiggle in the distance. There are untilled gullies and ridges tufted with broom, and clumps of olive trees, and grass as pale as straw. Then the countryside ends in a final wriggle of bluffs overlooking an expanse of glittering sea.

On the horizon are the hazy hills and mountains that mark the Sicilian coastline. We can see the conical form of

Mount Etna, pulsing smoke from its snow-covered peak. But it's just a detail, for to our left, across a range of olive trees and farmhouses, is another volcano. It's much nearer, and we find ourselves staring directly into its caldera: a chapped mouth breathing trails of steamy gas, which rise up the slope towards a crest of trees. It's the combustible focal point of Vulcano, our nearest island neighbour. In the local dialect it's known simply as *idu* — him. It's the legendary smokestack of an underground forge, the workplace of Vulcan, the Roman god of fire. The son of Jupiter and Juno, and the husband of Venus, he churns out thunderbolts, and armour and weapons for gods and heroes.

There are more islands in front of us, scattered like chance associates in the sea. One is Salina, which from our perspective looks like an extension of our own island. There is tiny Filicudi, where the locals lunch on spaghetti with sea urchin eggs and capers, and Alicudi, home to steep mountain paths and docile mules. They bulge like blue-cast breasts behind a muslin blouse, separated by a cleavage of sea.

We are both astonished by the view, and stand there for ages, mentally pinching ourselves. You don't come to a place to find what you already know, you go there to find something new — and we certainly hadn't expected anything like this. The view across the Tyrrhenian Sea is far more impressive than we could ever have hoped for, or could ever have been led to believe. And all for a third of our rent back home, with electricity included.

I squeeze Rohan's hand and shake my head in disbelief at our good fortune. What indolent times we will have up here on our terrace overlooking the sea, what grand meals under the stars …

Someone is calling out to me. I step towards the edge of the terrace and look down into the beaming face of a stump of a man. He has wide-set legs, good for straddling donkeys, twinkling eyes and bushy white eyebrows. Milky hair streams from under a cone of wool on his head. An icing of stubble clings to a face that could hold a day's rain in its furrows.

His name is Nino, he announces grandly in Italian, gripping my hand. 'It's short for Antonio, but no one calls me that.'

He is wearing patched trousers, the flies tied together with string. Two frayed T-shirt collars poke out from under a flannelette shirt.

'*La signora*?' he asks, enquiring after Rohan.

I don't know the Italian for breastfeeding so I point to one of my nipples and make mouthing gestures like a fish.

He looks confused, then slightly concerned. But he's obviously determined to make the best of things, because after a moment's silence he mentions toasting our arrival with *vino*.

He points to a barn beneath the family house, just across the laneway. He beckons to me to follow him, and lopes away with a springy step.

I find Rohan downstairs, just finishing up. She's keen to meet our landlord too and, after securing Louis into a pouch on her chest, we wander outside to join him.

Nino has waited until now to pull open the heavy barn

doors. He bows like a courtier and sweeps his hand across the scene to draw our attention to a gloomy interior. As my eyes adjust I make out ancient sickles and potato sacks, and cobwebby handmade fishing nets hanging from the walls. There are dusty jars on rough-hewn shelves, and grouped on the concrete floor are dozens of ten-litre demijohns sheathed in wickerwork.

'A man with as much wine as this fears nothing,' says Nino, as he tickles Louis under the chin with his stubby fingers.

He shakes Rohan's hand as formally as you like, with a cheeky grin, then turns to pick up a glass container full of yellowish liquid. He tugs out a ceramic stopper with his teeth, spits it into a hand, and snorts as he presses the neck against his nose.

'*Fuck-i-ne*!' he cries, and turns his head to see our reaction.

I'm taken aback by his pidgin English, and laugh, though really I'm more concerned about the state of the wine.

But, as if to salve my worries, he licks his lips, pours some into a tumbler and holds it up in front of my face. It looks like it's just passed through someone's kidneys. I contemplate it for a few seconds as Nino continues talking and rubbing a hand down his flannelette shirt. It takes Rohan's nudge in my ribs to make me realise I'm standing there like a tailor's dummy, not understanding a word he's saying.

I'm not a linguist, but I have a grasp of Italian and a smattering of Spanish to fill in the gaps, but what is coming out of Nino's mouth sounds a bit like garbled Russian.

He stops abruptly and cranes his neck, searching our faces with his twinkling brown eyes.

'*Dialetto*,' he explains at last, before dropping the dialect and skipping ahead in the open vowels of Italian.

'It's wine from my fields,' he says. 'Pah! It's a diabolical concoction. Last year was a bad one for the grapes. Pour it away if you don't like it.' His face contracts into deeper wrinkles and he flings out an arm, flicking his wrist as if he were casting the entire lot into the cactus bushes.

The smell alone is enough to choke me, but when a man's fate is fixed, he has to make the best of it. Besides, I'm foolhardy by nature. I bring the glass to my lips and take a tentative sip. For an instant I'm paralysed.

'How is it?' he asks, bringing his hands together in prayer.

It's good for removing barnacles, and if I had any sense I would have bolted to the bathroom right then and pushed my mouth under a running tap, or gone into a swoon to avoid another gulp of the terrible stuff. But instead I let out a feeble offering of politeness and squeak, 'It's fine.'

'You sure?'

'Yuah. Is gwood.'

'Not too rough?'

'Nuh. Is … ummm … vewy … umm …' I'm desperately searching for a word, something I can pronounce, which will tactfully sum the experience up without insulting our landlord on our first meeting. After all, he has probably crushed the grapes with his own feet, and bottled the juice by hand.

'I don't use commercial yeast,' he continues exuberantly. 'I let the wild yeast on the skins do their job. They give unpredictable results ... Who knows what flavour you can end up with? Go on. Take another sip.'

I blow out my cheeks and force open my teeth. But the second time around it isn't nearly so bad. My tongue still puckers, but at least I can taste something. A hint of lemon perhaps, or maybe it's the tang of my cauterised palate.

'It's, um, agreeable,' I say, with half-hearted optimism, knowing I've tasted as bad and gone back for more when there was nothing else to be had.

'Agreeable?'

'Yes. Agreeable ... and ... ummm ... well ...' I'm feeling cloth-headed already, 'quite effective.'

He crows with delight and claps his hands. 'Here. Take the lot then,' he declares, as he thrusts out the container. 'You and I will be great friends. Everyone else can't stand the stuff.'

Rohan laughs. Nino waggles a little finger in front of his fly. 'They say it tastes like someone's pissed in the bottle.'

But still, he grew his own grapes, and there was wine for him and his family, and more left over for friends and neighbours — if they could stomach it.

'It's not the best of wines, but you get used to it,' says Nino. 'You can drink until you are giddy and you wake up without the slightest hangover. Have as much as you want. Help yourself. Any time. You don't have to ask.'

I thank him for his generosity and he claps a hand around my shoulder. 'You can have lunch too,' he says. 'Right now, come on. Unless you have somewhere to go in a hurry?'

'Not us,' I say. 'We have all the time in the world.'

We find his wife in the kitchen. Immacolata is slim, in her late sixties. She's wearing a flowery pinafore over a flowery dress. Her kerchief has slipped slightly, revealing hair as black and shiny as the lumps of glassy volcanic obsidian that decorate the tops of nearby walls. I am drawn to her eyes, the colour of roasted chestnuts, and her dazzling teeth. They are probably false. Either way, the fine cut of her face shows she was a great beauty in her time.

Immacolata is certainly more reserved than Nino, and seems a little flustered, as if she's not used to people just dropping in, especially not two foreigners she's never met, with a baby vomiting breast milk down its chest.

Our hostess rushes around, attempting to rustle up some coffee cups and find an old cloth to clean up the mess that's congealing on her youngest guest's bib.

Meanwhile, Nino unscrews an old Grand Marnier bottle, and I take a seat at the kitchen table. I'm already preparing myself for the island equivalent of the boar and thrush pâtés of Provence, or some sausages spotted with peppercorns. Perhaps followed by duck with wild mushrooms, or a steaming rabbit casserole, just to be rustic. I imagine goat's cheese to follow, and almond and cream cake, to pre-empt the arrival of the digestives: exactly as endlessly described in those famous living-the-good-life-abroad books.

But then it strikes me. Apart from a coffee pot, there is nothing on the stove, which I notice is a very modern affair. The kitchen has cupboards, a gas cooker, a fridge and a sink, but while Immacolata prepares coffee here for guests, she never cooks here. The real work is done on a kitchen range out back. This room acts as a kind of parlour, a gentrification, to show visitors that their hosts are not peasants preserved in aspic, as you might expect if you met them out in the fields.

Immacolata returns, carrying a heavy pan. It's the first course and, as it turns out, the last: a mound of spaghetti, topped with chunks of last night's boiled potatoes, and a few fibrous artichoke leaves. Tossed with olive oil and plenty of chopped garlic, it's genuine, frugal food made from local produce that probably comes and goes with the seasons.

I look across at Rohan. Her Italian is better than mine, and she seems easy in their company. Louis is gurgling away contentedly. I sigh to myself. I'm really happy that this isn't Provence or Tuscany, and that these aren't wealthy landowners with a pad in the city and a place in the country for weekends.

But what's with the bottle of Grand Marnier?

'I've brought out something special,' Nino says coyly. 'Do you want to try? It's very authentic …'

Before I have the chance to answer he's pouring.

'Drink it slowly,' he says with an engaging smile, 'there's no hurry.'

I sip delicately. It turns out to be more of Nino's wine, just decanted in a fancy bottle.

Nino laughs out loud at the look of surprise he's conjured up.

Then the television goes on, and the volume is turned up to obscure the sound of our forks. It seems our hosts aren't much for talking, especially when it's time for the news.

We munch in silence through Palestinian bombings, American war plans, a child's murder in a town far up north, the weather somewhere else. As the screen flicks from one wretched scene to another, I can't help thinking about the irrelevance of what we are witnessing, both to our hosts' lives, and to ours. Not that it always seemed that way.

For years I'd gone to bed with a radio under the pillow, to catch up on the latest developments, and I habitually woke up fumbling for the thing again. Now it all seemed so trivial, and somehow polluting. I knew right then I wasn't going to miss any of it. I just wanted to be on this island, cut off from news of the outside world, with no television or radio, and no telephone for that matter. From now on we would rely on the old way for our bulletins: a letter with an exotic stamp. By the time it had weaved its way through the Italian postal system the news would be long cold, and distanced, just as it ought to be.

When lunch is finished we all make our way outside again. Nino wants to see the dog he's heard so much about.

I release him from the back of the car, where he's been largely contained since his accident last night.

Nino's quite taken with Tetley, despite him being bigger than he was led to believe. He'd once had an English

Setter he'd kept chained up next to the rabbits, he tells us. He'd almost thought of it as a pet. He thinks ours has probably gone soft by the way it refuses to cower when he raises his hand to it. It's obviously an inside dog too, on account of its thin hair. It will probably freeze if we keep it out in the cold. So he sets to, hammering out a chunk of masonry in one of his barns, mixing cement, and plastering in an iron hoop at the end of a chain.

As a concession, while the cement is drying, the dog can stay up on our terrace during the day. At night it can sleep at the bottom of the steps inside our house, as long as it's chained to the washbasin and can't get into the kitchen. Immacolata is especially proud of the tiles.

Though Nino might have a soft spot for Tetley, later that day it becomes clear his affection doesn't stretch to strays. Outside our front door and across the laneway is an impressive retaining wall made of huge nuts of volcanic rock stuck together with wads of cement and clinker. It holds back a ramp of scrubland that runs up a slope towards the sky. This construction is more than the height of a man. Because of this wall, the slope is tempered, and the effect is to make room for the concrete laneway and a set of houses and their outbuildings, which are made from blocks of the durable volcanic stone called *tufo*. While our house is painted white, most of the others are not. So, you have a grey concrete road, a high grey wall, and a scattering of houses, sheds and barns, all coloured grey. All this monotone could come across as ugly, but maybe it's the winter yellow wildflowers which soften the scene, or the light reflected off the sea that moderates the starker tones. Whatever it is, to my eye at least, the whole place looks like it's made out of marzipan.

I am upstairs on our terrace now, marvelling once more at the view. Rohan is putting Louis to bed for the sixth time today. Suddenly, I spot three puppies trotting down the scrubby hill above us towards our house, making their way slowly towards the top of the retaining wall. They have a clear view of Tetley, who is standing sentinel on the edge of our rooftop terrace, looking out for cats.

Noticing the intruder, one of the pups starts to bark. The others join in.

In an instant Nino appears in the laneway. He marches up to the bottom of the wall to glare at the offending beasts. Their barking begins to falter, before they start skulking back up the slope.

I'm impressed by the reaction Nino's presence has caused, but it's a trifling enough incident, and I would have forgotten it at once if I hadn't stolen a glance at Nino's hard-set face when he returned to the scene a few moments later.

The contrast between the jovial countenances I'd witnessed earlier that day and the look fixed firmly to his face now is so extreme that for a moment I wonder if I have misjudged him. The fact that he has a shotgun, and is raising it to his shoulder, only serves to reinforce my suspicions.

The puppies are almost at the top of the slope when there comes an almighty crack, and the first pellets begin flying towards their retreating behinds. The shot echoes through the laneway, setting my pulse racing. The puppies howl, and I rush to the edge of the terrace as a second shot rings out. Below me, Nino is blowing the smoke from the barrels of his gun.

Once he is sure his quarry has been vanquished he turns back towards his house. Then he sees me.

At first he greets me with a puzzled silence, as if he'd forgotten that we were living there.

'Did you hit them?' I blabber.

'The shots went over their heads,' he says calmly, after an uncomfortable pause.

He coughs. Then smiles. 'You're not allowed to kill those *bastardi* any more.'

The gunshots have woken Louis, and he's crying now. Rohan is comforting him as best she can. She rocks him in her arms for a while, but this only seems to agitate him more. She tries to feed him, but he wails louder than ever. She ends up strapping him into his buggy and wheeling him around and around the kitchen table, hoping that some movement will calm him. Stupidly, I try to talk through the day's events as she's doing this, but it's obvious that Rohan's too preoccupied to concentrate. So I wait my turn by feeding the dog and washing some dishes. Then Rohan retreats to the bedroom, to try her luck with putting him back in the cot, leaving me alone as darkness falls and the cold creeps in. And finally there's silence.

When I feel I've left enough time I inch open the bedroom door. They are both fast asleep, and it's not yet 6 pm.

Three

*Twenty years from now you will be more
disappointed by the things that you didn't do
than by the ones you did do. So throw off the
bowlines. Sail away from the safe harbor.
Catch the trade winds in your sails.
Explore. Dream. Discover.*

ATTRIBUTED TO MARK TWAIN

The days are chilly but the skies are clear and bright. One afternoon soon after our arrival, I leave Rohan asleep with Louis in her arms and sneak out with Tetley as quietly as I can.

We follow the laneway as it travels west above a falling slope of kitchen gardens. There are silvery olive trees and prickly pear cacti with paddles as big as oar blades.

I stop occasionally to take in my travelling companions: the misty outline of Sicily, the blueness of the Mediterranean, and the wide-open sky with its scent of salt. I breathe in deeply. Together they seem the antidote to the life I used to lead, just a short while ago.

We pass a few trees that I take to be figs, and before too long we come to a fork in the path. I choose the less obvious route and find myself on a muddy track leading past fields of feathery grey wormwood bushes and more dry-stone walls. These soon give way to more open country, created in a few broad strokes of the brush: a plain of shimmering meadow grass, khaki hills in the distance, a nudge of sea.

As I walk I contemplate my first few days here. Rohan's life now totally revolves around Louis. He catnaps. He feeds. He needs changing. He wants to play at 3 am. Rohan thinks he's still unsettled after the flight from Australia and the four-day car trip from Germany. Perhaps it's the change of environment too, or his new cot. Maybe it's just a stage in his life. Who can know?

Last night I slept alone for the first time since he was born, in the upstairs bedroom. We'd been short-tempered all day, and it eventually erupted into an argument. I'd tried to talk to her about something. But my voice was too loud. I'd woken Louis up, just as he was falling asleep.

I feel better today. I'm half-refreshed from the best night's sleep I've had in weeks. I realise we've been suffering from sleep deprivation, an effective torture technique. But now I can see things more clearly and I don't blame her for being so snappy. On the other hand, I don't feel guilty about leaving them today either. The strongest feeling I have is relief.

Now the track is shot with late winter flowers with sweet-waxy smells. It swings past a row of young olive trees, splits again, then carries me towards a man bent double over a patch of furrowed earth he's etched from the grasslands. He's wearing the same ragged clothes as yesterday, so there's no mistaking him.

'Nino,' I call out.

He straightens up and wipes his forehead with a shirt cuff.

'Just out of bed?' he teases, in a gentle, chiding tone. I see he is free of those symbols of slavery: the watch, the belt, the necktie. Perhaps he tells the time by the sun, then loses track of it again. I'm sure he rises when he feels like it: when the sky is white and violet and the songbirds are calling.

Tetley bounds up to greet him as Nino climbs the gentle slope and holds out a hand. Snuggled in his cracked palm are a few large seeds. 'Pumpkin,' he says. He snaps his hand closed again, to protect his seeds from Tetley's inquisitive snout.

I cling to something we might have in common. 'I love pumpkin,' I say as brightly as I can in my feeble Italian. 'Pumpkin soup is beautiful. Especially in Venice.'

He stares at me, and I immediately regret opening my mouth. It sounds like I'm putting on airs, like some arty-farty peacock from the city. I run a hand across my face, unconsciously trying to wipe away my foppishness as Nino weighs me up with his eyes.

'*Professore*,' he says, using the title some Italians give to those they might believe are more educated than they are, 'the pumpkins are for my daughter's sow, and to pound up for my hens. As for eating them in *Venezia* ... well, they do a lot of strange things up there, like building their houses on stinking canals. So it's not surprising to hear they eat pig food too.'

I laugh skittishly and that unnerving twinkle appears in his eyes again.

'You and I are going on a journey.'

'Uh ... sure. Where to?'

'We'll soon see,' he says, trying to repress a chuckle, 'after I finish up here.'

I watch as he drops the last of the seeds into a shallow drill. He covers them with soil, and marks the runs with canes cut from a nearby copse. When he is satisfied he places his hoe inside a low-slung nest of boulders topped with a sheet of corrugated iron. As I watch him, I imagine him lying on the mattress of old potato sacks inside, in his cosy bower, content as the rain beats down and nurtures his plants. I suspect he loves working with the land: planting the seeds he'd saved from previous years, turning up one morning to see the seedlings poking their heads from the ground. Nino is strong and fit, and shines with optimism. I believe all he needs to be happy is his health, the soil, the rain and the progress of his seeds.

'It's a good place to get away from the family. It's important, no?' Nino says.

'What is?'

'This!' he points a stubby finger at his lean-to. 'I saw you looking. What's wrong with you, *professore*? You're dreaming again.'

He winks, brushing his hands on his trousers. 'To every bird, his own nest is beautiful. You need a place to lie still sometimes, *professore*: a place like this, if your heart is in it.'

With this he hops up a couple of steps cut into the soil and plunges past some prickly pear and out onto the plain. I follow as he presses on quickly, with Tetley questing ahead, on the scent of lizards.

Nino's woollen hat and shaggy neck turn from side to side as he points out various landmarks. 'That hilltop … no, not that one — the big one! In front of you! With the white marker pole on top.'

He slows so I can catch up and walk beside him. He tells me the hill belongs to a friend of his who lives in Australia. He's coming to visit soon. And there, just past that clump of olives, that small storage shed, built from cindery volcanic stone.

'I used to store the grain from the harvest there. Oh, and those trees … yes, you're right, they *are* figs, how did you know that, *professore*? But they aren't so good; the ones nearer the house are better. And these are the hoof prints of the horse that belongs to the man who keeps pigs, just down the road from us.'

He pauses and waves his hand in an arc. 'But all this … this is mine.'

'*All* yours?'

'Well, my mother-in-law's, really …'

He's talking about acre upon acre across those creamy grasslands to our left, which seem to end in the sea, and at least as far as to those dangerous-looking tiers of rock to our right, which appear to lead up to some sort of plateau.

'But there's no one to work it now,' he continues. 'I have no sons. Only daughters.'

His brothers left the island in the 1950s, he tells me, to work in construction jobs in Melbourne. Everyone left in those days. Only a few hundred people remained on the island after the emigration. Imagine that, almost the entire population.

'I would have gone too. It was a hard life on the islands in those days. But when I applied to migrate they told me I couldn't take my girlfriend. We had to be married, but she wasn't ready for that at the time.' He rolls his hands across his chest. 'But I needed her ...'

'Immacolata?' I ask.

'*Si. Amore*. And then children. It was too late. I'd missed my opportunity.'

Instead they worked together in the fields. They bought a donkey, built their house, added rooms as their family grew, farmed wheat for pasta. But now he has the pension, and can buy spaghetti from the shops. He no longer needs a donkey to carry bags of wheat and flour around, which means he doesn't have to spend half his time collecting grass and herbs for it to munch on through winter.

'So life's a bit easier,' I say.

He shakes his head.

'Ah, but I'm old now. Still, there's always a rabbit to catch, or something to plant or prune.'

As well as I can in my rudimentary Italian, I tell him that I wished I were a man of the land too. I'd always wanted a piece of earth to call my own …

'You. A farmer!' Nino breaks in, slapping his thighs. 'You have to get up with the cocks, you know.' He throws up his head and crows. 'You can't just stay in bed with your wife all day. You need your strength.'

With that he takes off at speed, bounding along the track like a hound on a scent, with Tetley coursing in front of him. I try to keep up, but after coiling around a foothill at a fair clip, I'm forced to call for a breather.

'But we're not there yet, *professore*,' he cries, jerking his head towards the base of a cliff. In an instant he is gone again, cutting across a fold of waist-high grass. A few moments later I see him scuttling nimbly up a hemline of rock with Tetley on his heels.

I'm in a pickle. I don't like heights, and tackling dangerous-looking escarpments isn't my favourite pastime either. But, stupidly, I am determined not to belittle myself in front of this man. He's pushing seventy, after all.

I take the grassy slope easily and, at close quarters with the craggy incline, which I estimate must be thirty metres high at least, I valiantly cast out a hand. Parts of it tumble down onto my boots. Equally alarming is the discovery of large patches of cactus just above my head.

'Uh, just where are we going?' I call out.

'It's a short cut to my vineyard.'

'Is it dangerous?'

'*Si!*'

'Well …?'

But it's no use. I stand on the balls of my feet as Nino starts grappling with bushes and knocking down pads of prickly pear with clouts from his toecaps. For a moment I wonder whether to stake my life on the absurdly narrow rabbit run in front of me, or move along the ledge a little and seek out a wider path. But after a quick inspection I find there is only one way up.

My instincts scream out not to do it, but after feverishly trying to plot a way out of my situation, and getting nowhere, I check my unease as best I can.

Fallen rocks and exposed roots of gorse run across the track like tangled trip-wires. I inch slowly upwards and feel my stomach lurch as I realise I am moving out of bruises and broken limbs into almost certain death. It occurs to me too that Nino, with his stocky frame, low centre of gravity and bowed legs, is built for this kind of thing. But with my extra height and weaker legs, and a belly that tends to brush chunks of cliff face off when I get too close, I know I'm courting disaster.

But it's more difficult to retreat than go up now, and my cowardly qualities force me to continue clawing towards the crest in quarter-steps, with sweat dripping down my body, and pieces of volcanic mud buzzing past my face.

Nino and the dog are way ahead of me, and I shudder as they disappear over the wobbly edge of a bluff, leaving me to get on with it alone. I take another step, and my foot slips, tilting me sideways into a mud tier and a cactus bush. For a moment I totter on the brink, trying to keep my balance. Dislodged rocks turn in the air and crash off the cliff face. They vanish in a tide of dust. I cling onto the cactus as best I can, and then I realise my hands are hurting.

Steadying myself, I shuffle into a wider scratching and stop to pull the largest spines from my palms.

'That's it, *professore*,' Nino calls down, before reminding me he's an old man and I am still young.

'But you're a goat not a human,' I squawk, only to be rewarded with a bellow of laughter.

I look up. Dangers are everywhere. I step forward and grip a spindle of grass. It comes away in my swollen hand. I drive onwards, trying to dig my toes into the earth and succeeding miserably. I see only one faint hope of making it to the top and that is to grasp onto an ancient branch and hope it will bear my weight.

I try to use it as a lever, but just as I make some ground it snaps and slashes across my face, and my feet slip from under me. I crash back down onto the rabbit track and end up shaking and pinned, with my face pressed solidly against the dirt, trying to measure the distance to the ground below. Mistake. Getting dizzy. Never look down.

I know it's essential to take control of my limbs again, but when I attempt to lift a leg I feel it shaking in refusal. It takes several minutes to regain any semblance of composure before, bolstered by some critical encouragement from up above, I manage to work up some tolerable fluidity.

At last, with one final lunge, I pull myself over a knot of earth and crawl into the grass. With my last ounce of energy I flip over onto my back and lie there, sprawled flabbily at Nino's feet, like a great sweaty goat's cheese rimed with wood ash.

My throat is parched, my hands ache, and I can't feel my legs, but when I open my eyes I see Nino is as fresh and jaunty as ever.

'We could have fallen ...' I hear myself say.

He pretends distress and adds some theatrical trembling.

'*Si*. But I knew you were always behind me. I could hear the falling rocks.'

'Oh. That's fine then,' I croak.

'*Bravo.*'

Nino hitches his trousers higher with his thumbs then clasps my hand to help me up. 'You're strong, like me, and stupid too. You know, my son-in-law wouldn't have been able to do that. He wouldn't have even attempted it.'

I feel his eyes burrowing into me, and I wondered then if somehow I've gained his respect by following him up a cliff: this man with no sons.

Before I've collected my wits, we are off again, in single file, to tackle the final rise. Luckily it's an easy slope this time, and cresting it reveals a tabletop of pruned and leafless vines outspread before us. It's obvious by the shacks dotted here and there that it's a communal holding, and Nino confirms this by pointing to a section of the far side of the field.

'Those are mine. Over there,' he says proudly, as my heart pounds madly in my chest. 'Six hundred vines. Here, anyway. But it's only a small vineyard. I've got two others, about 3,000 vines in all. Later in the year, you will see. You can help me pick the grapes, in return for more wine — a different vintage, better perhaps. I need help to pick. I don't have a tractor, and no cheap labour. Not yet anyway.'

He finds this vastly amusing, but it has never occurred to me I'd have as much free wine as I wanted, and I won't pretend I don't welcome the offer. He can see it in my face.

'You be careful,' he says. '*Carni fa carni, pani fa panza, vino fa danza.*' Meat makes meat, bread makes a paunch, and wine makes you dance!

He's in his element as he bobs on the spot — and so am I. We've started off on the right foot, and though I'm not accustomed to people like him, I already feel a connection. It's like I've been sent a special guardian to guide me through my life on the island, and despite my aching hands I confess that I would have given up every conceivable luxury to be here with him now. But he has gone already, and all that's left is to follow him down a dirt path skirted with vines.

We reach the edge of the cliff that looks out to sea, and there we sit, saying nothing. I can see the island of Salina, close up: double black volcano domes with buildings perched like white butterflies around their leading foot. Leaving a port on its left-hand flank and coming our way is an *aliscafo*, a passenger hydrofoil, looking as big as a bath toy.

I imagine that long ago there might have been a farmer like Nino, who sat here like us; who saw the arrival of Liparus, the Italian king who would give Lipari its name. A few years later he might have noticed other boats coming too, borne swiftly towards the island by sheets tied to poles above the deck. It was the first time he would have seen a sail. On board one of these boats was Aeolus, a soothsayer, who had a gift for predicting the winds by looking into the flames. He would marry Liparus' daughter, and in time rule over the islands himself. After his death, white-frocked cultists would elevate him to the position of a god, and his domain would become known, for the first time, as the Islands of the Winds.

But intriguing landmarks out to sea tend to be extremely tempting to your average megalomaniac. As the centuries turned, in came Greeks, Romans, Visigoths, Vandals, Ostrogoths and Arabs. The resident population was thinned by daggers and scimitars, and in the year 836 AD the Saracens massacred just about everyone. Then, in 1544, the Turkish pirate Barbarossa deported the whole population — some 8,000 people — as slaves. It was left to Spaniards, Sicilians, Calabrians, passing stowaways and shipwrecked sailors to repopulate the islands.

It isn't surprising then that the isolated villages up in the Liparian hills each developed its own individuality, depending on who turned up and stayed. The population of Lipari is only around 11,000, but dialects differ across the island. According to Nino, even our little cluster of eight houses has its own local form, which differs slightly from the one down the road in the village proper, and there's another version spoken in the village nearest to the vineyards where we are sitting now. In the mix are various forms of early Latin, as well as Greek, Catalan, Arabic and various regional French influences.

Apparently, other things differed from place to place too. Nino tells me that several of Immacolata's dishes are considered specialities of our village, for example. The tomatoes are different too. Our village favours varieties of cherry tomatoes that grow nowhere else. Nino swears he won't eat any tomato that isn't his own, while people elsewhere wouldn't touch one of Nino's if their lunchtime depended on it. Even Arturo, Nino's son-in-law, grows his own varieties from seeds handed down from his father. Nino's are dry and tasteless, he says, not like the ones he grows.

Nino himself is grabbing my arm. 'We must go. Now!' he says hurriedly. 'Before we know it the fog will be upon us.'

I lean over the edge of the drop-off. Great streams of mist are rushing up the cliff face from the sea like ghostly upturned waterfalls. When I look behind me I see the whiteness already smudging out the vines.

I scramble up. Nino is off already, skipping across the plateau. I watch as he disappears like a fugitive over the edge, with Tetley at his heels.

For a moment I hesitate, then I feel the clammy air roll over me, and a spooky feeling causes the hairs on my neck to prickle. If I didn't know better I would have sworn I saw drowned sailors swimming in front of my eyes, borne inland on the mist, searching for their long-lost homes and families, and heard the distant singing of a siren out to sea and the heavy grey lids of ancient Etruscan tombs creaking open.

Fancy is a fertile thing and not to be seeded when you are alone on a hill and swathed in a shroud, so with a whimper I strike the track and retreat from that ghostly place, my head dipping below the cloud until at last I find a path. It's a far less daunting route this time, and I find Nino is waiting at the bottom.

We make our way across the plain side by side, and part in the laneway, in a chill wind, with the clouds howling across the moon and the sounds of a wailing child coming from our kitchen.

Four

The tragedy of life is not what men suffer,
but rather what they miss.

THOMAS CARLYLE

We've made up, and are sharing the same bed again, so I can get up in the middle of the night and help when needed. As soon as the light goes out Rohan turns on her side, away from me. When I try to cuddle her she shrugs me off. She wants sleep more than anything, she says. She's had a child pawing at her all day. Louis always wants to be in her arms; he cries as soon as she puts him down. She needs her space.

A typical night sees Louis going down at around seven and sleeping until midnight. Rohan then feeds him for an hour or so, followed by a lengthy attempt at burping. Then it's my turn to get him back to sleep. I start with some rocking, but he ends up bawling. Only bouncing up and down on the spot seems to help. When he's totally quiet, and I think I've finally been successful, I gingerly place him in his cot. This invariably wakes him up again, and I'm forced to pick him up once more. Three attempts later I've managed to move on a stage, and I'm stroking his head as he lies calmly beneath his blankets. Move my hand away too soon and his eyes flick open. Make the slightest sound and he's whimpering. The whole procedure takes about an hour, which is roughly the time he'll spend asleep before he wakes up hungry again.

No one told us it would be this hard. We thought he would be settling into a routine by now. A good one. But instead it's a struggle, and we're getting more tired as the days go on. Feelings of helplessness are creeping in. We are getting more and more unsure of ourselves. Rohan passes Louis to me and I pass him back again, neither of us really knowing how to stop his crying, or when to stop worrying about it and leave him alone to work things out himself.

We are sure about only one thing. There has been a conspiracy of silence among those who have had children before us. It is as though the truth is too traumatic to divulge to anyone who is childless, and is expecting pretty booties and adoring toothless smiles. Or else they bury reality deep within their subconscious minds, never to be revealed, in case their own traumas are awakened by discussing the memory of it all.

Not that it's difficult for everyone, of course. Some people appear to have it sorted out from the start, and know instinctively what to do. But for us it's a mystery, and we begin wondering if it's our fault that our child can't sleep. We are probably doing everything wrong, lavishly, and in unison.

We've now finished our third bout of battling with Louis for the night and, finally, both he and Rohan are asleep.

It's then that I hear someone hammering above our heads. A few dull knocks, a pause, a few more. It's just gone dawn on Saturday morning.

I fumble for some clothes discarded on the floor and make my way on tiptoe to the bedroom door. I open it as quietly as I can manage and creep out. Some workmen are starting on a wooden awning to cover our terrace.

It seems odd to be doing this in the cold months of winter, but Nino insists it will be essential when summer comes. It's a slow job though, with the coffee breaks and the conversations with anyone who is passing, and it'll be a few noisy weekend mornings until it's completed.

It soon becomes clear we won't be having a lie-in too often at all, even if Louis or Nino's builders allow us. This is largely thanks to our nearest neighbours, a portly family of three. Their house, garage and yard are downhill from us, just below our bedroom.

At five o'clock in the morning, Monday to Friday, they warm up their cars in the garage and yard in readiness for the big manoeuvre. Mother comes first. She guns up the engine and reverses it as fast as she can up their steep driveway and into the lane. The spare, driven by her twelve-year-old son, follows soon afterwards. Last one out is father's car, which needs to be inched out of the concrete garage and repositioned towards the slope with clunks of the clutch and shouted directions from the others. When all three cars are throbbing in the street, father honks his horn and drives away, stopping outside Nino's house to honk again for good measure. Then his wife begins shrieking at her offspring in a rolling, lolling tone that makes her sound remarkably similar to an agitated turkey. I presume she's ordering him back to the parking place, on the double — but I don't really have a clue as it's all in dialect. As is the tradition, the son takes offence, and counters with gobbles of possible abuse. When the procedure is completed they head back inside, and crash around, and screech, and gobble at each other some more, until it's time for mother to drive her stout son to school, a ten-minute walk away.

The procedure is reversed in the evening, when father returns home after a day on a building site. He honks his horn. Mother and son climb into their respective cars. They rev up the engines. They reverse. They shout for a while, then follow father's car back down the driveway and into the courtyard. Getting dad's Fiat back in the garage is a trigger for open hostilities, and we can still hear them at it when they close the front door. The bedlam only abates once they've clattered away their dinner plates, the leftovers are tipped on the driveway for the dogs, and everything is locked and bolted. This is the cue for their mongrels to start barking, which they do all through the night, until it's time for the roosters to take over the watch. It's the cacophony of the fisherman's quarter transported to the hills, and it's not what we'd expected at all.

They are only brief interruptions though, and with some positive thoughts we soon block them out.

While the weather is pleasant enough in the daytime now, as soon as the sun gets low, the cold begins to bite. We don't have a fireplace and we can't find an electric heater for sale. In the old days the locals probably slept with their animals to keep warm, but we only have a dog, and he isn't allowed in the house, let alone in our bed. All we can do is try and warm up with our arms spread wide over the gas stove, and go to bed at night with our jumpers on under five layers of blankets, like Nino and Immacolata across the laneway.

After toiling through the nights it comes as a relief to discover that our teething problems seem more surmountable in the light of day. Like a vampire, Louis tends to sleep best after the sun has risen, which at least gives his victims a chance to take a nap. Still, it's far from perfect, and we really need some advice.

Rohan is dubious about Immacolata's method for getting him to sleep through the night. She advises mashing up sweet biscuits with regular milk and feeding it to him in the evening. But he's just over three months old, and our only baby book tells us that he's far too young for solids. It also frowns on artificial sugars, and proclaims that cow's milk is best avoided until a child's at least a year old. But Immacolata insists her recipe will fill his stomach and stop him waking for top-up feeds.

Rohan politely agrees to give it a try, but she's seen the fat babies in town, pushed in strollers by overweight mothers with terrible teeth, and suspects it might be better to ask Justine for some guidance.

So, late one afternoon, just before dark, we combat the laneways in our shiny red car and head down the hill to Lipari town. We find the family crammed inside their tiny kitchen and, as soon as we enter, Orlando claps a hand around my shoulder and conducts me back outside.

'You're all invited to dinner,' he informs me solemnly as we walk towards the port. The women can stay home and chatter, about babies no doubt. He needs to get out. He's going mad stuck inside. The bar will do just fine.

We pull up some seats outside *Il Gabbiano* — the Seagull — on the landward side of a flagstone piazza running down to the sea. We're the only guests. The waiter is upon us at once.

Orlando introduces me. It'll help if I come here by myself, he says under his breath. If the waiter knows me I'll only pay the local price, instead of the tourist prices displayed on the menu.

I shake the waiter's hand, just to be sure he remembers me. Orlando orders. An *aperitivo*. Mine is alcoholic, his is not.

'I got drunk at sixteen,' Orlando tells me when I ask. 'I was sick in my bedroom, and then vomited on the boat. I told my father I was ill, maybe the influenza. When we went back home again my father found the mess in my bedroom. He screamed. He hit me! "A fisherman must never drink!" he said.'

Since then he has barely touched alcohol, which is a pity since you can buy five-litre flagons of wine in the supermarket down the road for a pittance, but probably wise if you have to get out of bed at three or four in the morning to winch up heavy baskets of shrimp in a dangerously rolling sea.

'How old were you when you started fishing?' I ask.

'Fourteen.'

'That's young.'

'I finished school.'

I bring up his son: 'Do you want Luca to work on the boat too when he's old enough?'

Orlando shakes his head. 'I want more for him. Maybe university. Fishing is dead.'

'Why?'

'Too many problems,' he shrugs.

I'm just about to ask him to elaborate when we're interrupted by the first in a stream of people he knows. He nods his head as they saunter past, or fires off some rapid dialect if they choose to make more of the situation. No one takes any notice of me, and Orlando doesn't introduce me. He's too cool for that. He only tells me who they are when they've gone. 'That one's my friend,' he says. 'That one works in the fruit shop. The short one is a fisherman too. That one's a *bastardo* … don't trust him.'

Then he spots someone else he knows strolling across the piazza. He excuses himself, gets up, and leaves me nursing my drink and some peanuts. At least it gives me the chance to appreciate my surroundings.

At this time of the evening the piazza leading to Marina Corta, the short harbour, is magical. The lights from cafés pick out pots of geraniums on shadowy balconies and shutters folded back like wings: some blue to keep out the mosquitoes, and others green to ward off the flies, depending on which you dislike most.

Directly ahead and looking out to sea is the statue of St Bartolo, the island's patron saint and the fishing fleet's mascot. Just to its right, and further back still, is a causeway that leads across the black shallows to a high-walled breakwater. This shelters the miniature port and the flaking yellow form of the Church of Purgatory, which is glowing now like a beeswax candle. From here the piazza's flagstones lead past a small pebbly beach and meet a rise of cobbled steps. They climb up to another church, also lit by lanterns. Dominating the other end of the piazza is a towering natural rock rampart, glossy with uplights of its own. These prominent high cliffs fold and crinkle upwards towards a summit topped by an imposing citadel, a stronghold flecked with columns of cypress trees.

With the wall of rock on one side, the buildings behind, the church in front, and the steps leading up to the other on your right, the place resembles an amphitheatre, with the acoustics to complement the experience. I can hear the growls of the motor scooters, more guttural than normal; the gentle swish of the sea against the slipway is louder than it should be. Though I'm quite a distance away, I can just about pick out the rumbling exclamations of some grim-lipped fishermen squatting inside their long boats, run aground for the winter on the flagstones.

If I dared to get closer I'd see that the bright stripes of paint running along the flanks of the boats are chipped and wormed and the hulls are pooled with water. I'd see the old salts playing *briscola* with a deck of cards marked with coins, cups, swords and cudgels; and I'd smell the thick tobacco smoke from their *Nazionali* cigarettes, which only leave their lips when it's time for a replacement.

If I turn around I can see the alleyways of the old town, with their small, tight-fitting houses bivouacked with generations of the same family. They are flat-roofed to collect water, and buttressed together across the divides with arches to protect them from earthquakes. It all sounds romantic, and it is, and best of all there are no tourists around to spoil it. It'll be months before the Germans are disgorged from their cruise ships, and the Swiss arrive wearing their lurid ski jackets and carrying those alpine poles they like to walk around with, as if they're expecting to confront the Matterhorn around every corner. Winter means there are no Italians from the mainland either. We'll have to wait until August, when they'll come in their tens of thousands.

'Remember you said I could fish with you?' I ask, when Orlando returns at last.

'*Si*. It's possible.'

'Great. But when?'

'The season starts in the middle of March,' he says, 'but April is the best month. Lots of *gamberetti* come then.'

But there must be things to do beforehand, I reason. 'Where's your boat now?'

'It's been out of the water since December. We'll have to repaint it soon.'

He tips his sunglasses off his nose to better see someone passing by.

'I can help,' I suggest. Doing something practical appealed to me, after years of using my mind to make a living of sorts.

Orlando nods his head: 'I'll let you know when we're about to start.'

'Are you looking forward to fishing again?' I ask.

'It's hard work,' he says without a hint of a smile. 'Very hard; and dangerous sometimes. But I need it. I can't stay at home. It makes me go crazy.'

'Crazy', 'dangerous', 'hard work' — these were experiences I tended to avoid if I could help it. But we have limited savings and I need some work, even if it's just to supplement our living costs with some seafood. As Orlando had suggested.

'He eats like a *morena*,' Orlando announces, as he watches his son ripping the flesh from a palm-sized fish with his teeth. 'You know the *morena*?'

'The moray eel,' I guess. I've seen them displayed on the fish stalls near the ferry port, alongside fresh sardines, octopus, and small stripey fish that look far too beautiful to eat. Hacked into chunks, with yellow and black slimy-looking skin, the *morena* looks like a chopped-up snake.

'Dangerous creatures,' he says. 'They get into our baskets and will bite off an octopus' arm and swim away with it, and then come back later for another one. Sometimes we pull up an octopus and all its arms are missing. Compared to a *morena* an octopus is *stupido*.

The *morena* just comes and goes when it feels hungry. The octopus just sits there eating the bait, thinking life is easy.'

He takes another fish off his plate, rubs some olive oil over its flank with a sprig of parsley, and bites into the meat above its central line. He leaves the undersides. They're too bony to fuss with.

Their toddler, little Beatrice, is crying now, and Luca is banging plates and knives. Louis is wailing to be fed again too. Orlando winces and quietly makes his exit.

'He's probably going to lock himself in the bathroom,' Justine tells us as she comforts her daughter. 'He loves the kids, but he can't take the noise.'

Justine has changed so much. Four years out of Australia and her bleached blonde hair has returned to its natural auburn. She's put on a little weight, her gestures are more exuberant, her kisses on the cheek have doubled, and she wears more make-up than she used to. Little by little this Italian outcrop has moulded her into one of its own.

She tells us that she was entranced by those first evenings under the stars, with the boats twinkling in the moonlight. She and her fisherman laughed. They walked hand-in-hand along the edge of the port, where the children jumped and squealed bare-chested into the water. Then, before she knew it, she was a mother too.

It's an unfortunate fact that romance evaporates when there are nappies to change, and you are short of cash, and the house is so small you have to sleep in the same room as your child, and there's cooking and cleaning to do, and you have to put up with twice-daily visits from your mother-in-law.

When a second child came the money got tighter, and the house seemed even smaller. In winter it was cold and noisy outside. In summer it was hot and noisier still. By the time evenings came Justine was too exhausted to care about stars or boats or walking hand-in-hand. She just wanted to sleep, alone, without being disturbed.

'At least I didn't have any problems learning Italian,' she says gamely.

It came naturally to her, and now she speaks fluently, without an accent.

'But I'm still a foreigner as far as the locals are concerned. They think I've got an attitude.'

She admits she's high-spirited, and abrasive sometimes when she thinks things aren't right. She's very attractive too, and I'm not surprised when she tells us she's caught the eye of quite a few of the island's males.

'Have you met the butcher yet?' she asks with a wicked smile. 'He's known around town for his tasty chickens.'

She laughs again.

'He knew I was married. I had kids for God's sake. But that didn't stop him. It's second nature to an Italian man to flirt. He knew nothing would come of it, but that didn't stop him looking at me for too long or giving me a cheeky comment.'

That was dangerous enough, she informs us. Jealousy is an admired quality here, and there are eyes everywhere. Every married man is on guard for the marauding male. A Sicilian proverb states: 'a smart man doesn't give his wife a lot of freedom'. Folklore warns that a virile stranger will have his way with your wife as soon as your back is turned.

To prevent this, a wise husband should never let another man into his house, unless he's family, or at least well vetted; which just about counts me in as far as Orlando is concerned.

He must also stop his wife from working outside the home, unless she's at his side in the fields, or working in the family business. She can't visit a café, either alone or with her girlfriends. She's forbidden to leave the island, even for a shopping trip. Her husband might be cuckolded.

'One of the hardest things I've had to get used to is Orlando's family and friends sending reports back to him, even if I'm just walking around town.' Justine says. 'It's not his fault. They're just protecting him. It's just the way it's done. I've even seen children acting as runners.

'In general, the more attractive a woman is, the more likely she is to leave the islands for good,' she continues. Beautiful women bring trouble, they say, so an island man usually marries the least attractive one he can find. It's no secret that some of Orlando's relatives voiced their concern when he announced he was going to marry Justine. It wasn't just because she was foreign, and might run off back home, as most of them do — much more importantly, she was far too pretty!

Rohan tells me on the way home that her talk with Justine about Louis hasn't helped much. Her own children were relatively easy and slept quite well from an early age. 'You'll just have to muddle your way through it,' Justine concluded. 'In the meantime, you should try the pizza place near you. There are plenty of good-looking waiters up there. They might help take your mind off the baby for a while.'

The pizzeria has a reputation for good food too, so a couple of days later we decide to visit. As soon as we arrive a suave-looking waiter pounces.

'*Che bel bambino*,' he announces gleefully. 'What's his name?'

'Louis,' Rohan says.

'*Lui* ...' the waiter repeats slowly. In Italian, *lui* means 'him', and it occurs to us that we can't go around referring to him as a pronoun ... it'll make us sound stupid.

Rohan tries again. 'Luigi,' she says, remembering the Italian equivalent.

The waiter is delighted and claps his hands. He has an uncle named Luigi! 'Luigi, *Madonna*!' he squeals, and gathers up a few baby fingers to press to his lips. He turns to a raven-haired young woman behind the till, and calls out, 'Maria, Maria, come and look. A baby.' He repeats himself, raising his voice even louder so Giulia out the back can hear too.

Both women drop what they're doing and scamper over. They gather around, uttering a flurry of *oohs* and *ahhs*.

'Ask what his name is,' the waiter implores excitedly. 'Go on ... ask ... ask ...'

'*Come si chiama?*' the raven-haired one pipes up, desperate to know but unable to prise herself away from the baby's eyes.

'Luigi,' Rohan says again.

There are more squeals. He's the star attraction of the night, and they take him off our hands for almost the entire meal. He's paraded around the room, held up to the television flickering and blaring away in a corner, taken on a tour of the kitchen, and rushed down the road for someone's mother to look at. It's only when we're almost finished that they return him to the table for his first taste of real food. Although we still feel he's too young, they've noticed he's been chomping his mouth in mimicry whenever he notices someone eating, so the time is right they declare, and before we can interject the waiter has dipped a finger into the remains of the tomato sauce on my plate and has rubbed the rich paste across our baby's lips. He follows it up with a smear of red wine from the dregs in my glass.

Louis seems pleased with himself as the flavours sink in, and the waiter and his workmates are beside themselves with delight ... and it's then I notice the colour of Louis' eyes. What with the drive to get here and the day-to-day procedures, I realise I've barely had time to look at him closely for a while. I don't know when they changed, but now I see his eyes are startlingly different from my memory of them. In northern Europe they were grey; that particularly dull North Sea hue that's reflected in the winter light and the cloudy skies — but now they're a striking Mediterranean blue.

Five

If the North Wind takes to blowing,
it will rain for a week.

SICILIAN PROVERB

One minute my underpants are drying nicely on the line and the next I'm being pelted by hailstones. It's something I'd never have imagined could occur on a Mediterranean island. But what surprises me more than anything was that it came on so rapidly. Ten minutes earlier the warblers were singing in the cactus groves and the sun was shining overhead. We were sitting on the terrace, reflecting on how we seemed to be living out a dream, and how in our hearts we'd always suspected our life on this island would run contrary to the experiences of the writers and poets who'd forged the mythology of the Mediterranean. But here we are, sure now that what they'd put down in words was true. Another glass of wine is called for, to toast our good luck. I walk downstairs feeling euphoric. I pour some of Nino's wine, take a sip, and catch my breath.

Just then I'm interrupted by a frantic pounding on the front door.

I find Immacolata pressed in the doorway. She greets me in a faded dress and torn stockings. I smile. She looks taken aback at my composure, then bolts out a torrent of high-pitched dialect. I grin stupidly. Then I notice the panic in her eyes and the fact she's jumping up and down on the spot, frantically pointing up in the direction of our terrace. Still puzzled, I step outside to take a look: but all I see is our whitewash wall, and a bird of prey circling lazily in the deep blue sky.

When I turn around again I find Immacolata's already hobbling back down the laneway, favouring her good hip and holding on to her headscarf.

It strikes me that her strange demeanour might have something to do with the hawk up there. Perhaps she thinks it's about to swoop down and carry off the baby or something. Maybe that happens around here. It's only when I'm back in the kitchen that the potential seriousness of the situation strikes me with a terrifying blow. While I've been idling down here anything might have happened upstairs. Perhaps Immacolata had watched as the half-completed awning toppled over, crushing Rohan and Louis to death. But no, I would have heard something. Or perhaps she saw one of them fall off the other side of the terrace, and land in the neighbour's courtyard and, finding me grinning like an idiot, she's been forced to rush off to get someone with some sense to deal with it.

I take the steps in threes, and burst back outside with my heart drumming madly. I find Louis gurgling to himself on a blanket and Rohan unpegging the washing.

'Immacolata ...' I gasp.

'Yes, I got the gist of it.'

'Of what ...?'

'She's telling us to get the washing in. Look, she's back up on her terrace over there, waving a tea towel at us and pointing at the sky. I suppose she thinks it's going to rain.'

'Well, uh, it doesn't look like there's going to be any rain to me.' I take a deep breath and slump down in an alcove, feeling the relief you do when your partner and baby haven't plummeted to their deaths.

Two minutes later I'm plugging a large plastic ventilation shaft in our kitchen with plastic carrier bags to block out the howling wind. I join Rohan and Louis under the kitchen table, sure the windows are about to be smashed in by hailstones the size of eyeballs.

For the next two weeks we're trapped inside. It rains torrentially. The wind snaps branches off olive trees and strips them of leaves. Boats launched too early in the season are torn from their moorings and dashed against the shore. Our washing hangs over the backs of chairs, and on almost every flat surface, getting mustier by the day.

When we do have a chance to step outside we emerge into a spooky backdrop of mist. We're in the clouds, and can barely see a few feet in front of us. It's a soft, spongy light, and it could be romantic — if we had a fireplace to curl up in front of; a rug to cover the cold, hard floor tiles; a dimmer switch for the dazzling fluorescent light; and a baby who didn't keep us awake all night. We try to make the best of it. We cook up thick bean stews to keep us warm, hibernate in bed whenever we can, dream out loud about the summer to come, and stare through the glass terrace doors for ages, willing a volcano or the sea to appear, all the time reminding each other this isn't England, despite the cold and the fog.

We make it to town only once, to stock up on supplies from the supermarket. The mist might not be a problem down here, but the wind and rain are still bad enough to keep most people indoors. We find the shelves almost empty, the bread shop running out of flour, the fishmonger closed. The streets are deserted, and huge waves are crashing against the sea walls. The ferries from Sicily have been cancelled, so the island's cut off, and we're all alone. And *la depressione* is taking its toll on the inhabitants.

It's a peculiar island phenomenon, this so-called depression. We hear reports that some of Orlando's brothers have suffered from it at one time or another, and rumour has it their mother has too. It can strike anyone, at anytime, though more often than not it creeps up during the worst of the winter weather, when you can be confined to the house for days on end.

It starts with uneasiness, then moves into despair. The island feels smaller. You feel hemmed in. You look around at your relationships. You question your life in general. Some people are struck down by the hopelessness of their situation, the futility of things, their isolation.

There's only one known cure: you must leave the island, head to Sicily, and be admitted to hospital. A week should do it, along with a series of injections. You shouldn't feel ashamed when people find out, which inevitably they will. After all, *la depressione* is far too commonplace to have much stigma attached to it. It's discussed openly, as well as behind people's backs, and comes up in the most normal of conversations.

In fact, on our visit to town I asked someone I'd just met if he'd ever been abroad. 'Well, not exactly abroad in the strictest sense,' he said. 'But I did spend a nice few days over on Sicily last year.'

'Really, where?'

'Oh, you probably don't know it … it's the mental ward at Messina General.'

'Ahhh.'

'Hardly ever saw a nurse, except when they came to give me the needles.'

Eleven days into the storm the stone walls in the laneway come down in the downpour and block the road. We're entirely cut off now.

Sometimes we spot Nino darting past, dripping with water, but for some reason we never follow him into his house, and no one appears to see how we are. Which in truth is not too good. We are just hanging on now. Perhaps everything's exacerbated by not enough sleep and the almost inhuman demands of our baby, but one day I wake up feeling lonely. As much as I try, I find it hard to remember what my wife was like before Louis took up her entire life. Then, unnaturally for us, the accusations begin to fly.

'Why don't you help?' she asks.

'I do! I was awake all night with him, and I babysat for a bit yesterday ...'

'You're the boy's father for goodness sake! You're supposed to spend time with him. It's not babysitting when it's your own child. It's not a favour to me.'

'I know ... that's not what I meant ...'

'What do you mean then?'

'Well, it's just that I don't feel part of a relationship any more. It used to be *us*. A couple. I thought having a baby would bring us even closer. But I just feel like I'm by myself. Alone.'

'You talk about feeling *alone*! I've got no time for anyone, not even myself. It's hard for me. You just lie around moping.'

'Because you're always on edge, even when you're asleep.'

'Because you start clomping around. You can't seem to realise that if he wakes up after only a few minutes it'll all start again. I just want to be unconscious.'

I try when I can. I cuddle him, I change his nappy when I notice it needs doing, I take him away from her and play with him, I try to put him to sleep. But he's feeding constantly and seems to cry out for his mother when he's tired. I feel unable to do more, and I'm beginning to have doubts about us coming here in the first place. At least if it were hot we could lie around on cushions on the terrace together, eating grapes, and dozing. As it is, it's just too cold, even indoors. And our house wasn't built for comfort.

The days continue, with lengthening intervals of sunshine between the squalls. To give Rohan time to sleep I try going out for walks with Louis in the buggy. But someone always spots us, and slows down their car, or runs out of a house. 'You can't take the baby out!' they cry, thrusting their arms up to heaven. 'He'll freeze to death.' I try pointing out he's dressed in four layers of clothes, has a hot water bottle in his buggy and two thick blankets. But they won't have any of it, and order me back inside.

On a couple of occasions I go out alone with the dog, far into the countryside, and up to the summit of the tallest hill. Then I catch the flu, which means I feel even sorrier for myself. I know I have to fight hard for sympathy from my partner at the best of times: she soldiers on when she's sick, whereas I tend to wallow in my illnesses, like most men.

'I have enough on my plate without having to be a mother to you as well,' I hear her mutter.

'I don't want you to be my mother!' I croak. 'I just want you to see that I'm ill!'

But it's difficult to empathise with each other when we're in survival mode. We've become desensitised to the basic things we had in our relationship. And resentment builds when we respond to each other's needs with less and less interest. Before, we would have picked up on the clues, but when we're overwhelmed, we can't see them any more. Laughter is submerged by piles of washing, and intimacy by the undervalued feeling that each of us has.

When Nino sees me coughing on the terrace, trying to hang out a few bibs and baby jump suits in a break from the rain, he clucks noisily and blames it on my impulsive walks. He's heard from someone that I've been spotted heading to the hills on days meant for staying safely at home. It's the *colpo d'aria* that made me sick, he says mysteriously: the punch of air. When I ask him to explain he tells me the winds are at their strongest and most dangerous in the hills. I was lucky to have just caught the flu. I could have been paralysed, or killed.

My battle with the flu stops me from going into town when Rohan suggests it one bleak afternoon. But Rohan reports back. Justine's upset, I'm told. Orlando refuses to leave the house. He just lies on the couch all day, while she's expected to do the housework and look after the children. It's causing arguments. He insists the housework is her duty. He'll be out on the boat soon, when spring comes, and then he'll be working hard enough to please her. Until then he's not going out, and mumbles something about the things he might catch from the wind in the alleyways, but refuses to elaborate.

A few days later I'm rugged up in several layers of clothing and tramping along the sodden tracks, deep in thought. My flu is abating at last. The soles of my boots are gathering a thick platform of mud. The rain does not bother me now that it's lost its intensity.

I take the route Nino first led me along but, this time, instead of climbing up the cliff face that threatened to do me in, I veer away and follow a gentler path. There's only one real uphill stretch, and once over the brow the land tumbles down — and there in front of me is the sea again, with Salina dominating the foreground. It looks so close you could almost lean forward and pick off the houses between your thumb and forefinger.

I'm gathering pace again. I wind downhill. And there is Nino's *casetta*. It's not much more than an oblong two-roomed storage shed made from blocks of volcanic *tufo*, like most of the buildings on the island. Inside is a plank bench. One of Nino's old jackets hangs on a nail. On the dusty floor are empty bottles, stacks of dried reeds for Nino's baskets, and stakes for plants.

The *casetta* is set in a landscape of cactus, hay and high red cliffs. Just behind it are a few bare-branched plum and apricot trees, and in front, facing the sea, are rows of dormant caper bushes. They end in a stretch of grass, nibbled short by rabbits. Beyond this is a broken edge of land that slides down into a dangerous-looking ravine. At its base, far below, the land turns to pasture, and more cliffs, before falling into the sea.

I'm drawn by its peacefulness. It's a place for new ideas. Ants crawl across patches of deep red earth. The only sound is the breeze, and the call of crows. I take to coming here whenever I can, sometimes daily. I read, and I try to write. I have a vague idea about a novel, but nothing comes when I place my pen nib to the paper. I find myself thinking of Louis instead, and the impact he's made on our lives. The closeness I thought Rohan and I would feel for each other after sharing his momentous, exhilarating birth doesn't seem to have happened. These days our relationship is based on practicalities, and we don't have the time, or perhaps the skills to nurture the real essence of what we had together. I can't remember the last time we swapped loving words. And it's difficult to make even short-term plans when the needs of a baby are so immediate. I can't help thinking that everything seems out of perspective: that the simplest things can feel like an ordeal. Going out used to mean five minutes to get your shoes on. With a baby it can take more than an hour, by which time you've often lost your impetus.

I love Louis like no one I've loved before, but I feel guilty that I'm not enjoying every second of being a parent, and guilty too that I can't seem to work out when Rohan needs my help. I try to anticipate things. I try to take Louis off her hands whenever I think about it. But I can't breastfeed. I can't stop him crying. And it makes me feel inadequate. Sometimes, I feel the easiest thing to do is to absent myself as much as I can, so I don't get in the way. It's wonderful that we've got a dog that needs walking, so at least I have an excuse. And Rohan doesn't want to take Louis out into the country so often when it's cold and drizzling.

Bit by bit the days grow longer, but the chill of winter remains in the air. One evening, as I'm coming back from a quick walk with the dog, I spot Nino walking up the laneway, bent double under a load of sticks. Later, as we're warming our hands on the flames from the gas cooker, there's a knock on the door. It's Nino again. Their house needs heating, he tells me, and they've run out of bread. So tomorrow at dawn they'll solve both problems by baking some loaves on the big wood fire. The heat it generates will keep the place warm for days. We're welcome to join him, he says. He knows from the letters he gets from his brothers in Australia that they don't do things like this in places where they can afford to waste electricity.

It's still dark when we get up and cross the laneway. Louis is awake and fed. He's kicking in his pouch on Rohan's chest, a woollen hat on his head and a blanket tucked around him. It's a tonic for us all to be going out together. We find Nino in the shadows of his courtyard, using a machete to chop thin branches of *erba bianca* — the 'white herb'. We know it as wormwood, or artemisia: a bitter-tasting perennial named for Artemis, the Greek goddess of the hunt, and of both childbirth and chastity. She carried a bow and arrow made by the god Hephaestus, or Vulcan as the Romans called him, in the forge beneath Vulcano.

The Romans knew Artemis as Diana, a name you come across all over Lipari, on hotel signs, pizza menus and archaeological sites.

I had a faint recollection that you could distil wormwood to make absinthe, the hallucinogenic liquor once popular in 19th-century France with people like Oscar Wilde and Vincent Van Gogh. They believed its effects, which include surreal, obscene dreams, inspired their work.

'Could we make a drink out of it?' I ask.

'*Certo*. Go ahead. It'll probably kill you,' Nino says nodding vigorously. 'I'll get my sickle and we'll go and cut some more. It would be an interesting experiment, *professore*.'

I observe his little dig cheerfully. I'm happy today. This is why I came here, to be with people like this, to learn, to do things out of the ordinary.

It takes Nino a couple of minutes to bind some herb sticks with bark cord, and fasten the resulting broom head to a crooked wooden pole. When he's finished we follow him into the parlour room, and out through a side doorway into the cookhouse proper. We come across a small gas cooker, a washbasin, and an enormous brick fireplace set into a wall.

Their youngest daughter, Allegria, is here already. She's a stout, spectacled woman in her mid-thirties, with a glitter of perspiration on her face. She thrusts out her hand and says hello, before she turns to fuss over her children: teenaged Emilia, and a four-year-old boy called Fabian. She adjusts their headscarves to keep loose hair from falling in the dough, then wipes her sleeve across her forehead.

Immacolata appears, dressed in a pale blue pinafore and knitted stockings. Her job is in front of the fire, and she's just in time for a load of twigs that Nino drops at her feet. She bends down with a wince and a hand on her hip, picks up a small bundle, and shoves it into the fireplace. They explode into flame, and the heat forces us all to take a few steps back.

'That's incredible!' exclaims Rohan in astonishment at the heat. She jumps back with Louis in her arms.

'*Certo*. It's been burning all night,' Nino says. 'You have to have the right temperature to make bread properly.'

'Do you use a thermometer to measure it?' I ask stupidly.

There's a peal of laughter. 'I'm not a nurse,' he says. 'Put your hand in and see how hot it is for yourself. No? OK, I'll tell you. It's the wood. You have to use the proper mixture of wood. Olive mostly, white herb and mulberry. Then you have to stay up all night and keep feeding the fire when it gets hungry.'

'And you stayed up?'

'Of course. You wouldn't find these two,' he nods mischievously in the direction of his wife and daughter, 'missing out on their beauty sleep. Look at these wrinkles.' He uses both hands to paw at his cheeks. 'I don't spend the nights dreaming like some people.'

Immacolata toys with a dangling earring and flashes her perfectly white teeth. 'But I dream only of you,' she says with a giggle.

Nino snorts with laughter. They're obviously devoted to each other. They show it all the time: holding hands, rubbing each other's shoulders, bantering ... 'She's the queen of the house,' he'll say frequently, and he's 'the master of the land. This is how it should be.'

The flames have died down by now, and the bricks inside the fireplace are glowing white-hot. Immacolata is reaching for more sticks when the formidable form of her oldest daughter blocks the doorway. I recognise her, just, from a wedding picture on the wall in our bedroom. Paolina is beefier than back then, with an imposing bosom and arms good for pounding dough and giving headlocks. The children retreat into a corner as soon as they see her.

'Let's get to it,' she barks, rolling up her sleeves, and we trail behind as she bowls through a couple of swing doors and into the kneading room.

Here we find a rough, home-made bed base, with a thin straw mattress peeking out from below a pair of crisp white sheets. On a table nearby is a smooth wooden trough.

Paolina hauls a large sack of flour off the concrete floor and nearly knocks Rohan off her feet as she swings it towards the table. She pours some into the trough, and bullies young Emilia into fetching some water. 'Come on, come on, jump to it,' she bellows, 'and fix that headscarf, your hair's poking through.'

Emilia hurries to the sink and fills a plastic bowl with water. But it's too heavy for her and water splashes over its edge as she struggles to lift it.

'Watch it!' Paolina shouts, as Emilia's glasses slip down her nose. She tuts loudly as Emilia holds out the bowl unsteadily. 'It's not even full! What am I supposed to do with this?'

She grabs it anyway, and pours it slowly into the middle of a heap of flour.

'Fetch me some more, a full one this time!'

I see tears magnified behind Emilia's thick lenses, but her mother and grandmother say nothing, and I notice that Nino has bolted.

Then Paolina turns her eyes on me.

'Stand closer,' she menaces, in a voice like a gravel crusher. 'You can't expect to see anything back there.'

I trip forward like a frightened schoolgirl, with my head going like a nodding dog.

More flour, some yeast and more water, and Paolina judges it's time to squeeze it together until it congeals and begins to flake.

Emilia pours in another slop of water, and Paolina fists the dough like a boxer. She pummels away for several minutes, barely working up a sweat, and when she's sure the dough is beaten she manhandles it out of the trough and carries it across the room, bent backwards with the weight.

Thunk! She drops it down on a wooden board.

She sprinkles more flour. Batters the dough a bit longer. Tears off pieces the size of boxing gloves. Then carries each lump back to the trough for Allegria to press and fold some more. When she's content that the dough is the right texture at last, Paolina whips into the giant dough balls with a knife, rolls sections out into snakes, then twists and cuts again. Each serpent has produced six knobs of dough just the right size for bread rolls. She orders Emilia to deposit them on the far end of the bed, and cover them with a top sheet.

'Not like that! I told you to line them all up. They're all over the place. Now, see that batch at the end, move it over a bit, yes that's right.'

Once the rolls are done it's time for the loaves. Paolina cuts more dough, and weaves some into plaits. In Sicily and the Aeolian Islands, bakers are famous for sculpting dough. They make nativity scenes, the faces of saints, swords, crosses, palm fronds, sheep and fish. Each locality has its distinctive forms, often linked to a religious event or the veneration of a local patron saint. Paolina's offerings are made with feeling and appetite, and come in the shape of hands with one raised finger; or of breasts, complete with pointy nipples that she joyfully tweaks for the laughter it brings.

As I watch her work, I wonder how we ever got ourselves into the position of spending good money on industrially manufactured, plastic-wrapped pseudo-bread with its various dough conditioners, firming agents, anti-caking agents, preservatives and emulsifiers.

The bread needs an hour to rise, so while the sisters clean up, Immacolata prepares coffee. When it's ready we retreat to the formal kitchen, where we find Immacolata's mother, the Nonna, sitting quietly on her favourite chair. She's ninety years old and only speaks dialect; but she's intent on telling us the story of her life.

Allegria is called for. She can translate the dialect into Italian and some broken English.

We find out that before the war the Nonna worked in the pumice mines near Aquacalda — an hour away by foot, she tells us. The mine belonged to her husband's uncle (you can see the ruins of it today on the coast road, near the ones that are still working). They use the pumice for soaps, metal polishes, building materials and talcum powder. So much of the finest white dust ended up on the sea floor beneath the mines that the water is as green as an emerald.

But the Nonna had no time to appreciate the beauty she was helping to create. She'd set out before dawn, with a stick to ease the uphill climb, her way lit by a lantern. She would meet her husband on top of the hill, coming back from the night shift. She'd give him a bag containing his dinner. He'd kiss her on the cheek before walking home alone. Soon she'd be hacking away at the pumice with a pick.

All was to change when war came. Her husband was sent away to fight the Russians on the Eastern Front, while she raised five children, and poultry, and tended a small field of wheat. So many people, snatched from their land, were desperate for food. She sold beans, meat and bread. Eggs were hatched, chickens raised. Soon she'd saved enough money to buy another patch of dirt, and then more still, this time with a few olive trees.

Her husband was a broken man when he returned. But over the years, he still had strength enough to help her enlarge the shack, room by room as each child came. He died years ago, and now she lives in a back room. Immacolata looks after her, and Nino supplies her with food from the land.

It soon becomes clear that the old woman adores Louis, and she insists on holding him, while reminiscing about her own children when they were young. She vomited for the entire nine months of her first pregnancy, she tells us. The child was born weighing little more than a kilo. She'd delivered it herself. In those days there wasn't a doctor on the island, and midwives had to be fetched from Lipari town by donkey.

The fire has died down now and the dough has risen. It's time to bake. Nino inserts the brush he's made into the fireplace and sweeps the ashes away, and the room fills up with a pungent smell of herbs. The *erba bianca* will add a distinctive bitter taste, he tells us. It also increases your appetite.

The doughy loaves and rolls are already in the baking room, ready to be placed on a wide wooden paddle and put into the oven. A few minutes later and they all come out again. They end up in a couple of large wicker baskets. Some will be shared out among the extended family and eaten fresh over the next few days, though most of the rolls are broken into pieces and go back in for a second baking. They end up hard and crispy and will last until the next baking day in four weeks' time. The locals dip these in minestrone, and Nino takes a few hunks out into the fields with him to plunge into a glass of red wine. Otherwise you can soak them in water, and then leave them to dry a little. They'll taste almost as if they've been freshly made.

Immacolata gives us an armful each, and a couple of fresh loaves too, and as we walk away we feel like we're taking some of the warmth of the oven with us, back to our place overlooking the sea.

Six

Our life is frittered away by detail.
Simplify, simplify.

HENRY DAVID THOREAU

In March you can gather wildflowers in armfuls. First up
are the canary yellow sour-sob bells that cover the roadside
verges and mass beneath the olive trees. Then, as we rush
towards spring, tiny bright sequins pop up around rabbit
warrens and alongside country tracks, and wild sweet peas,
iris and pink field gladioli emerge among drifts of wild oats
and the pale beehive seed capsules of great quaking grass.
Sometimes on our walks, we strike out across the sea
bluffs, crushing dense mats of tiny sweet alyssum flowers
beneath our boots, sending wafts of honey into the air. At
night, when it's black and cloudless, we're struck by the
brilliance of the stars, the boat lamps in the darkness, and
the electric flashes of storms hovering over Sicily.

It's the end of winter, and imagination flourishes. When we look at leafless vine-arbours we see shade and grapes. In our minds the air drones with cicadas. There's the scent of jasmine and pine, and tangy hot skin.

In anticipation of the companionship summer always brings, Nino places an upturned log under the white mulberry tree, so passers-by can sit down for a chat and stretch out a hand to pluck a few creamy berries. Among the first to rest here is an old man who lives in one of the houses in our little group. He sits with Nino, content to watch the chickens scrabbling for fallen fruit and flicking dust over their glistening red feathers. Sometimes we spot his housekeeper, a Polish woman, paid to look after him by his family in Australia. Nino winks slyly when she's out of earshot. He's sure she takes care of the old man's needs in more ways than one, he says with a mischievous chuckle.

Next to pull up at the log is Maria, who lives just down the laneway. She's well over eighty. She wears shoes made from two bits of leather she's stitched together herself, and stashes a sickle in the cord of her housecoat. We see her most mornings, leading a giant, shaggy donkey that she ties to a fig tree in a little stretch of pasture near our house. 'It won't last long,' Nino observes one day as it trots slowly past with its head bent. 'That *sceccu* is over forty,' he continues, using the Sicilian word for her ragged grey animal. 'But she loves it so much that she'll end up feeding it porridge with a spoon.'

In town the air is still, and warming up. People are sweeping their steps, pulling back the shutters, and greeting each other as though they've been away for months. There's optimism about, as if the approaching spring could herald the best summer they've ever had. Strangers, who see us as the first tourists, greet us like the swallows that are flying in across the sea, and waiters in newly opened cafés try out their overblown prices and wait for our reaction. A frown and they give us a discount. No response and the prices are set for the summer.

The fishmonger's trying his luck too. Justine's gone out of her way to introduce us so we'll be charged local prices, and that's his cue to demand more than it says on the receipt. It's a tax dodge, he explains with a grin. If we're pounced on by the *guardia finanzia* and asked how much we paid, he expects us to lie and show them the false receipt.

I'm not sure this is a good idea. From what I've heard the *guardia finanzia* are tax clerks with military uniforms and sub-machine guns who have the right to walk into your office at any time and perform an unannounced audit, or hold you up outside a shop and demand to see your docket. The fishmonger touches his nose when he sees my smile falter. 'We're all in it together,' he says.

There are several reasons why Italians of all classes regard the idea of revealing their full income and paying the necessary taxes as laughable in its naïveté. You can argue all you like about Italy being a relatively new country, and about most people believing that most officials are corrupt, but if you look at it from the theory of an apple then it all makes sense.

If you and your close relations are the pips, your extended family is the core, your friends the flesh, and your local community the skin, then everyone else is an outsider. You can afford to give outsiders a bit of a nibble on occasion, but if you allow them all to take the bite they are after then the apple would be gone before you knew it.

Elsewhere in town, Louis is the centre of attention. Several times a minute we hear an intake of breath and a '*Che bello*!' as we walk down the street. Hands reach for his, or stroke his hair. Rough-looking ferrymen pinch the flesh on his arms, and small-hipped mothers, who barely come up to Rohan's shoulders, comment on the shape of his skull. 'It's round!' they squeal: and compared to the conical crowns of their babies it is. 'How ever did you squeeze it out?' these women cry with their hands on their cheeks. '*Mamma mia.*'

In time we can predict their more usual questions, and our responses become automatic. 'A boy,' we say before they even ask his sex. 'Yes, he's heavy too. Yes, you're right, he does have a round head.' And we learn not to bite at adverse comments. 'He's too hot to lie on that sheepskin! In this weather! Where are his shoes? He's barefoot! *Madonna*!'

The sun seems to have affected some people more than others, and the most obvious change occurs to the woman in the bakery. On our rare trips to her shop in winter she'd been sour-faced and distant. Now she's obsessed with Louis, and rushes outside when she sees us coming. She stuffs pieces of roll in his mouth and plays with his fingers, telling us over and over how sweet he is, and how she'd like to steal him away. Now she's out in the fresh air she might as well light up a cigarette. 'Isn't it funny,' she says, 'how he pulls a face when I blow smoke into his eyes?'

Down at Canneto, the island's most popular beach, the larger fishing boats have spent the winter up on wooden stocks. Among them is the one I hope to be working on soon: the MSS *Levante*. After a season's fishing and a winter in dry dock its paint has faded, and worms have left trails in its wood. But from the beautiful curve of its hull and its sturdy decks it looks like a vessel we can rely on.

It's mid-morning now and unshaven fishermen with large Roman noses and skin the colour of ripening olives are crawling all over it. One is halfway up the side of the hull on a ladder, with a paint tin dangling from his mouth. Two more are on deck working with brushes, and Arturo, the oldest of Orlando's brothers and Nino's son-in-law, is sitting on the pebbles, smoking a cigarette.

My feet crunch over the shingles as I walk towards him, and he greets me with a slow, almost embarrassed smile. I look at him carefully. He's a stocky man with a five-day growth, unkempt speckled grey hair, and a face beaten about by the wind. He half-reaches out his hand, and folds it gently around mine, as if he's shielding an injured bird ... and I like him immediately. Next in line is the second oldest, Rocco. He has proud, almost cold eyes. He shakes my hand in a pistol grip and turns away without a word. There's a nod from red-cheeked Raimondo, the youngest, who's brushing orange paint onto a short wooden plank, and a little bow from fat Giacomo, a silent, unassertive fellow with an innocent grin.

The brothers have been working as a team for many years, and I wonder how they'll accept me as part of the crew. From what I've heard from Orlando the money's tight. Their father owns the boat, and takes a sixth share from the sale of the catch, despite never fishing alongside them himself. In a good week they can make a decent wage, but the cash is whittled down by bad weather and the long winter lay-off, when the crustaceans scatter and retreat to the depths. Orlando might have only promised the odd bag of shrimp, a few small fish, or an octopus now and again — enough to keep some food on our table — but I know I'll have to apply myself from the start, to ward off any suggestions I might just be on a working holiday, or worse still, a freeloader.

So when an old coffee tin filled with thick grey paint comes my way, I grab it, greedy for as many experiences as I can get. I start on a section of the tall railings running around the boat's bow. I paint for an hour, moving as quickly as I can, determined to impress them, to show them I can be an asset. All this time I barely look up to admire the surroundings. But when an oily *espresso* appears I stretch my back and finally take a good look around. It's an impressive sight. Behind us is a curve of apricot buildings lit by the sun, with balconies of geraniums above the arched doorways of *gelaterias* and bars. Banking up beyond are barren-looking hills and sudden drops of land overgrown with reeds and red oleander. Whitewashed houses are chalked up here and there, and all look down on the boats and the beach, and across the pale blue sea to the island of Panarea.

On a clear day, like this, you can see the lonely volcanic cone of Stromboli too, suspended above the sea by a thick cord of smoke. It has a violent nature, this powerful volcano, and on moonless nights you can watch it from the beach, pulsing hot and red in the darkness. Sometimes the boys fish around its coastline. They pull up their baskets as the lava shoots out of the caldera with tremendous booms, before slugging down the volcano's ravaged flanks, to splutter in the sea. Stray rocks and boulders have almost sunk the boat before, so they stay as far away from this upheaval of a coastline as they can. But when the shrimp are gathering in the shallows you have to take your chances.

The boys are sitting or leaning now, puffing on fresh cigarettes. Orlando hands out some tiny *biscotti* hinting of vanilla and covered in sesame seeds. They're dull to taste, and dry, but perk up and soften when poked through the reddish-brown foam which floats on the surface of our coffee shots.

The mood onboard is almost joyful. They see this boat as their saviour. Not only has it long protected them in the physical sense, it has also insulated them from having to leave the island to seek out a job, as so many have been forced to do. It also keeps them sane. With winter just about over they will soon be at sea, and then they'll be liberated from their wives and children.

'All she talks about is shopping,' says one, shaking his head. 'She's always spending money and telling me what else we should buy.'

'They think we're rich,' says another. 'And the kids cry with their hands outstretched or their arms around my legs and tears on their cheeks! Making noise, always making noise.'

For most of the fishermen, the days when they are waiting, and not working, are empty, like living a half-life. The weeks pass changelessly. They have nothing to do. They're restless, bored. So they quarrel with their wives and scold their kids. When you are out at sea you can see the bad weather coming, but with kids and wives it's constant turmoil. For these fishermen, their preferred home is their boat.

I don't tell them about my life up in the hills, and they don't ask about how I'm coping as a father. I'm not sure what I'd be able to tell them anyway. All I know is that when Louis lies on my chest I feel like he's part of me. But he's a part I need to escape from too, sometimes. I find it just so overwhelming. Rohan told me last night that she's desperate for a break too, a lengthy one, but Louis refuses to drink breast milk from a bottle, so she can't leave him too long, and he seems hungry most of the time. He's reliant on her, and she has no choice but to live her life through him. As for Rohan and me, at least we're still friends, even if we are tending to paper over the cracks.

Arturo is amused by the revelations coming from his brothers, even though he's heard them so many times before. He's different, and everyone knows it. He likes his family life, and the little vegetable plot where he grows his tomatoes. But Arturo's dabbling in the mud is starting to upset some of the others, and Orlando, who has never planted anything, is particularly worried. 'He spends too much time in his garden,' he says. 'When we need something doing on the boat, or someone to help fix the baskets, he's hardly ever there. I think we're losing him.' And he shakes his head. 'You're either a farmer or a fisherman,' he continues. 'Gardening and fishing don't mix. It's like pasta. Put cheese on a seafood sauce and you end up with something that's neither one thing nor another, just confusion.'

I chuckle to myself as I listen to his concerns. From what I've heard, Arturo's garden is tiny, and though he might help Nino from time to time, in an amateurish sort of way, it seems silly to be so concerned just because he grows a few tomatoes on a miserly plot of soil.

'I like the idea of farming too,' I say. 'You know Nino's offered us some produce if we help him out now and again?'

Orlando tries not to wince. 'You must choose,' he warns, but when he sees I can't fathom the significance of what he's saying, he smiles, and tells me I'll find out for myself. Then he directs me towards my next task: the anchor.

I take to it gladly, and as I work my brush I find I'm contented up here on this wooden deck. Life is simple: paint and sea, the rattle of pebbles on the shoreline, the sun on my neck, and the coffee still lingering in my mouth. I feel as if I'm painting my own giant model of a boat, like the ones I made from kits of plastic as a child.

When the anchor is finished Orlando moves me on again, this time with a tin of blue paint for the aft deck. I work rapidly, brushing and dabbing, steadily moving towards Rocco, who's working on the port side. We reach the stern together. I stretch and smile, happy with my progress. Rocco ignores me, calls out to Orlando for a cigarette, then sends me down the ladder to help Arturo with the dirtiest job of all.

I find him squirting hydrochloric acid over the propellers beneath the boat, to remove a build-up of rust. We attack them together with scrubbing brushes, holding our breaths and ducking out now and again to escape the fumes.

'*Basta*,' Arturo says when we finally wash the acidic foam away with buckets of seawater. 'Enough for a day. It's almost lunchtime.'

The boys clean up methodically, picking up rubbish from around the boat, slowly passing up tools and buckets, and pulling down the ladder. The paint on the railings and the internal skirting will dry while we eat and sleep. Tomorrow we'll come back for the engine room and the deck. There's no need to hurry, there's no pleasure in being impatient. Each job has its allotted time, and none is more important than lunch, which Orlando is organising on his mobile phone. 'We'll be back in ten minutes,' he says, simply, and rings off. There's no need to say anything more, and when we arrive at his place Justine has the pasta *al dente* and on the plate.

The MSS *Levante* is finished by the end of the week, a day earlier than planned. I'd like to think it was because of my help, but Rocco soon dampens my cockiness. I'm fast, he says, just not thorough enough. He juts his chin in the direction of the sea. He tells me that whenever he looks at me I'm always gazing out across the water and dreaming. I'm a little put out, but when I raise the issue with Orlando he tells me straight that Rocco likes me. It's just that he's careful, and wants me to know my place. An apprentice who gets cocky over his painting might do the same when he's letting out the shrimp baskets, and before I know it, I'll make a mistake, get my arm caught in a rope, and be dragged overboard and down into the depths. The sea's brutal. Lose concentration for a second and it'll have you.

Two days later the boat is ready to launch. When I arrive at Canneto the boys are milling around on the pebbles, getting ready to remove the wooden stocks that have held the boat up all winter. A large mechanical digger is approaching the MSS *Levante*'s stern from the sea, with the teeth of its scoop pushing a long, indented wooden rail as wide as a house plank. Slowly the rail slips beneath the boat, an inch or so below the base of the hull. More pushing and it's soon poking out past the end of the bow. The boys knock out the stocks with heavy mallets and the boat settles down on the rail, then the digger moves around to face the water. The scoop is lowered again, and slowly the MSS *Levante* is edging seawards. At the last moment Rocco hauls himself up the ladder and climbs onboard. The rail digs deeper into the clear water and the loose pebbles beneath, and the MSS *Levante* lifts itself up and begins to float. Rocco starts the onboard engine, and we watch it slowly turn, a bobbing clown, with its salmon pink cabin, red and white hull, and skirtings coloured a Mediterranean blue. Rocco will steer it around to its summer port, in front of the cafés in Marina Corta. They won't go fishing until they're sure about the weather. Until then there's plenty for me to do up in the hills, and Nino has asked us to help dig up the potatoes tomorrow morning. We can have as many as we want. If it's a good harvest we might have enough to see us through summer.

We leave the house before eight and soon find Nino swinging a mattock with a basket half full of potatoes behind him.

'Ah. Here at last,' he says, wiping his brow with a dirty shirt cuff. 'I've been searching high and low for you. Where've you been? It's close to finishing time.'

'We were in bed.'

'A bad night,' Rohan adds, looking down at Louis, who's smiling sweetly in his buggy. But today promises adventure, which makes us both happy.

'You should spend less time under the covers, then you'd get a better night's rest,' Nino laughs, pleased with himself as he jiggles his hips.

I smile, as I'm expected to, though in truth I yearn even for a kiss from her. I'm not even sure what Rohan would do if I tried. She'd probably push me away. I've asked her why we don't kiss any more. She told me I always seemed to be sick — either getting over something or coming down with something. She was exaggerating, of course, but there was some truth in this. She had no space in her life for illness. With a baby to look after round the clock, getting sick would just mean she had to do it all while feeling lousy. I understand her anxiety and it makes perfect sense. But I miss her.

She is so in love with him. It's a love affair, with all the hardships that any love affair entails. But physically, emotionally, intellectually, everything going to Louis has been ripped away from our relationship.

'At least *he's* got energy,' Nino hurries on, pointing at Tetley, who's straining at his lead, desperate to get at the potatoes in the basket.

'He's always got plenty of that,' Rohan says.

'Release him,' commands Nino, with a wave of his hand.

'He'll go straight for the potatoes. He'll think they're balls.'

'Then give him a taste of this first,' he says, picking out one from the basket and throwing it our way. When it lands at my feet I notice it's bright green, turned toxic by exposure to the sun.

'Go on, *professore*,' Nino calls out. 'Let him have a bite.'

I unclip the lead from Tetley's collar. He pounces, and almost as soon as he's grabbed the potato he's dropped it again.

'It's poisonous, and he knows it,' Nino says. 'He won't go near a potato again.'

The dog rushes off, still eager to show off his retrieving skills, and returns a while later, this time with what looks like a gnarled piece of root in his mouth. Slowly he lets it fall across my boots. I recognise the significance of his offering. I've seen plenty of them around, so there's no doubt about it: it's the trunk of one of Nino's caper bushes. And by the look of it it's really old. Tetley must have ripped the thing straight out of the ground.

I look up, alarmed by my discovery. Fortunately, Nino has his back to me.

My hand darts down, and I toss the caper plant over my shoulder and into a thicket of bramble, just in time.

Nino turns around as Tetley scurries off again.

'Are you watching or not?' he asks.

'Of course,' I respond, but there's something in my tone, and my cough, that makes him suspicious. He keeps his eyes on me for a second or two then turns around again to demonstrate once again how he uses the mattock's prongs to pull up the potatoes. A few creamy tubers appear. Most are as small as eggs, but two are large enough to cut into decent-sized chips. He knocks them towards us with the blunt end of the tool. 'You just pick them up and throw them into the basket,' he says. 'Not too difficult. When it's full, fetch another from my three-wheeler up there on the track.'

I work beside Nino on the plot, upturning dozens of potatoes, while Rohan sits on a rug and rattles toys with Louis. I look over at them occasionally as I work and, each time I do, I'm struck by the fact that he is my son, part of me, and that my beautiful wife chose me above everyone else. I start to feel like the companionship I'm missing might not be gone forever.

Digging up potatoes is hard going, though I'm enjoying the smell of the earth and the thuds of the mattock. But in the end Tetley's excited barking starts to become a distraction. He's probably spotted the caper plant in the bushes and can't get at it, but when I finally walk over to investigate I'm startled to find a huge black snake. It's curled around a branch sticking out of a thicket.

My instinct is to grab the dog by the collar and run, but then I realise the brambles are protecting us, and that the snake's jaws are busy pinning the hindquarters of a rat, which is squeaking in panic and desperately struggling to get away.

I dash back to the field to get the others.

'What is it?' Nino asks.

'*Serpente*,' I say, excitedly.

But before he's reached the middle of the potato patch, Nino spins on his heels again and wanders off in the opposite direction.

Rohan is soon beside me, with Louis in her arms. She's as entranced by the spectacle as I am.

Nino reappears before long, carrying a long cane pole he's cut from a patch nearby. He gently pushes the cane towards the struggling creatures. I'm convinced he's going to move a few branches away to give us an even better look. Or maybe he's going to help the rat escape.

Instead, he judges the length, flicks his wrist, and the end of the cane whips gently across the snake's upper vertebrae.

The reptile drops the rat and begins to thrash and coil around itself. A few seconds later it slips off the branch and crashes through the bramble bush.

I stand there in disbelief, then turn to Nino, and find him proudly holding the cane out for our inspection. I notice the bark has been stripped away just below the tip, leaving a bright-green notch where his sickle has been at work.

'What happened?' I ask.

'The sap is poisonous,' he responds. 'It causes paralysis on contact.'

'Will it die?' Rohan stammers.

'*Si. Morto.*' Dead already.

I stand for a moment, too shocked to be indignant about his disregard for life. The only excuse he can possibly have is that the snake is venomous but, when I ask him if it is, Nino shakes his head. All the island's snakes are harmless, he says. They barely have teeth.

'Then why did you kill it?'

He curls up his lips in a grimace. Sometimes when he's sleeping out here — he points to his corrugated shelter — he can hear them, the *serpenti*, slithering. One time he woke up with one sliding across his face. There are thousands of them. Especially in spring.

'How can you rest and dream in a place if it's full of snakes?' he asks. 'This place is for me, not snakes! It's come from me. It's grown out of me.'

I'm struck by this, but any thoughts to pursue the matter are swamped by regret. If I'd only known, I would have kept the snake secret, to protect it. I try not to judge Nino too harshly. I'm an outsider. I haven't earned the right to criticise.

So we continue working, until the potato patch is stripped and the baskets are full and loaded in the three-wheeler's tray.

Nino zips off. We follow on foot.

Back in the laneway Rohan decides to leave us. She's tired after such an eventful outing, and Louis needs changing. I offer to do it myself.

'Don't worry. You do the next one,' she says. 'I know you want to spend some time with Nino.'

She nods towards her chest, where Louis is kicking wildly in his pouch. 'I'd better go. He's really on the nose.'

Back in the barn below Nino's house we sort potatoes. Those too small or bruised or green or damaged by the mattock are put aside for the chickens. The rest are laid out in various sizes to dry on the floor.

We can help ourselves to as many as we want, Nino says, when we are finished: to anything he grows, in fact.

'*Grazie infinite.*'

'You might want this though,' he says, and reaches down into his trousers. He pulls something out, and I recognise it at once. It's the caper plant from earlier. He must have found it somewhere, or maybe Tetley brought it to him when I wasn't looking. My jaw drops and I ferret for excuses: 'I … um … well …'

He waves two fingers in a chopping motion, diplomatically gesturing to me to cut my explanation short. Instead, he scoops out a few bright blue crystals from a small tin box, throws them in a bucket, and carries it over to a tap. He adds some water and drops the ancient stick into the mixture. When he's sure it's impregnated with the chemical he winks — I'm forgiven. 'The plant was generations old,' he says. 'Probably time to plant a new one anyway.' Then he tosses the green-stained stick towards the dog, tied by the lead to a hitching ring once used for donkeys. Tetley jumps for it instinctively — but from then on, in the dog's mind at least, every warty stick he sees in the fields tastes of the algaecide that Nino uses to clean his water tanks.

Over the next couple of weeks we see plenty more snakes: black ones and green ones, all on the lookout for a mate after a long winter's hibernation. They rustle through the drying grasses that nuzzle up to the pathways and sun themselves on the country tracks. There have even been times when I've turned a corner too quickly and almost stepped on one. Rohan hates them, but she rarely comes out with me on my walks with the dog, especially if I volunteer to take Louis along with me for an hour or so. She prefers having some time alone, to reclaim something of herself.

Seven

Know'st thou the land where
lemon-trees do bloom,
And oranges like gold in leafy gloom;
A gentle wind from deep blue heaven blows,
The myrtle thick, and high the laurel grows?
Know'st thou it, then?

GOETHE

Lunchtime is spent on our terrace, with ragwort flowers in a jar between us. They are simple weeds, their yellow centres crawling with tiny beetles: but no well-bred rose could be grander. Tonight we have a chunk of *Piacentinu*, a sheep's-milk cheese flavoured and coloured with saffron; a handful of small salted capers; oregano leaves torn from their stems just minutes ago; a lemon from Nino's tree; some local olive oil, pungent and green; and clusters of wrinkled tomatoes from Nino's barn, where they've been hung all winter to air. Easy meals like these, with a glass of wine and a clump of bread, are all we need on a slow afternoon like this.

Unusually, Louis has had a good night. He was up just twice, and we had nearly five hours' sleep. The change in us today is remarkable. We are positive for once. We see a way out of the tunnel. Maybe it was just a stage that Louis was going through: perhaps one of those growth spurts Justine mentioned a while ago. Perhaps that was why he was so demanding. The relief that he might be over it is palpable.

The only thing missing on such a glorious day is seafood. It seems logical that on an island, with so many boats around, fish would be cheap. But everything turns out to be more than twice as expensive as back home, which makes seafood a delicacy and something to look forward too. Even though we've agreed to take our local fishmonger's dodgy receipts, we guess we're still paying above the odds.

The fishmonger spent years working on a fishing boat in southern Australia before returning home, so we feel we can use the comparison to ask him straight out why our squid rings cost so much, despite the lower standard of living here.

'You have to pay the fishermen,' he says, 'and the wholesaler, and then there's us. The other shop might be a little cheaper —' he's referring to the competition around the corner '— but it's nothing more than a clearing-house. They keep their fish in salt water! Ours is on ice, so the fish is much better quality. But water's expensive, you see

— they ship it over in tankers from Italy because we have no lakes or rivers — and you need water to make ice.'

It seems a bit of a lame excuse, especially since I know the boys complain about the money they get for their catch, but we're forced to swallow it. Justine shops here, and she introduced us, so now we're committed. We've been warned it would cause great offence if the fishmonger heard we were shopping for seafood somewhere else, and even Justine might lose her discount just because she introduced us.

But one day we come close to dropping him once and for all. I am standing outside the shop, minding the buggy and the dog, while Rohan queues inside.

After a while she hurries out, with no fish.

'What happened?' I ask.

'I just watched a woman in front of me buy a large snapper. I saw him ring up the till and hand her a receipt. Then I went to buy a fish half the size, and he tried to charge me twice as much as her!'

'What did you say?'

'Nothing.'

'Why not?'

'I didn't want to make a scene.'

'So you just walked out?'

'What else could I do?'

When we mention the incident to Justine she tells us it happens all the time. There's nothing underhand about it. Perhaps the woman works in a shoe shop and gives him a good deal on slippers. Or maybe her husband's a mechanic and once fixed his scooter for free. You never know. The fact is, we don't have any produce or favours to swap, and even though we live here, and have gained the fishmonger's trust enough for him to ask us to break the law for him, we'll continue to pay the fixed price until we can offer him something more solid than helping him dodge tax, which is in any case expected of us as members of the community.

At least be glad we're getting fresh stuff when we buy from him, she adds: because he knows us he won't try to pass off anything that's on the turn. 'Anyway, you're supposed to be going out with Orlando soon, aren't you?' she reminds me. 'Then you won't have to rely on the fishmonger at all.'

Yes, but when? The boys have been out there for over a week now, from the middle of the night until lunchtime, pulling up baskets of shrimp from around the coast of Filicudi. The problem is, Orlando is convinced the sea is too rough for me, and the journey too long and hard. From three in the morning to three in the afternoon the boat pitches and rolls, he tells me. It's a battle all the way. You use all your energy just trying to stand. He sways when he's back home, standing in the kitchen. Sometimes they even lose control of the boat.

I'm disappointed, but he tells me they'll be fishing around a closer island soon, and if the weather stays good I can join them. In the meantime, he says, why don't I meet him down at Marina Corta tomorrow when the boat comes in?

I arrive early. The harbour is crowded with boats. Little squid hunters are lined up beside tuna and swordfish catchers, their decks loaded with bales of red fishing nets.

I linger around the shallow water's edge, watching tiny fish pick at the filleted skeletons on the bottom. Then I sit on a mooring post flecked with thick globules of dry blue boat paint and look out at the horizon. A short time later I see a vessel approaching at speed. As it grows nearer I deduce from its bow waves that it must be an *aliscafo*, but as it grows larger I recognise the pink cabin. It's the MSS *Levante*.

It skirts past the hydrofoil terminal and runs behind the breakwater and the Church of Purgatory and the motor slows as it nudges into port.

The boys look wretched. Their hair is tousled and dark bags hang under their eyes, but some of them still manage to give me a cheery wave as they draw closer. Raimondo throws out the anchor. There's the rattle of chain, a puff of black smoke. The smell of warm engine and old fish fills the air. Excited gulls jostle overhead.

For a few seconds the boat drifts as the boys make up their minds where to moor. Then Arturo clunks the engine into reverse and turns the boat around. He threads it between two small boats and Orlando lurches forward and steps out onto the wharf. Raimondo throws out a mooring rope.

'How was it?' I ask eagerly.

'We're happy,' Orlando says wearily, with a cigarette between his lips. 'We've got plenty of shrimp, and lots of cuttlefish, and some squid and octopus.'

'Good money?'

'*Si*. For once.'

He turns away abruptly to help Rocco and Arturo unload the catch. There are six large boxes in all, covered in towels to hide the contents from anyone who might be too interested in their business, and some heavy plastic shopping bags.

A carter loads up the boxes and wheels them across the piazza to the storeroom. Orlando beckons me to follow, to watch the weighing in a building at the edge of the square.

The wholesaler whips away the towels and the boys stand there, silent and expressionless, as the buyer casts his eye over the orange-striped shrimp.

They'll be sold on from here, mainly to the island's restaurants, where they'll be added sparingly to creamy dishes and feasted upon by the wealthiest islanders and the first of the tourists to make it this far south.

'You must try one raw,' Orlando says as he collects a few shrimp that have fallen on the floor. He pulls the head off one, squeezes the flesh out of the carapace with his fingers, and slips it into his mouth. I'm initially reluctant, but follow his lead, and as I chew I'm nicely surprised. The shrimp is as sweet as a grape.

'I have to stop myself eating them out at sea,' Orlando says, 'otherwise I'd eat them all.'

In the last two boxes are varieties of fish so small it's hardly worth gutting them before they're fried. Some are thin and silvery, others more bulbous and banded with pinks and tangerines. They have gaping mouths and large clear eyes. The most striking of all though are those streaked with lemon. You wouldn't see prettier creatures on a coral reef, and it seems a pity they've fetched up here, headed for somebody's fork.

Then one of the plastic bags is thrust under my nose. Inside are grey octopus hoods, and glistening, slimy arms and tentacles. I glimpse the stiffened bodies of cuttlefish in another, and the bulging black eyes of dozens of squid. There's a conger eel too, and at least one ribbon fish, though there could be more. It looks like a long thick strip of silver foil, bent into coils, with fearsome teeth.

The wholesaler weighs each bag and box on a set of scales and when it's all tallied up he shakes Arturo's hand. The money will be paid and divided up at the end of the month. Until then the boys will have to rely on their savings.

While we're here, Orlando suggests, I should take a look in the chilling room. In the meantime Raimondo will stock the boat with tomorrow's ice and bait and the others will clean up. He's told them all I'll be turning up, so they're sure to understand if he takes off a little early.

Orlando pulls open a heavy door and directs me inside. There, laid out on hessian sacks on the floor, are twenty blue-fin tuna, and two swordfish — juveniles, but still impressive creatures, with gigantic black pupils and vicious-looking sabres.

'A trawler brought them in this morning,' Orlando tells me, 'after a week out at sea.' He admits they're small. They could well be the last ever caught off the islands.

'A few years ago the European Union tried to get the swordfish fishermen to stop,' Orlando goes on. 'They offered them money, lots of money, to make their nets smaller. They thought it would stop the dolphins and whales being killed.'

It was a gold rush. Almost everyone on Lipari who owned a boat demanded a claim form. Vessels that hadn't gone after swordfish for years were suddenly piled with old nets, and it's said that several small rowboats sank under the weight.

All the fishermen had to do next was to determine what the EU's proposals 'really' meant. Sure, it wanted them to change the size of their nets, but what exactly did they mean by 'size'? After a lot of deliberation it finally occurred to them what they had to do. They would announce, as one, that they agreed to the EU's demands. They would change the size of their nets, in the interests of the environment. All they wanted was the money up front.

The bureaucrats in Brussels were delighted. They'd expected the fishermen to put up a struggle, but there'd been hardly a whimper. It was another job well done.

The money was handed out. Cash was pooled and whole families suddenly became wealthy. Larger boats were ordered, with more powerful engines to take them further out to sea, and the old nets were discarded as agreed. Then everyone bought new ones.

The nets were the same length as before, but the mesh holes were smaller. It was an interpretation of 'smaller' that the EU had overlooked.

Finer mesh meant the fishermen could catch all sorts of fish they'd missed before. As for those dolphins the bureaucrats were so worried about, well, everyone knew they were eating the sea out of fish. How else could you explain the bad catches people were getting? Healthy dolphins raided the nets all the time, making large rips in them in the process. Only the sick and the old couldn't escape, and were pulled up dead. In the old days the sharks would have taken them anyway. So, because the sharks had ended up as cat food long ago, the fishermen were only acting as a stand-in for a natural predator. That's how they saw it anyway.

So the fishermen did well out of it, and the EU was made to look foolish. But recently, the latest in a long line of Italian governments has sided with the administration in Brussels, and instructed the police and coastguard to intercept every boat. Fines and net confiscation would follow a warning, and boats were being stopped all the time. The swordfish fishermen were irate about the treatment of course, and planned to march through the streets. I'd witnessed one such protest that morning: a few dozen men, women and children, armed with placards and powerful coffee, milling around a café.

Orlando was concerned about these developments. If the swordfish industry collapsed then there might well be a rush on to start making shrimp baskets. Then the livelihood of his family, and those of his brothers, would be threatened too.

As for *my* fishing aspirations, Rohan thinks they're as romantic as I do.

'But when are you actually going to do it?' she says over dinner that night. We were almost always around each other, and I think she was starting to see too much of me.

Eight

Alas, I think I am becoming a god.

Titus

Arturo's taken me under his wing. One morning, at the tag end of a storm, he comes up to the hills to teach me about the winds. I'll need to know all about them if I'm to be a fisherman.

Raimondo turns up too, and we sit together under Nino's mulberry tree discussing the change in weather. Raimondo thinks it's the result of the *Ponente*, but Arturo blames it on the *Maestrale*. He points into the wind. That way's Salina, he says. The waves are breaking against the shore at a 45-degree angle and your neighbour's stockings are flapping in a certain direction on the washing line, so it's definitely the *Maestrale*.

It became obvious yesterday afternoon that there would be no chance of fishing today. Watching the clouds come in across the sea has become one of my preoccupations. I often follow their approach from miles away. Sometimes the clouds are lumpy and pale, nudging towards fair weather, other times they're long wispy streamers, high in the sky: white mares'-tails made of ice. The worst is when they form murky sheets, before crossing the sea in chutes of rain. Last night's downpour was so heavy it dissolved newly ploughed ridges in the fields, and mined away at the dry-stone walls until boulders came crashing down in the laneway. Now, with the sun starting to warm up, the place is steaming like a pan of mussels.

The boys had driven up on the back road, a route we try to avoid as much as possible. In parts it's even narrower, and far more precipitous, than our laneway, as I'd already found to my cost. Twice I'd managed to grind our shiny red car into the walls. Now all four doors are scratched and badly dented. The damage will cost thousands to repair, but we know there is no point. It will probably just happen again. Besides, this way at least we look like locals, if you ignore the German numberplates.

Rohan took both collisions surprisingly well, seeing them for the accidents they were. It's one of the things I love about her. She doesn't blame people for things. She told me once that everything breaks in the end, so there's no point getting upset when it does. I would have been less forgiving, I'm sure.

Arturo sends me off to fetch a piece of paper and a pen. When I return he plots the points of the compass in wonky capitals: *Nord, Nord-Est, Est* ... Then together the boys direct me through the winds.

There's the *Tramontana*, which blows from the seven stars in the constellation of Ursa Major, and the north-eastern *Grecale*, which once filled the sails of ancient Greek vessels as they set off to trade in the Mediterranean. From the direction of the sunrise comes the eastern *Levante*, and from the southeast and the deserts of North Africa the dusty *Scirocco*, the Syrian wind. 'It's dangerous,' Arturo says, shaking his head.

Neither boy remembers the name of the south wind at first, until it comes back to them, yes, the *Mezzogiorno* — the half-day wind. Arturo scoffs as he crushes the dead end of his cigarette with his boot. 'It means "mid-day". It's what the northern Italians call us southerners. They say we work half the day and sleep the rest of it.'

'Some of us get up with the sun every day and work until it goes down again,' butts in Nino, who has just arrived back from the fields, dragging his heels like an overworked donkey despite it being only breakfast time. He wanders over to his kitchen garden, sits on his haunches, and watches a line of ants crawling up the trunk of his lemon tree. If he's fortunate they will lead him to some sap-sucking scale insects, which he can crush between his fingers. As usual I'm taken aback by his hands: gnarled old creatures, as callused as olive trees, tattooed with decades of dirt.

Arturo puts a match to another cigarette and continues with the lesson. There's the gusty *Libeccio*, which usually brings squalls and thunderstorms. 'It's from the southwest, from Spain.'

Then there's the western *Ponente*, or *Ponte* as Arturo writes, which comes from the direction of the setting sun.

Finally the *Maestrale*; the cold, dry northwest wind, which varies in intensity from summer breeze to tempest, and which is still bringing streams of wispy cloud towards us from the sea.

For a moment I imagine Arturo wetting a finger and putting it above his head to feel the wind before setting out to fish, but when I put this to him he laughs at my ignorance. It's far more complicated than that, he says.

'You can tell by the currents and the white caps on the waves. And when we have the chance we look at what Stromboli's doing. When the volcano is more active than normal, and you can see the lava flowing out, it always means bad weather, the next day, or the next.'

'Before we put out to sea we always look at the volcano to see which way the wind is blowing,' Raimondo adds. 'You have to look at the colour of the smoke too. And when Stromboli shines like a lantern, we know either a *Scirocco* or *Maestrale* is coming. And when Sicily and the other islands look closer than normal it means the weather's changing, probably for the worse.'

I've noticed this phenomenon myself. Some days we're astounded by how close Sicily looks. You can almost look into people's windows from our terrace, and can clearly make out every ridge and fold of the mountains. At times like this it's hard to believe that the 'mainland', as they refer to it, is two hours away by ferry. The effect is caused by a combination of low pressure and wind.

'Are there any other ways to tell what's happening with the weather?' I ask.

'In the summer, when the sea mist caused by the humidity has cleared it's a sign there's a strong wind out there,' Arturo continues. 'Then we won't take the boat out at all. We'll just mend the baskets.'

'Or just sleep,' notes Nino, who's been listening in.

Sitting here, absorbing the moment as we crowd around this tiny piece of paper torn from a notebook, I begin to feel a connection with these fishermen. They are teaching me about something as basic to them as rain is to Nino. And there's no better classroom, I think: up in the hills on the island of King Aeolus, lord of the winds. It's a poignant moment, and as Arturo passes me the page of names and compass points, the *Maestrale* lets out a sudden burst and the paper flies across the laneway.

It lands at Nino's feet. The leaves of the mulberry tree rattle in the wind. '*Cattivo tempo*,' Nino announces. Bad weather. But it's just what he wants. It might rain again, and it will do his seedlings good to have a drink before things dry up for the summer. Still, he's taking no chances. He hands the boys a bucket of dishwater he's been storing in the workshop. 'You'd better start on the lettuces, boys,' he says. 'That's what you're up here for isn't it? A spot of farming for a change.'

'Well, umm ...' There's no use arguing. Arturo obviously enjoys himself up here, but you can tell from Raimondo's face that he's unimpressed. In any case, there's no fishing today and if they do Nino a favour he might let them store some engine parts in his shed.

I stand by as the boys lug the buckets of dishwater into

the garden. They stop in their tracks as they register the lettuces already soaking in pools of rainwater.

Nino taps his temple with a clumpy hand, his smile flickering.

'*Acqua salata*,' he says under his breath. Salt water. 'The salt's got in and rusted their brains.'

In Lipari town the locals are cleaning up storm damage. Pots of herbs and geraniums lie shattered on the ground and police are directing pedestrians around some masonry, which has fallen from the first floor balcony above the butcher's shop. Most of Marina Lunga is flooded. Wooden fruit boxes are floating around, and Giuseppina is wading through the extended puddle with her green silk ball gown hitched up high and her running shoes tied by the laces around her neck.

Giuseppina is one of the island's strays, like the three dogs that follow her around. She's said to sleep in abandoned cars, but even so she insists on holding pizza from the bins with her pinky cocked. Giuseppina makes a few euros in the summer months from selling obsidian, the translucent black rock which sometimes forms when lava spills into the ocean. Being much harder than flint, obsidian was once favoured for knife blades and arrowheads, and in Neolithic times it brought wealth and trade to the islands. But these days it's just a shiny rock found in lumps all over the island, and you can't make much money from it. So café owners donate coffees, which Giuseppina can drink at the bar — if she keeps the dogs outside and promises not to lift her skirt above her head on hot summer days and use it as a fan. Some of the customers have choked on their *brioche* when they've seen she doesn't wear underpants.

Another of the island's characters we meet from time to time when we pluck up the energy to take Louis into town is a tubby man with long, lanky trails of dark hair hanging below a scabby bald patch. Spend long enough on the island and you'll bump into him everywhere; way up in the hills, loitering around the beaches, and roaming around the town centre. He walks and walks, and only breaks from dialogues with himself to greet acquaintances with a deep and resonant '*Buongiorno*'.

When it's not him on your path it's Football Man. He's as thin as celery and always wears shorts and a soccer shirt cut diagonally by the strap of his brown leather satchel. He has a faster and more determined pace than Mr Buongiorno, and only slows down when he's forced by his compulsion to clean the pavement of a cigarette butt, plastic cup or café napkin with kicks of his boot.

On the mainland, people like this would continue on their way until they ended up in other towns. On a very small island they're back where they started in almost no time. Stick around and they can even become your friends.

One of those we're soon on good terms with is the 'Supermarket Detective'. Apparently, he just turned up at the supermarket one day and began packing shelves. Nobody asked him to, and no one has asked him to stop. He doesn't get paid, but it gets him out of the house. He patrols the aisles, working with a cold, brisk efficiency to ensure tins face the right way, and buggies don't block the thoroughfares. When he meets us in the street after work he always nods and croaks hello. After all, we're regular customers, and we're generally in control of our buggy.

Once, when the stresses under the surface are rumbling, and we are squabbling over something too silly to even remember, Rohan loses concentration and runs the buggy into one of Giuseppina's dogs. It's been scratching itself on the pavement outside the supermarket's entrance. When she hears the dog yelp Giuseppina comes running. She bares her teeth, she flaps her dress, she throws her bobble hat onto the ground, and damns our family to hell. We are just about to make a run for it when the Supermarket Detective steps in. He instantly defuses the situation by threatening to ban her from the bins out the back. She skulks away, but her threats remain in our ears. From then on we cross the road whenever we see her coming. We laugh about the incident afterwards, but in truth we both sometimes feel as unhinged and unbalanced as some of the people we meet on the streets.

My mental map of Nino's territory is expanding like ink on blotting paper. On our countryside walks we come across caper plants and grape vines, garlic and onions, beans and peas, olives and zucchini. There are pear trees, almonds, figs, and rosemary and carob. What Nino can't grow or find wild, he barters for with his excess produce. If he needs petrol for his three-wheeled *Ape*, he'll exchange eggs and rabbits with the owner of the local service station. A sickle needs sharpening? A metal worker gets a handful of onions.

Today it's nice enough for a picnic, and we lie in one of Nino's fields. This one is going fallow, and we are cocooned from the rest of the world in grass reaching up to our bended knees.

Louis is playing with a wildflower. He's changing so quickly, growing up. He laughs when I pretend to munch on his tummy, or when I hum his favourite tunes and dip him up and down on my knee. He screeches, and blows raspberries, and bubbles and grunts, and he hates it when I cough — he bursts into tears every time.

'I can hardly believe it's only been five months since he was born,' says Rohan. 'He feels like a part of me I've never been without. Who'd have ever thought I'd be this maternal?'

I'm not quite sure how to respond, so I stay silent.

'I'm glad you're bonding with him now,' she continues. 'I was worried at first you weren't. I thought you might be able to reconnect with me if you learned to love him as much as I do.'

'Well, of course I love him,' I say, somewhat sharply. 'You can't pressure someone into bonding. I didn't know what was expected of me, that's all. I suppose I'm just getting used to it now.'

We both go quiet. Instinctively I know this conversation could end up in an argument. We might be having a picnic together today, but in the grand scheme of things we were each going it alone. And I didn't want to contemplate where that could end up.

Louis is demanding attention now. He's pulling at her hair as she lies amidst the grass and flowers of spring.

She turns towards him and swings him up onto her stomach. I watch them together; I see that no one can make her as happy as he can. They are tied together by an umbilical cord.

'You look like you were made for each other,' I say at last.

With that Louis rolls off her chest and plonks himself into the grass between us. She arches an arm and encases him, and I grasp her hand and hold it.

A cloud has passed, for the moment at least.

We head back home as the sun is setting over the sea. It's a perfect pink-orange ball, and it colours the layers of cloud that are stretching from one end of Sicily to the other.

The following morning I walk out onto our terrace into another fine day. There's the MSS *Levante*, dropping baskets around our part of the coastline. I stand on tiptoes and wave both arms above my head, unsure if they can see me. Later Orlando says the crew spotted me easily against the backdrop of a whitewashed wall, and I inform him as delicately as I can that I'm upset he didn't tell me he was fishing nearby. I remind him again that I still haven't gone out, and I've been on the island for weeks now.

The problem now, it seems, is with their fishing licence.

'We can only take four people on board at any one time,' he tells me. 'But five of us go out every day. If we're caught we're in trouble. We're always looking out for the police.'

'Why don't you just get a licence for five people then?' I ask, confused. 'Or six, including me?'

'It's too expensive. The more people you have named on the licence the more money it costs. Because they're after the swordfish trawlers, they're always stopping us.'

'But they must know who you are by now though?' I say. 'And they can see you've got shrimp baskets not nets ...'

He throws up his hands. 'But they keep changing the police. They rotate them, and bring in people from all over Sicily, and even Italy, so they can't be bribed. They're all suspicious, and are told to stop everyone.'

Sometimes it's the *guardia finanzia* spot-checking licences, he says, or the *carabinieri*, supposedly looking for drug smugglers — they're not so bad because you can always give them a bag of shrimp and they'll go away — and other times it's the *guardia costiera* checking if the vessel they've picked up on their shore-based radar screens is, in fact, a boat, and not, say, the corpse of a floating whale. Any excuse, just as long as they make their presence felt.

'So what do you do when they come to check your licence and they see you have five people on board?' I ask.

Orlando shakes his head sadly.

'Giacomo,' he says. 'He has to hide below decks, in the engine room. He hates it, but he's the only one not registered. Oh Marco, it's so hot down there and very noisy, and the boat rolls in the swell. You must have a strong stomach. Sometimes he crawls out after they've left and he's sick over the side, and he has much experience of hiding.'

Poor old fat Giacomo. He suffers from claustrophobia, and tears run down his cheeks when he's forced to squeeze through the deck hatch and clamber down into the bowels of the boat.

'There's not enough room down there for anyone else,' Orlando continues. 'Give it a couple of weeks. Things will be much different then. The police will get bored.'

I don't ask why he hadn't mentioned the licence before we moved to the other side of the world. Maybe he just didn't think it through.

A few days later I'm on his case again, with a renewed bout of questioning about shrimp baskets and boat parts, as we sit with our coffees at *Il Gabbiano*. I tell him I'll pay for a licence, but he tells me it'll take months, maybe even years to come through. It's the legendary Italian bureaucracy at work. Italians seem to have official paper and stamps for everything, but they mostly fail when it comes to actually communicating laws and regulations with the general population. Islands of administration seem to exist without any real connection with each other, and you often have to visit three or four of these islands before you even know you are in the right archipelago. The result is long lines of confused Italians in every post office, government department, hospital and police station wondering if they are in the right place, or in the correct queue to pick up an essential, but incomprehensible, document.

'Look. Maybe I have an idea,' he says. 'We could try talking to the captain of the coast guard. He might be able to write us a letter giving permission for you to be on board, until we get around to sorting out a proper licence. If there's trouble we can show the note. Anyway, it'll soon be summer, and you can come fishing every day without anyone's permission: there are too many boats around then, lots of them taking tourists out, and it's too hot for the police to work.'

'Great. But until then, it looks like I'll need permission from the captain. When do you think we should go?'

'Maybe tomorrow. I'll give you a call.'

Three days later and Justine passes on a message via Nino's telephone. 'Orlando says to meet him at 4 pm at our house. It's time to see *Il Capitano*.'

I sling a leg over the back of Orlando's scooter and we roar noisily through the narrow alleyways. We buzz past fruiterers, fishmongers, pizza restaurants, and unoccupied café tables running alongside the brown sand marking the undeveloped edge of the ferry port. We pull up at a concrete shack with a smelly bin outside. In front of us is a splintered wooden entrance with a hand-scrawled sign in blue crayon. 'Use other door,' it reads. But as we stand there it opens anyway, and a young man with dark cropped hair, three-day growth, and wearing a pressed white uniform appears. He looks surprised to see us hanging around.

'You need some help?' he asks in an offhand tone. He had the bored contempt that goes with officialdom in these parts.

'*Si*,' Orlando responds with a blush that proves he's not used to dealing with authority. 'I'm a *gamberetti* fisherman. This is my friend. He wants to come aboard the boat and see what we do.'

'Do you have a licence to take tourists?'

'No, just for fishing.'

'I see. So what do you want us to do?'

'Maybe you can write a letter saying he can come on board in case anyone asks us out at sea.'

'*Il Capitano* will have to decide. You'd better come in.'

We make to follow him into the building but he stops us with an outstretched hand. 'Use the other door.' He retreats through the doorway and slams it shut.

We find the second entranceway is secured by reinforced steel. Orlando presses a button and a moment later the same man answers and waves us inside. He's already figured we're trouble and calls for a more junior officer to deal with us.

Orlando relays the request again. This officer listens politely and strokes his stubble. 'Come back tomorrow,' he says. 'Around 10.30 in the morning.'

Outside again, Orlando announces he'll be out fishing the next day, but tells me to take Justine with me to argue my case. We will have to discuss our strategy over pizza.

The next morning, with Justine armed with Orlando's registration number and stern advice to treat *Il Capitano* with the greatest respect, we head back to the office.

Just as we arrive we come across an old man slumping out. He looks us up and down. 'Why are you here?' he scowls.

Justine explains.

'Forget it. This office does nothing,' he says. 'You have to visit the one in the main street to get anything done.'

We go inside anyway, where a uniformed official finally confirms we've wasted our time.

But we are on a mission. So we walk back into town, to try and secure an appointment with *Il Capitano* himself. We ring a bell, state our business, and an officer tells us to wait in the corridor. An hour later we are ushered through into an office with a pleasant courtyard view. Behind a solid wooden desk, a man weighed down with gold braid is signing papers with an exaggerated flourish. 'Sit down,' he says without looking up.

We sit, and shuffle uncomfortably, until he's finished and ready to hear our story.

Il Capitano nods, and checks Orlando's licence number in his books. We were right to come to him, he says, even though he's a very busy man.

He concludes there is no such thing as a document to allow me onto the boat, and confirms that if I were to apply to put my name on the licence it would have to be sent to Palermo. It would take at least two years to be approved. He can't give me direct permission himself either. But he suggests that if I'm ever asked what I'm doing on the boat I should say I've talked to him, *Il Capitano*.

'No one will stop you from,' he coughs, '*observing* the fishing, for as long as you like.'

He can assure it.

It's lunchtime by the time we arrive back at Justine's and the water for the pasta is soon bubbling on the stove.

Orlando sits down to lunch soon after, still smelling of bait and the sea. We tuck into spaghetti in *salsa bianca* — a paste of onions, tomatoes, capers and basil — with fried *melanzane*, anchovies, olives and tuna. There are crusty bread rolls too, and glasses of cold beer.

Orlando is quick to question Justine about our meeting. He knows she can be blunt at times, and needs to be reassured that she showed *Il Capitano* the respect a man in his position expected. But when she's finished relating her tale he's happy enough with the outcome. Then he stumps me by asking if I'd felt the earthquake that morning.

'Oh yes, I was going to ask you,' Justine pipes up.

Just after dawn the boys on the boat had watched uselessly as boulders tumbled into the sea somewhere below our house in the hills. They knew precisely what it meant. They rushed for their mobile phones to ring their wives back home. They heard the earthquake had rocked Lipari town, and had filled the alleyways with people in their nightclothes. It was a nasty shock, but up in the hills we hadn't felt a thing. When we had the chance we slept like the dead; nothing could raise us.

Orlando is full of admiration and Justine claps her hands in delight.

'If you can handle an earthquake in your sleep then maybe you won't have any problems if it gets rough out there,' Orlando says. He takes a sip of his beer, his only one for the week, and looks me in the eyes. 'You want to come tomorrow?'

'Tomorrow. Are you sure?'

'*Certo.*'

'What about the weather?'

'*Perfetto.*'

The boat will be heading to Panarea. Close by. They're leaving at four in the morning, on the dot. I should meet them next to the boat. If I'm late they'll go without me.

That night I set my alarm clock for three; time for a coffee like the locals, a shower, the drive down to town, and the walk through the alleyways to the boat. I can hardly sleep. I'm going to sea at last.

Nine

They went to sea in a Sieve, they did,
In a Sieve they went to sea:
In spite of all their friends could say ...

And all night long they sailed away:
And when the sun went down,
They whistled and warbled a moony song
To the echoing sound of a coppery gong
In the shade of the mountains brown.

EDWARD LEAR

I'm up before the alarm under my pillow goes off. Mercifully, Rohan and Louis are still sleeping.

I make my way gingerly down to town and park the car as near to the port as I can. Then I stride through the narrow cobbled alleyways towards the water. Apart from my breathing and the echoes of footsteps, the town is still.

The cars and the trucks and scooters of the day are gone. The roads look wider, and the shops more solemn now that their outdoor stalls and pavement signs have been taken in.

I find most of the boys onboard, pulling on oilskins and matching yellow boots. Everyone's here except Arturo, who turns up late without an excuse. Orlando mutters something under his breath, before hauling in the buoys and weighing anchor. Arturo lights up a cigarette, makes himself comfortable, and guides the boat out. Then someone turns on the deck lights, and the boat explodes in oranges and blues.

As the lights of Lipari draw slowly further away, one of the crew fumbles with matting for the deck: some old sheets of rubber and a couple of coffee sacks to stop us from slipping on the spray. Another pulls up a hatch and clambers down into the engine room. He hands up a short wooden stool, then three more.

The crew pair up and start packing purses made from plastic garden netting with slices of defrosting sardines. I watch them for a while, before taking my chance when Raimondo gets up to hunt for cigarettes.

'Marco,' Orlando cries out plaintively. 'You don't have to do it.'

'But I want to,' I reply, and I'm soon greasy with fish and guts and the saline is stinging my fingers. We don't talk much. By the time the stars are fading in the sky we are washing our hands with water hoisted from the sea, relieving ourselves of a crust of flesh, scales and salt.

The sky is paling now, and I can make out little white houses along the coastline of Panarea.

'Just point the boat at the far end of the island, to the right,' Arturo announces rather too trustingly when I join him in the cabin. 'We'll be going around the other side.'

He walks out, leaving me to nervously take the wheel. I've never driven a boat before, so for a while I do nothing but stand there, motionless. Then, gaining confidence, I jiggle the wheel a bit, and notice the island drift off to one side. I turn the wheel more forcibly, to change the orientation, and we start off on a lazy circle. I desperately wrench the thing back to the same point I thought it had started from and by sheer chance the island floats back to a central spot, and stays there. It seems best to just let go, and hope Arturo will come back before I run the boat aground.

Thankfully, a few minutes later he's beside me again, twiddling with the depth sounder above his head. He takes another cigarette from a packet — one of five on the dashboard — and lights up.

'*Bravo*,' he says quietly, before relieving me of my captainship. 'You seem to be getting the hang of it.'

I leave, and stumble outside. The clouds are turning orange, and seagulls are flying low across the water.

Before I even have the chance to sit down and regain my composure I'm poked in the ribs and a sudden cry of '*Delphini*!' goes up.

Everyone's fingers are pointing me in the direction of the dolphins, which are rushing the boat with extraordinary speed and flipping out of the water to reveal the dusky stripes on their flanks.

'The first this season!' Arturo shouts excitedly from the cabin. 'Look at them, Marco! See! There's more over there!'

They're a marvellous sight, and we watch as they do a final communal breach, then slide away in the direction of Stromboli and its spreading violet trail of smoke, until they're indistinguishable against the colour of the sea.

A while later Orlando spots a buoy. The boat turns with the seagulls towards a marker flag bobbing on a raft of plastic bottles.

'It's the wrong one,' he explains with a frown as we draw nearer. 'We need to find the buoy with the flag on the other side of the line. We have to work against the current. The ropes and baskets could get tangled if we start here.'

'What would happen then?' I ask brightly. I have no idea what he's talking about.

'If things go wrong we might have to cut the rope. The baskets would sink and we'd never find them again. But it would be the only way to save the boat.'

'Oh. So the baskets are all joined together on one long rope?'

'*Si.*'

'How many of them are there?'

'A hundred on one rope, and there's another hundred on the seafloor out here too!'

The light's improving rapidly, but although Arturo runs the boat to-and-fro, we still can't find the second marker.

'Perhaps a hydrofoil ran across it,' surmises Orlando, 'and sliced the rope. It's happened before. Or it could be looters. Someone might have raised the baskets during the night, then cut the float and left it to drift away.'

He looks concerned, and calls out to Arturo to run the boat back towards the first flag, even though the current is coming towards us at a fair pace.

Arturo brings us full astern, backs up towards the flag, and leaves Raimondo to pull the float onboard. He unties it. After guiding the end of the rope over a roller fixed to the stern, he hauls it across the length of the deck towards the cabin and winds it around the spool of a mechanical winch.

'Stand beside me, Marco,' Arturo says, leading me to the back of the boat. 'It's a good view from here, and it's safe — unless the rope snaps away and knocks you overboard ...'

I gulp.

'Don't worry. Giacomo is right here too. He'll grab your legs before you go in.'

I glance towards Giacomo. He's holding a knife in a gladiatorial stance, with the other hand resting on his protruding stomach. I notice he's wearing yellow rubber washing-up gloves with the fingers cut off.

I'm far from comforted.

The winch grunts into life. The rope tightens and strains, and slowly more comes aboard.

By now the sun is above the horizon and I'm staring down into clear green water. Soon I can make out a faint, almost fluorescent tinge of something solid rising towards me.

It's the first time I've seen one of the baskets and as it jumps clear of the surface with a hiss and gush of water I'm surprised how big it is. Two people could just about touch hands if they put their arms around it, and it would reach up to their chests.

Arturo makes a grab at a side rope and helps lever it aboard. Once the basket is freed Rocco upends it and tips the contents into a trough of water at his feet. It's a pitiful catch, just a handful of shrimp. It hardly seems worth it.

Rocco re-baits the basket and hands it back to Orlando, who ties it to a railing at the bow.

Soon we have four baskets aboard, and the bottom of the trough is skittering with shrimp: enough for a reasonable lunch.

In the fifth basket there's a small *morena*. The eel slithers out onto the deck, glistening yellow and black with its mouth flaring. Rocco reaches for a club and smacks it over the head, then hoists it by the tail end and throws it overboard.

I wince, but there's little time to feel sentimental. The next basket is coming up rapidly, and now it's aboard and being detached from its rope. Inside is a sturdy grey eel as long as my leg. It beats itself about on deck, before lying quietly, gasping for air.

'It's a *dronko*,' Arturo says. 'Too small though. We'll salt it up and use it for bait.'

More shrimp arrive. Then the first octopus. Giacomo gathers it up and wiggles his knife in the flesh between its eyes. He places it neatly in an icebox.

In other baskets there are more eels, then a *scorfano*, a dull orange scorpion fish with poisonous spines.

Arturo lets out a breath and points towards the next basket in line. I see something large and black. It's an *astache*, a huge black speckled lobster with massive claws. It'll fetch a good price. Into the icebox it goes.

Within seconds another basket is tantalisingly close to the surface. The rope whines, and creaks, and mews out loudly. Arturo's brow is rippled like beach sand. He flicks a hand sign in the air, and the winch judders and coils flip free. The rope cracks like a rifle and snaps firm again, spraying us with needles of water. The basket falls away into the depths.

The current has pulled us too far over, off line, and Raimondo has to reposition the boat. The boys attempt to bring the basket in again, and again, and for the next ten minutes the winch struggles, the rope screams. Tension rises, curses fly, layers are stripped off, cigarettes are chewed through, and a new plan is called for. Arturo suggests using the boat as a pulley and dragging the remaining baskets along the sea floor. It's agreed, and the engine is suddenly roaring, and diesel smoke is billowing around us. We try again, and this time, to sighs of relief, the basket tumbles on deck.

Inside is another *dronko,* but this one's gigantic. It fills half the basket and bares its giant teeth at us as it's unloaded. It's obviously far too dangerous to be allowed to thrash about onboard. It could take our legs off. So Rocco picks up his club again, and I watch with a kind of appalled fascination as he bashes it repeatedly along its spine.

And so it goes on, basket after basket: a few fish, a few prawns — some come up empty apart from the odd starfish or unlucky hermit crab. Just as soon as the last basket's up and emptied they all go overboard again, and we're just about to set off to find another lot languishing somewhere on the seabed when Giacomo lets out a garbled cry. He points a finger from his rubber-gloved hand. We all turn to look, and see a boat speeding towards us from the island.

It's the coastguard for sure, and Giacomo's face pales as he considers the prospect of another lock-down in the engine room.

But not so fast. There's an animated debate as all eyes peer in the direction of the approaching craft. Someone's noticed there are fishing rods onboard. Finally Orlando identifies the intruders. The boat belongs to some old school friends. They're obviously just after some bait.

They pull up alongside us with cheery waves.

Orlando scoops out handfuls of shrimp, and passes them over in a plastic bag. It's about four good baskets worth; which equates to an enormous amount of labour. I'm surprised that the brothers seem happy to be so generous.

'Why did you give them so much?' I ask when I get the chance.

'It's their island,' Orlando explains. 'We can't be here all the time to keep an eye on the baskets. They'll let us know if anyone tampers with them.'

'It's like Nino giving the local metal worker some tomatoes in case he ever needs his sickle fixed,' adds Arturo. Or some bags of capers to the doctor in return for a prompt referral to a specialist in Sicily should the need arise.

The sun is basting by the time we've found the second load of baskets, and with the rise in temperature the conversation becomes more spirited.

It's clear there's a great camaraderie among the brothers, and obvious love. Raimondo laughs and banters with Arturo, Orlando occasionally joins in with a joke, and Giacomo offers a gentle smile as he slowly unties the twine from the old bait holders and throws the remains of the fish to the birds.

Only Rocco doesn't join in. His role is too gruelling for him to spend too much energy on talking. Instead, when he's not working he stares blankly at the flapping, clattering eels around his feet, and the hermit crabs as they scuttle around hopelessly searching for shade.

When the process starts again, I take over from Arturo, pulling the baskets onboard until my arms are numb and my back starts to ache. Halfway through the second load Arturo sees I'm struggling and tells me to rest, up on the roof, where I can lie stretched out and watch the brothers at work below.

I've always done my best thinking when I'm doing nothing much. Now, as I drift away from the fishermen below, my mind is full of thoughts. I'm doing something magical with my life now. I'm *living* again. I feel my spirit can range wide here, out at sea. I don't know if I can make a go of fishing, but at the moment it's good enough that I have the opportunity. Then I think of my writing, and how I haven't done any yet, and promise myself I'll press into action as soon as I can. I don't fancy my chances of getting much done with Louis in our house in the hills, so I mentally stake out the *casetta* and its stone step, where I can ponder and scribble until the sun goes down, with a flagon of wine by my side. Selfishly, it doesn't occur to me that Rohan might have something to say about this, but in my defence I'm caught up in the moment.

I jump down off the roof and set to work again, keener than ever to experience everything I can. I help Arturo with the winching and, fuelled by my enthusiasm, he takes to explaining as much as he can about our surroundings.

He points out a restaurant high on a cliff and beaches you can only reach by boat; he runs through the names of the fish as they come in; and tells me of the shark they once caught, and about the tall-topped tuna boat he once went out on. 'A man always used to stand on the end of a long spit set out on the prow,' he says, 'to harpoon the fish. You always tried to kill the female first, because the male would hang around. But if you killed the male first, well, the female would just swim away —'

'Like a woman,' Orlando interjects. 'It's universal.'

My task now is to help Orlando with the fish. We line up the largest ones head-to-tail in a crate, and grade the others.

Orlando throws the useless ones to the seagulls, and I watch them for a while above the frothy trail spreading out behind us.

I'm getting philosophical. I can't help thinking about those tiny specks of fish I've seen schooling along the edge of the wharfs; how from newborn fry they spend their lives hunting scraps and dodging enemies, floating, swimming, suspended night and day, getting slowly picked off. Until, at last, there's only one: alone, but bigger, and in deeper water now. Then one day it swims into a basket, and is hauled up, and the difference in pressure blows up its swim bladder, so even if it escapes suffocation, or the seagulls, it's doomed. But of course, that's just the way it is, and has been for thousands of years. Apart from the addition of plastic and oil, little has changed for the fishermen or their catch.

We pick through the shrimp, throwing away urchins, bits of sea sponge, and a hermit crab with eggs around her belly.

The haul is far from impressive. The boys will make some money out of it, but Rocco decides they can only afford to give me shrimp for a discount. So Raimondo weighs out a kilo, and Orlando insists on paying for the share.

By the time we tie up we're all looking forward to bed. But first there's lunch at Orlando's place, and it's pasta, of course.

While Orlando washes up in the bathroom, Justine corners me.

'So, did you enjoy yourself?' she asks.

I tell her it was an amazing experience.

'But it's not hard though is it?' she says. 'I mean, Orlando always comes home and says he's exhausted, but I think it's really an excuse not to do anything around the house.'

I look at her incredulously. She must see I'm so tired I can barely speak, but when I tell her this she puts it down to my not being used to it.

'But it really is hard work,' I insist, trying too hard to convince her. 'It never stops. They work for ten hours with barely a break. They're tired to start off with …'

'Really?' She's mocking me, and I'm still not sure why.

'Haven't you ever been on the boat with him?'

'Only once. But they only put three or four baskets out, to give me an idea, really. They said it would be too hard for me if they did all of them. I told them they should try looking after children all day.'

'But Orlando's told you what they do all that time out at sea, hasn't he?'

She shakes her head. 'Nope. He doesn't like to talk about work. Whenever I ask him about it he just tells me I wouldn't be interested.'

'Oh. Anyway, it really is hard work. Take it from me.'

'Sure. By the way, you've caught the sun — you're going to have to moisturise.'

I only realise it now that she points it out. My cheeks feel hot. My forehead's a bit sore, and I'm sure my nose is glowing.

Justine quickly fries some shrimp and adds them to a tomato sauce. She plumps it all up with chunks of twice-baked ricotta and spoons it out onto plates of spaghetti.

'Thanks, Orlando,' I say earnestly when I've finished and I'm ready to leave. 'For everything, including the shrimp.'

'What are you thanking him for?' Justine asks, raising her voice and playing at being offended. 'I'm the one who cooked them!'

Back in the hills, I try and outline my experience to Rohan, but she's distracted. There are things to do, practicalities to look after: a nappy to change, surfaces to wipe, clothes to fold. I'm handed Louis while she mops the floor tiles. I tell her about the dolphins. She asks if I have any seafood for dinner tonight. I tell her I don't. She moves to the bedroom to collect some dirty washing from the floor. I tell her I have to sleep, but try one last time to tell her about my day. But I've picked the wrong time, as I often do.

Ten

*The traveller sees what he sees, the tourist sees
what he has come to see.*

G K Chesterton

In a state of excitement Justine tells us her mother will be
arriving in the next few days. She's not sure how long
she'll stay, but it'll be a few weeks at least. Rohan is
looking forward to it, and so am I. Kerri is an earthy, no-
nonsense Australian, and her stay promises to do wonders
for Rohan.

For the past couple of weeks I've been going out fishing
with the boys almost every day, and there are only a few
hours we can spend catching up between my afternoon
sleep and bedtime again.

Coping with a young baby on an island where there are
no mothers' groups or baby health clinics, and where
everyone else has an extended family to help, is turning

out to be far harder than Rohan had expected. And, because I drive the car down to town during the night and leave it there while I go out on the boat, it makes it difficult for her to get down to town. All this is making Rohan feel lonely.

She's tried spending time with Immacolata, but she's had a staggered start. She's called on our landlady several times now, but she always finds her in the middle of cooking or cleaning. Immacolata stops what she's doing, self-consciously tucks the stray curls of hair back into her headscarf, and insists on preparing *la signora* a formal reception of coffee and biscuits. Rohan encourages her to carry on with her tasks, and even offers to help, but Immacolata always refuses.

'I know it's silly, but the conversation is so polite, and it makes me feel like I'm intruding,' Rohan says. 'It just feels so formal.'

I think I know what she means, and I suggest that they just have to get used to each other.

We talk for a while longer. It's a good conversation for a change. Usually, our time together goes something like this: Rohan tells me what the baby had for lunch: milk. And dinner: milk. And what came out of his mouth: vomit. And what he did subsequently: nothing much, apart from crying and sleeping, a bit of staring, and some more crying and sleeping ... And what she's spent her day doing: not much. And what she's been thinking about: can't think, brain dead.

'Well, I got up, earlier than normal,' I might say.

'Yeah, I heard you.'

'Went fishing over at Panarea.'

'Yep.'

'Hit my first *dronko* over the head.'

A frown.

'Orlando's taken over stabbing octopus ...'

'Nice. What else did you do? (*God, when can I go to bed?*)'

'I don't know ... umm ... we caught some shrimp. Not too many ...'

'Did the boys say anything interesting?'

'I don't know (*ummm*).'

'What do you mean you don't know?'

It's a strange thing, but the more I go out on the boat, the less the brothers feel inclined to speak Italian. It's got to the point now where they speak almost entirely in dialect, even when they're asking me questions, and it's only when I shrug my shoulders that they realise their mistake. It's just that I've become so familiar, they say in apology. They forget I can't speak Liparese. They make an effort for my sake for a while, but quickly revert to their native tongue. I've tried getting around it by continually asking questions in Italian, but it's surprisingly easy to run out of intelligent enquiries during a ten-hour trip and you easily start to sound stupid.

'What does this do?'

'It's another piece of wood for sitting on.'

'Oh. And this blue fish? We haven't caught one of those before. What's it called?'

'A Blue Fish.'

'Oh.'

'And this? I know we catch it every day, but I've forgotten its name.'

'A *blubblubblub*.' (Unintelligible dialect.)

'That's what I thought you said. Can I have a sleep on the bunk bed in the cabin?'

'Good idea.'

'Righto.'

So there's not really much to talk about when I come home with the odd bag of prawns and an occasional fish.

We try to liven things up a bit by packing Louis up and heading to town for a pizza, but neither of us is getting anything like the right amount of sleep, so though we enjoy the change we worry about falling unconscious at the wheel on the way back. We return early.

When Louis is catnapping we attempt to string new words together in Italian, with workbooks and notebooks spread out in front of us, but after a couple of attempts we give up: Rohan finds the process too exhausting. Reading doesn't work for her either. She falls asleep after just a few lines.

One of the only things we accomplish as a couple is sticking some felt pads onto the bottom of the chair legs in the kitchen, to stop them scraping on the floor tiles. When we've finished we turn the chairs the right way up, sit on them, and begin pushing backwards with our legs. We glide around the kitchen, remarkably soundlessly, for longer than any psychiatrist would recommend.

Kerri arrives in the nick of time, on the back of Orlando's motor scooter.

I fill her glass with beer and she drains it in one go. She pours herself another one before asking, 'How are you going?'

Rohan looks at me, and I look at her. 'Ummm …' we both say in unison.

'I don't want to bag you out or anything but it sounds like you don't have a clue!' she says when we tell her about putting Louis to sleep.

She's a mother of two, and her son in Australia has two young ones as well, so she knows what she's talking about, she tells us. She immediately bans our desperate attempts to get Louis to sleep via exaggerated pogo-ing on the spot for hours. Instead he's fed, kissed goodnight, put in his cot and left to close his eyes himself. At first the screams and sobbing are heart-wrenching, but eventually the wailing ceases, and there's silence. A few days later and he has the hang of it, and goes down relatively easily. Our sleep is still broken, but we've got hours more of it now. Rohan is a changed person.

With her life again in some sort of order, Rohan talks about joining Kerri and Justine down at their favourite café for breakfast. Kerri leaves early every day and walks down to Lipari town. It's more difficult for Rohan. By the time she's sorted Louis out it's already getting late, and she can only use the car in bad weather, when the boat is in port. On days like these I sometimes go with her, but today she's making the trip alone, while I walk the country with Nino. His pockets are full of a mixture of seeds: lettuce, chilli, pumpkin, beans, and who knows what else, which he presses into the soil, spontaneously, whenever he thinks he might appreciate finding something worth picking one day.

Rohan recounts the events of the morning when she comes back home. She started off by strapping Louis in the baby seat and driving through the country lanes leading to the main road to town. Her mind flashed through everything she might have forgotten: money, the baby's drink bottle ... would she be home by one o'clock or should she have packed him some puréed fruit for lunch? Oh, the photos would be ready, but would she have enough cash to pay for them? She wondered if she should get in line at the post office to buy stamps for the letters. It's not so urgent. She hasn't had time to write them yet.

Justine and Kerri were already sitting with their coffees when she arrived. A waiter rushed up to take Rohan's order: a chocolate *cornetto*, and a *Caffe Americano*. Kerri and Justine each had a *treccia*, a plait of dough filled with sweet apricot jam, while Justine's kids had a *brioche* filled with ice cream. Between reining in the children, replacing dummies and breaking up *brioche* into bite-sized pieces on demand, the women managed to scrape together the foundations of a conversation. But, as usual, it didn't get started properly, and the children were restless.

After breakfast Rohan attached herself to Kerri and Justine's routine. First to the supermarket; a battleground, with little Luca demanding a treat, a cake, or the latest giveaway stuck to the front of a packet of breakfast cereal. Then on to the bakery for bread rolls, followed by the fruit stall. They always went to the same places, even though there were plenty of others. Then it was back to the house in the alleyway, where Kerri drank coffee and talked, and Justine cleaned and cooked lunch.

Rohan tells me that she feels she has found some semblance of normality with these women. And now, for the first time in ages, she has something to tell me that doesn't solely involve our child.

In return I tell her about my dilemma. It concerns the potatoes Nino said we could take whenever we liked. I'm torn between trespassing on his good will and the prospect of just a few more for dinner. I don't want to be seen to be taking too many and abusing his generosity, but the temptation to raid his barn is far too strong. I find myself looking around me, and sliding the bolt as quietly as I can. I load my haul in a tuck of my T-shirt, and like a thief I steal out again. I always admonish myself, and pledge to buy some of our own next time we're in town. But his potatoes are so flavoursome, and they encourage me to dream about how wonderful it would be to buy some land of my own and plant a crop myself, and to be able to offer something I'd grown to Nino in return.

Kerri decides to buy a car. She wants to put it in her daughter's name so Justine can have it to get around. It will free her from the confines of the alleyways. A few days later Orlando hears through a mechanic about a Rover for sale. The owner runs the petrol station, and he's reluctant to part with it. Like everyone else who owned a car on the island he'd bought it new, and had intended to keep it until it fell apart. Then he'd probably remove the number plates and dump it in the countryside, or leave it in one of his fields for his dogs to sleep in. But because he considered himself a modern man, he was willing, sadly, to let his faithful old Rover go, at an early stage of deterioration, to someone who would care for it.

In Italy you don't just pay someone for a car and drive away with it. You need to consult a lawyer. There are plenty of documents to be signed and witnessed too. The process can take around three months to complete. But probably because he knows the radiator is just about to blow, the owner agrees to 'loan' the car to Kerri until then. With the full payment handed over, of course.

The Rover gives Justine more freedom than she's dreamed of. She's no longer restricted to the centre of town. She can drive up into the country, or to any one of the island's beaches, in theory whenever she likes.

Our house is quickly tacked on to the daily routine, and each afternoon Justine drives her mother back up to the hills, and stays until the sun goes down. They sit on the terrace, drinking beer, while Luca tears around after Tetley, then kicks his football, and tests his mother's patience. Rohan listens intently to Kerri, who has plenty of advice about bringing up children. Then Luca's noise wakes Louis, who is sharing his downstairs sleeping quarters with me while I have my post-fishing nap, and soon I emerge into the sunlight too.

When the talk isn't of babies, it turns to men, and more particularly to Orlando. I hear how he gets upset with his son when he plays with a ball in the alleyway. 'He thinks only wild kids do that,' Justine retorts, 'but it's a great place to play, I say. No cars. It's safe. But when one boy is out there then another one appears, and before you know it there're fifty thousand of them running around, and they're all screaming and carrying on, and then they fight. I know all kids do that, but there's an old lady nearby who doesn't like the kids running around and Orlando gets upset when he thinks the neighbours are thinking bad things about his family ...'

And now someone's pulled up the anchor on Orlando's father's rowboat and has left it to drift. Orlando only spotted it by chance when he wandered down to Marina Corta for an afternoon coffee. He was livid when he came home and took it out on Justine. He's developing an ulcer, she tells us, from the stress of it all.

'He's angry about this and that all the time: it's noise here and noise there. I told him: "Your environment is eating you away". Because where we are you hear everything; it's noisy all the time — you've heard it,' she continues. 'We've got three little boys who live right near us and they always cry, you know, they're three little boys cooped up in a tiny house, of course they'll go crazy.'

She reminds us of the motorbikes revving their engines, and the toilets flushing, and the arguments drifting in from down the way, and the mosquitoes at night in the summer, and the gossip. Now there's a feud going on between her and Rocco's wife, Rosalia, who lives upstairs, and isn't too easy to ignore. Little Luca keeps knocking on her door or something. But Orlando can't see it. He thinks everything is perfect. He has his brothers, the boat, the cafés. All close. He wants a quiet life, and he doesn't understand why all he's getting is stress.

And so it goes on ... day after day ... becoming more and more revealing, as Justine's relationship with Orlando unfolds. I hear she'll leave him, not for silly little reasons, but if he doesn't shape up a bit. 'I know he does a lot for me,' she says. 'He works hard, but he needs to make me happy, and the kids. I'm not like these island women. They don't mind living in these little houses. They love it, the confusion, people coming by. If you said: "Rosalia, will you swap your tiny house for a big house up in the mountains," she'd say no, for sure. They just don't like outdoors. They love it inside ... He knows that I'm different. One of the things I told him was that I have to get out of that house. I know we can't afford to buy another one, but we can rent ours out, and rent another in the country. He's agreed, but whether or not they're just words I don't know. I need to have a little outdoor bit where the kids can play. It doesn't have to be a garden, just a little yard or something.'

If she could she'd move away for good. Life has come full circle. She found the island, and now she wants to go back home, to escape from here. She'd be gone in a flash. But in her heart she knows Orlando wouldn't survive over there in Australia. On the island he's got his own business, a boat with his brothers and his father. What would he do if he followed her, and left for good? Work in a factory? Swap the sea for somewhere that's nowhere? Wilt, and wait to die, like a hermit crab brought up in a shrimp basket and left to crawl out of its shell on a hot summer's day and die on the deck?

Justine's diplomatic, to a point. Kerri is far less forgiving, especially when it comes to the island's men and the traditional roles she feels are enslaving her daughter. She finds it hard to believe that Orlando's stressed. He goes off on a boat when the weather's nice and comes home to a freshly cooked lunch and a siesta, and a wife who looks after the children. What possible stress could there be in that?

I learn a lot, but I begin to feel guilty. In the early mornings I'm out with the boys in a man's world, which Justine and Kerri have never been shown, and which Orlando refuses to talk about. And here I am now, in the late afternoon, privy to complaints about the man I fish with.

After four weeks of this, seven days a week, what began as a noisy but complementary part of our immersion in the local culture has started to feel like an invasion. I feel my life in the hills is being compromised somehow, and our house has mutated into the epicentre of an expatriate community.

'If you don't like it, then tell them,' Rohan says one day when I voice my objections.

'Do *you* like them coming here every day?'

'I don't mind it. But then we have a lot in common.'

'You mean children.'

'Yes.'

'But Louis is mine too. It doesn't mean I want to spend three hours every night comparing notes.'

'Well, then tell them.'

'I can't.'

'Why not?'

'I don't know how to. Surely they should be a bit more sensitive? Why don't they just give us a couple of nights off a week?'

'Ask them! The problem with you is that you think everyone should read your mind. Stop taking it out on me, I've got enough to deal with without you being angry about them coming up here. If you're upset with them then do something about it.'

But I'm only getting snippets of sleep, and I'm not confident enough in myself to be laying down rules for others.

So I start bolting down the laneway as soon as I wake from my afternoon nap, and it's a great relief to pass Nino's tomato plantations, and munch on a few plums and the last apricots off his trees as I go, and to thrust through meadows now flooded with poppies and fennel, and the ghostly flowers of asphodels on tall, slender stalks. I usually end up beside the *casetta*, my placid eddy, where jolts of blue anchusa flowers are rushing to seed before the hot weather comes.

Over the past few months I've noticed the sunsets moving across the sky, from right to left. It began by dipping orange behind Salina's double cones, now it drops as red as a pomegranate into the open sea. The metallic intensity of the Mediterranean in late afternoon, and the almost imperceptible movement of its surface, always takes me by surprise. Often there's the faintest smell of sea in the air; you can just detect it above the spiciness of the plants and soil. If you cup your ears you might hear it too; but sometimes it's hard to know if it's the sea or just a breeze running through the grass. I sit here, in a comfortable daze, weighing small rocks in my hand before throwing them to Tetley, waiting for the sunset, watching the tiny paper sailing boats as they slowly move across the dazzling surface of the sea.

On one visit I take to wondering if I know anyone who would love this place as much as I do. Only a few people come to mind, and though they might all find pleasure in it, it occurs to me that the only person who really, desperately appreciates this place is me. I've found the most idyllic place I can imagine, where my mind can wander expansively, or focus in on the tiny details of the landscape. I watch ants as they scurry across the loose red dirt around me, and find true beauty in a flower: a simple weed, but a lightning bolt of fresh colour that nothing unnatural can match.

I find myself staring at a sailing boat, and notice the sea is shimmering like a sheet of fish scales in the late afternoon light, and I theorise that there are islands where you'd least expect them. In a way, that boat is one, and our hamlet too. Both are entities unto themselves, distinct from the landscape surrounding them. The same goes for every house, and every family. And we're islands too, floating ones: all of us moving towards and away from each other like waves, mooring for a while, then setting ourselves adrift again.

I'm in a frame of mind to contemplate my life but, as I do so, I begin to realise that I'm starting to feel capsized again. I could blame the language barrier on the boat, and a kinship system I don't belong to, for stopping me from getting as close to my fellow fishermen as I'd wish, but I'd never have thought that I'd start to feel so alienated from my family in the hills, and so impotent to change things.

I've read about it of course: the first-time father, who gains a child but loses his partner. The woman who channels down into her child, leaving the man to coast along as best he can. But I thought I was too smart and sensitive for that to happen to me. But here I am, with the women rafted together around their common ties of children, and I'm beginning to flounder.

I try taking my mind off the situation by working again to improve my Italian. (It's funny what you do when your marriage is falling apart.) In my meetings with Nino I've noticed there are plenty of words I don't understand, and sometimes it's only through a lot of effort and plenty of gesticulating that I am able to figure out what he's going on about. All I can offer him are simple words and basic, halting sentences. It amuses Nino, and he bangs the side of his skull as if to knock the words into my head, then counters my dumb expressions with volleys of double meanings and naughty innuendo. He delights in exploiting my ignorance, and laughs aloud when he sees I'm blank to his good-natured banter. I quickly learn to stifle my embarrassment, because it just sets him off all the more when he's got me pinned down. But I'd do anything to be able to retaliate with well-timed parries, or silly jokes of my own.

I'm aware that some words, like shotgun, trap, maim, and snap — as in 'snap the rabbit's neck' — are not so useful in polite exchanges in the more pleasant quarters of Rome or Venice, but they're handy when you're in conversation with a peasant farmer. So, I start pacing the kitchen, repeating the words aloud over and over again in a bid to fix them in my mind. 'Maim, maim, maim ...' I say, in Italian. 'Shotgun, shotgun ... bullet, bullet ...'

Not surprisingly, Rohan is convinced she should stay as far away from me as possible, which doesn't exactly help things much.

When I confide in Nino a little, and tell him we sleep in the same room as Louis, and I try to help around the house as much as I can, and that we're not getting on well, he slaps his forehead and announces that I'm a fool.

'First off, *professore*,' he says, 'it's better for you to sleep in one of my sheds and to work with me in the fields. A woman has her duties, and a man has his. They shouldn't interfere with each other. A man must be strong, and a woman too. But undermine each other —' he points a finger at his eye '— and look out, you'll make each other weak, and then you won't respect each other any more.'

Whatever Nino says, I'm convinced that some of our problems could be resolved if only I could wrestle Rohan away from her female companions for a while, so that we can spend some time as a family. I'm worried about upsetting Justine, because I like her so much, but the easy camaraderie I'd expected is wearing thin. I just wish she'd only come up a few days a week instead of every afternoon; at least then we could have our sunsets on our terrace again. Taking away our sunsets is worse than theft.

I drop a hint to Kerri, but she appears not to understand, or doesn't want to, and replies that it's just part of the routine: Justine and the kids always come up in the afternoons, and that's that.

Another two weeks pass and nothing changes. Then

while I'm out one day Kerri announces she's returning to Australia, on the next plane, to see her boyfriend and sort out some problems they've been having between them. She'll be back, she says, in three weeks' time. Maybe she'll bring him too, she says.

The day she leaves I stay for drinks with Orlando after fishing. I've noticed he's been looking a bit glum recently too. But when I ask him if anything's wrong he says he's fine. I'm determined to get to the bottom of it though, especially when he orders a Campari and gin, then quickly follows it up with another. I've never seen him drink more than a single glass of beer before.

He downs his second drink just as rapidly as the first, lights up a cigarette and mentions his wife. I had an insight into how marrying Orlando had affected Justine, but I had often wondered how marrying a foreigner had impacted on Orlando. It turns out that living around the foreigner's mother might well be more of a challenge.

He likes a quiet life, he tells me. But when Justine's mother comes over she puts things into his wife's head, gives her big-city ideas that only mean trouble if you're living on a small island. Now when he wakes up in the afternoon Justine's not there, she's up in the hills instead. It used to be a good time to see his kids, before they got tired and went to bed. Now he and Justine are arguing all the time. He hardly sees his family, and when he does Justine's always spouting on about some new idea she's picked up from Kerri. The latest is a holiday over in Sicily, driving around in the car. Kerri wants to pay for it. But imagine it: two women alone. With *his* children. They don't realise how dangerous it is over there. There's so much confusion: so many cars, so many people, bandits, murderers. They could be kidnapped, knocked down on the roads, killed. He might never see his children again.

He's overreacting, but I can see he's genuinely concerned. Foolishly, in hindsight, I tell him I'm also glad his mother-in-law's going home for a while. I'm finding it difficult, I say, to live in the same house with her now …

As the words come out of my mouth I realise that if someone asked me to put my finger on exactly what's brought me to this conclusion I couldn't. It's not one particular thing, it's a series of them: some remarkably trivial. It would make me sound stupid to mention them aloud. But others are more profound. I'd come here for a sea change, to escape the world I'd got used to — to see if I fitted in here. But Kerri is just visiting. She has no greater purpose than to spend as much time as she can with her family before she returns home. And while that plan is admirable in itself, it isn't exactly compatible with mine.

I'm here to get to the heart of the island by letting it wash over me; to sit under an olive tree; to get to know the tracks in the countryside almost as well as those who've walked them all their lives; to stare at flowers; to feel the sea inside me, day after day; to experience the spirit of the place. Only then will I begin to understand if I can be truly happy here.

Kerri doesn't see things like this at all. Her life is in town, in the café and the shops, and in her daughter's house. She functions best when she has an unfailing rhythm to her day, and the poetry of wildflowers and olive trees don't fit into the schedule. So, fundamentally, we haven't much in common.

I take pains not to bring Justine into my confession to Orlando, and there are no real insults or condemnations: it's just a general overspill of my feelings of discontent. When I'm finished I feel relieved. After all, he, of all people, must understand. When it comes to his mother-in-law we're both in the same boat, sort of.

But he says nothing in response, and just nods his head, finishes his drink, and makes his excuses. He's late for lunch, he says.

On the boat the next day he barely speaks to me. When I ask him to join me for a drink before we head off home he refuses, and as I'm walking back to the car I hear Justine calling out. She needs to have a word. She tells me she's heard I've been criticising her mother. She doesn't mind, it's up to me what I say, but Orlando's deeply offended. 'He won't cut you in the street,' she says, 'but there's no point in trying to apologise either. It'll go in one ear and out the other.'

I'm flabbergasted. I'd sat there and listened to him roll out *his* criticisms, and now I'm damned. I thought I was expressing myself to a friend. Worse, there's no comeback. He's even passed his message on through Justine.

'He won't say anything to you because he doesn't like confrontation,' Justine says, as if she's reading my mind. 'That's just the way they are.'

It's the final straw on top of a difficult few days.

Just as I'm about to put the car-key in the lock I spot two large yachts tied to the dock. One flutters a Union

Jack. Aboard is a flaxen-haired woman in her early thirties. She's sitting on a plastic chair, sunning her bare legs, with a cup of coffee beside her on a table and a cigarette between her fingers. I watch her, and for a moment I imagine myself sitting beside her on deck, sipping on a martini, before we hoist sail and get under way, leaving this island behind …

I'm usually shy at times like this, but something pulls me towards her.

'Are you English?' I ask as I wander closer.

'Yes,' she says, flashing a smile. 'And you?'

I nod my head and ask her what she's doing here. She tells me the boat she's on is travelling in convoy with the one beside it. She works for a company in the south of France, which delivers new yachts to wealthy clients throughout the Mediterranean. The one she's on now will stay in Lipari, and the day after next she'll sail to Croatia on the other.

It sounds incredibly romantic. Idyllic even. A floating island, with drinks. I find I'm envious of her freedom. She has no commitments to make her stay, no conflicts on land — she can just take off and be out of here. I want to go with her, but I know I can't.

'Will you be coming to Lipari again?' I ask.

'I hope so. I just love these islands. I wish I could stay.'

'What, for a few weeks?'

'No, you know. Live up in the hills or something. To see the sea from the island rather than the island from the sea.'

'I want to be like you,' I feel like shouting. 'I want my freedom again!' But nothing comes out, and I drive back to the hills alone.

Eleven

Home is where you hang your head.

GROUCHO MARX

My happiness is at its lowest tide, and I've broached the idea of splitting up. The words came from somewhere deep inside me, when on the surface you'd never have guessed they were coming. I had no idea Rohan would be as shocked as she was — I thought she'd accepted the inevitable as much as I had.

'I've never felt any less love for you,' she tells me, 'even though I love Louis. Before he was born I felt that you and I were closer than ever. But how can I give more when I already feel I've given over most of my life? I've committed myself to this relationship. I thought you had too.'

'I just don't know,' I say. 'It feels like we have no other choice. We just don't get on any more. We never talk. We just don't seem to be right for each other.'

The words are coming from my mouth, but I'm somehow dissociated from them. It's as if someone else is speaking, but I know it's my voice, and I'm not entirely sure I trust it.

'Maybe it's not you or me,' I hear her say, 'maybe we're just not the right partner for each other. Maybe we *would* be happier apart.'

I know she's been thinking this for a while now, just as I have. We can easily blame each other for being wrong or extreme, or inconsiderate or unsupportive, but maybe all this is happening because we just don't match up any more. It's all so difficult to work out though, because we're not in the ideal circumstances. Perhaps we should spend some time apart, to think and reassess, to trial what it would be like to live separately, permanently. But where? We're stuck on this island, in this house, spending too much time together.

We lie in bed that night like corpses, too scared to touch each other, stuck in our own little shrouds. We are both doubting our compatibility, after so many years, and I know what she's thinking as she stares into Louis' face; it's the same question as mine — does he know we're breaking up his family?

I realise Rohan fears raising Louis on her own, and she feels sad when she thinks about him growing up without his mother and father together, loving each other. We both wanted so much more for him: more than either of us had as children. It's a tragedy, a failure. But we realise too that we're in too deep. It feels like quicksand. We're suffocating.

Sometime in those long hours, when it's as dark as cuttlefish ink, I try to stretch my mind back before we had Louis, but I can barely remember anything from then. There's a mist over my brain; a placenta pulled over my memory.

'You only care about yourself! You never think of anyone else but you,' Rohan cries. 'You spend all that time lazing about, staring at your navel. Get real and see that there are things to do around here — instead of just getting sozzled all the time.'

'That's not true! You know that's not true. You're always trying to put me down.'

Our unhappiness is erupting. We are face to face, screaming, belittling each other with insults. I'm backed into a corner when she tells me she'll take our child, and I lash out with a slap, catching her on the cheek. She hits me back, and pummels on my back with her fists as I turn away to protect myself. She gathers Louis up. I see his face: he looks at me, his huge eyes unknowing. The door slams. I hear the engine start, and I'm left alone.

I pace the kitchen. I fill a glass with wine and gulp it down. Feverishly I fill another. A few minutes later I'm striding through the darkness towards the *casetta* with my dog, and a flagon of wine swinging in my hand. I have never felt so alone, so unwanted, so desperately small and hopeless. A useless, insignificant blight on this world.

The moon is out and I see my legs, marching, working by themselves, heading towards the cliffs, the dog a shadow in the darkness. I am there before I know it and swig from the flagon once more. I look over the edge. I could jump.

No one would care. I could. I could. But what would happen to the dog, to my poor Tetley? Would he follow me over? Would he know the way back to the house? Should I throw him over the cliff first? And with that thought my heart breaks at last. I can't do it, not to him. I feel useless, pathetic, a mockery of myself, as I stand there ashamed of myself for lashing out at Rohan, for contemplating death.

In the end, it's my trusted hound that saves me. He turns away and returns with a rock. He drops it on my shoe. I pick it up with tears in my eyes and throw it with all my might over the edge of that dreaded cliff. It disappears into the blackness. I strain to hear the crash as it hits the ground, but hear nothing, only emptiness. Everything is still. Waiting.

I drink again, but I notice my desperation is gone now. Still, I laugh almost maniacally. I stagger, exaggerating the walk of a drunk and laughing at myself for acting the fool. But my mind isn't right. I'm not used to this. I'm usually so much more in control of my life.

I find myself walking back along the track, towards the village. Then suddenly I'm here, outside the front door, and a decision has to be made. There is no car. But there is Nino's shed. I slip inside, tuck myself up in some potato sacks and force my mind to clear itself. I sleep fitfully, with Tetley beside me, my only friend. I awake around six, frightened that Nino will find me here, and will ask too many questions. Questions I won't be able to answer, because I don't know the answers.

Sometime during the night Rohan returns. There's a lock on the bedroom door, possibly put there by someone who knew the benefit of keeping out children. Now the door is firmly closed against me.

I live alone for days. We are both stubborn and refuse to talk. We edge around each other, and cry alone at night. Neither of us is good at apologies. Then comes my voice in the darkness, as I leave my place on the sofa and enter the bedroom just as she's turned off the light: 'You still want to split up?'

'I don't know,' she stumbles. She's still angry.

'Neither do I.'

The next day Rohan announces that she's leaving. She's taking Louis to Germany, to stay with her mum. She doesn't know how long for. She just needs to get out of here, and away from me. She needs to think by herself for a while.

I'm too crushed by events to even think about trying to persuade her to stay. She buys air tickets that morning from a travel agency in town, and the next day she's gone.

I miss them both immensely, but I know our separation is the best thing for all of us.

I spend much of my time alone. Walking. Thinking. I can't face the fishing boat.

When she returns at last, after ten days away, she tells me she had a good time. She went places, saw things, and thought: 'Marc would like this …'

But she didn't miss me too much all the same.

I can understand. Constant parenting had meant we'd lost our friendship and intimacy. And now we're on the brink of divorce.

In a last attempt to save our family, we conclude that there's only one thing to do. We have to figure out what attracted us to one another in the first place. So we agree to sit apart, in the kitchen, and scribble away. My mind flies back to when we first met. It was my last night in Australia. I'd outstayed my visa and the government had politely asked me to leave. Her friend was taking over my room, but he'd arrived a couple of days earlier than expected. Then she'd turned up, dressed in her tennis gear. She was tall, with long dark hair, and striking features. She looked me straight in the eyes, and gave me a smile. I was smitten, and literally lost for words. But I was leaving, so what could I do?

For the next nine months I was marooned in Britain. The money I'd saved in Australia soon ran out. I couldn't get a job, however hard I tried. My optimism dwindled. Then, one day, I received a letter from Australian Immigration saying they'd approved my application for residency. And with the last of my cash I fled.

On that first evening back I called her up. We had dinner. We kissed in the car. Two weeks later we moved in together.

'You were intelligent,' I hear myself saying as I read from my list.

'I liked your accent.'

'You enjoyed travelling. I couldn't think of anyone better to travel with.'

'You were interesting, and interested; so many people aren't interested ...'

'You liked camping and walking. You challenged me in my reading.'

'You were at ease about talking about your feelings — sadness, broken hearts.'

'You listened to me back then.'

'Let's not argue.'

'I'm not. It's written down here ...'

'If you say so. What's your next one?'

'It's your turn.'

'I liked the fact you were interested in so many things and you weren't cool and pretentious. You liked David Bowie and ELO for God's sake.'

'It was a long time ago. But we shared the same interest in history, in food.'

'You're kind.'

'So are you.'

'The black satin sheets were a turn-on.'

'I borrowed them for the night.'

'I wanted a serious relationship. I'd never had one.'

'I wanted one too. I always wanted one. I like being in a relationship.'

'You've got one.'

'So have you.'

We make tentative steps: a few words here, an offer to make a cup of tea there. We are overly polite. Walking on glass. But before long we are talking constructively for the first time in ages. And then we kiss. And it feels so special, so strange, like the first kiss I've ever had.

I promise to cut down on the fishing and to take Louis off her hands more often. Rohan will attempt to include me more, and teach me the things she's learning.

Encouraged by each other's responses, we both start to flower again. She laughs. I smile. I even catch myself singing in the kitchen as I cook one afternoon. But we're still left bewildered. How had we let things get so bad? The stacks of good-life-abroad books I'd read made no mention of times like we've just experienced. It's all olives and lunchtimes in those worlds, and the worst things that happen are problems with the plumbing. All those glossy pictures you find in those lifestyle magazines, showing swathes of bougainvillea, plump inviting cushions, and stone tables groaning with lemons are just that: a still picture, a reflection of life that exists momentarily and out of context. They never depict the realities of life, the fact that you bring yourself and your attitudes with you to your exotic new world, and that problems are bound to crop up, because that's the nature of things.

Twelve

*Seed ground that has been fallow, not ground
that has just yielded fruitfully.*

SICILIAN PROVERB

It's well into April now and the caper plants have been
growing at a terrific rate, putting on an inch or so each
night. Now these low mounded shrubs, with their small
round leaves and backward-hooked spikes, are the size
and shape of cartwheels, and the first tiny green flower
buds, the capers themselves, have popped out on the fresh
new tips.

To celebrate the first small crop, Immacolata brings
over some capers she's soaked in brine for two days, then
boiled up in more salted water. She's added them to a
pesto of olive oil, garlic, balsamic vinegar and oregano to
make *insalata di capperi*, which we eat with some salted
anchovies, bought out of a giant barrel in town, and a

wedge of ricotta. Someone has sprinkled this with pepper and baked it in a wood-fired oven until the outside is charred and the inside is sweet and smoky.

They say it's the volcanic soil and the salt air that make the capers from the Islands of the Winds taste better than the ones we usually find in supermarkets, grown in huge crops in North Africa and Spain. It's sometimes difficult to know what you're getting, though: Nino reckons the caper factory on Lipari is importing capers by the truckload from Morocco, which they pickle and jar and stamp 'produce of Salina' — the island where they grow the best capers in the world. He can always tell an Aeolian caper, he says. 'They're grey and succulent, while the imports are green and taste like vinegar.' Blowing a raspberry with his backside thrust out, he insists the authentic version provide a more effective cure for flatulence.

It's Nino who wakes us early on a Sunday morning with shouts of '*capperi, capperi*!' I find him waiting for me in the lane, rubbing his hands, with a white cotton pouch to strap around my waist. He's about to tackle the caper bushes on the slope behind the chicken coops. Allegria forgot about it yesterday morning and didn't turn up, so they're behind schedule. She's here now though, with her kids, ready for work.

The problem with capers, Nino says, is that you need to pick a bush clean every eight days, otherwise the buds get too big and tough. 'But what if it rains?' he asks. 'Or you want to go for a walk? Or drink a glass or two of wine under an olive tree? Or a stranger or friend wants to talk? Well, the capers can wait. You shouldn't put work ahead of your natural impulses.' But as Allegria is a bit more methodical in her timing they could do with an extra pair of hands — meaning mine — and we might as well get cracking before the sun gets too hot.

Rohan is half-hoping she can go back to bed, and when Nino sees her loitering behind me in the doorway, unsure of whether to join us or not, he makes up her mind for her by waving her away with his hand. It's not that he doesn't trust her, he explains, it's just that women shouldn't help with the harvest.

Rohan looks over my shoulder at Allegria, who is busy strapping on a pouch. But she doesn't press the point.

I pull on my shoes and follow the others as they vault a rock wall and scramble down a bank of dirt. The first caper bush we come across is bobbled with flower buds. Those nearest the tips of each spoke are as small and round as a shotgun pellet, while the ones further up are the size and shape of a thumbnail.

While Nino scuttles off to strip another bush, Allegria grabs hold of the end of a tendril, straightens out the natural whip, and rolls her thumb and forefinger over a bud, which seems to be enough to loosen it from its stem. She catches it in her other hand and moves onto the next. In three seconds flat she's stripped the tendril clean and the capers are in her pouch.

At first I'm useless at it. I straighten a tendril and get spiked straight away. I flick a caper into my palm, then another and another. Then they tumble into the dirt. I try again, with one eye on Allegria, and before long I'm proudly holding out six perfectly plucked capers in my palm.

Allegria smiles wearily and moves on to another plant, much larger and denser than the first. 'It's more than a century old,' she tells me as we set to work on it. 'Now it's cropping hundreds of capers a year.'

It's peaceful out here and the job's not too demanding, and as we pick and drop the buds into our pouches, and the children watch intently and try their hand at it too, we have time to get to know each other a little better. Allegria tells me about an education push by the government in Rome to get women from remote areas into the workforce. She took advantage of it and studied tourism, but like many well-intentioned policies thought up by bureaucrats from the big cities, it was doomed to fail in a place where traditional roles are still the norm.

'What job can I do that allows me to start at ten so I can take the kids to school, and get home to make lunch?' she says, resigned. 'And because school finishes at midday, six days a week, I have to look after the kids all afternoon, and supervise their homework. Then there's my duty to my mother. She needs more help than ever now that she's getting old. I have to look after the Nonna and help Nino when there's work to be done on the land. Arturo wouldn't have liked it if I'd got a job anyway.'

'But at least you have each other,' I say. 'I don't think I've ever seen a closer family.'

'We have to be like that. Working on the land means you have to be loyal to each other. One person can't do everything. You have to rely on your family.'

'Living in cities has taken away a lot,' I say, thinking back on my life. 'Families are broken. People hardly see each other any more.'

'But what do you do for food? ... I mean ... well, I suppose you just buy everything. You don't have to plant things and share them. I guess there's no need if you just get paid in money.'

'It's sad, isn't it? I guess that's one of the things I'd hoped to get here ... you know, a sense of community.'

'A family?' she laughs.

'I hadn't thought about it like that.'

But as I shuffle around to pick more capers her comment starts me thinking. Maybe I hadn't come here seeking such closeness, but now that I was here I recognised how much I'd missed it in some of my own relationships. I had fleeting contact with both my parents in England, who were divorced and remarried, and I barely saw my sister. At a push I could tell you the sex of her children, but I wouldn't know their names.

Partly this was because I'd spent so much time living abroad, but I knew it was my culture too, nudging me away from home, to stand on my own two feet. My education encouraged me to achieve, and the city pushed me to focus on money. The talk was about nuclear families, as if it was normal to have such restricted relationships within a larger family, and you passed your aged ones off to nurses and carers because your life was too busy, your mortgage too big, your career too important to spend the time to look after them yourself.

It was true we'd 'started a family' with the birth of Louis. But this term, which we take as read, described a concept alien to these people. They already had family. Generations of it: up and down, spreading sideways through marriages and down through births. Tens of them — hundreds sometimes — connected to each other so tightly by blood and the Church that it was impossible to wriggle free, even if they wanted to. How then, could they *start* a family? It was an absurd concept; one only applicable to orphans.

A warning shout from Nino wakes me from my meditations. The soil's loose on the terrace I'm standing on and it could easily collapse. There's a clump of prickly pear below, he points out. He'd like to see me hopping around with a backside like a pincushion but it would be a waste of a morning if everyone had to spend it pulling out the spines.

I smile and move away, stabbing my toes into the soil to show I'm gripping on tight. I realise how much I'm coming to like him, this chuckling old man, who's holding out a sunburned hand and slicing off a piece of caper plant and waving it in front of me, showing me, unprompted, like a father instructing his son, the best way to propagate them.

'You strike new capers in November, from cuttings,' he tells me, coming closer. 'Forget about seeds. Growing caper plants from seed is *stupido*. You never know who the *papà* is. It could be some miniature plant that grows in the rocks that's doing the fertilisation. Think of a caper like your soul. A caper needs to meet its match to prosper.'

The caper plants you see in the wild, trailing down the dry-stone walls, rely on ruin lizards, he says. They have a taste for the ripe caperberries; the bulbous red fruit that appear after the caper has flowered. Seeds get stuck to the rims of their mouths, and if fortune has it they'll be rubbed off when the lizard darts into a crevice. They grow well in the dust that builds up there, brought from Africa by the *Scirocco* wind.

The lesson over, Nino gets back to work, and I do the same, happily warming myself in the rising sun and the heat of the labour.

It takes us nearly two hours to collect all the capers, and by the time I've finished my pouch is heavy with buds. The sun is bringing out a sweat by now, and we're glad to retire to the shade of one of Nino's barns, where I take a seat on an upturned basket as Allegria pours the capers onto a cloth on the ground. 'We'll leave them here for at least a day,' she says, 'to cool from their time in the sun. Then Nino will sort them into different sizes: the smaller ones taste best; the bigger ones are more bitter, and are crushed and used on pizzas.'

'Or even used to mask the flavour of rotten meat or fish,' Nino says. 'What are you laughing at, *professore*? Even the most reputable restaurants do it.'

But before they can be eaten the capers have to be cured, he says, and a week or so later I ask Nino to show me how it's done.

'You yes, her no,' he replies, jutting his nose at Rohan.

'Why not?'

'I told you before. She's a woman.'

'But so is Allegria.'

'But she's my daughter. I know her.'

'You know Rohan.'

'Yes ... but ... well, it's a little difficult ... I mean, how will I know?'

'Know what?'

'Well ... if she's, umm ... well, you know ...'

'What?'

'*Menstruating.*'

It sounds like Nino is having us on again, but from the look on his face we know he's serious.

'Well, I'm not,' she says.

'Are you sure?'

'Positive.'

'Well ... all right.'

But we can tell from the tone of his voice that he's not entirely convinced.

Nevertheless, he turns his back and trundles off down the laneway and ducks through an opening in one of the walls.

We follow him towards an outhouse, but before Rohan's allowed inside he questions her again.

'You must understand,' he says, 'I can't afford to let you in if you're menstruating. Or just about to. It would ruin the capers. My family depends on them.'

The taboo regarding menstruation dates back to ancient times. In the 1st century AD, Roman natural philosopher and historian Pliny the Elder noted:

Contact with the monthly flux of women turns new wine sour, makes crops wither, kills grafts, dries seeds in gardens, causes the fruit of trees to fall off, dims the bright surface of mirrors, dulls the edge of steel and the gleam of ivory, kills bees, rusts iron and bronze, and causes a horrible smell to fill the air.

In the 21st century, Nino still sees no reason to risk disaster.

'I'm *definitely* not menstruating,' says Rohan, trying to conceal her despair.

'Well, OK … but stand well back and don't touch anything.'

I share a look with Rohan.

Inside the outhouse there are several large plastic drums full of capers and sea salt. The salt draws out the moisture, he tells us. After a few days the saline juices, the *salamọia*, start to collect in the bottom of the drums. After a month in these containers, commercial packers will seal the capers in sterilised jars with more brine and vinegar, but on the Islands of the Winds they're left to dry off for a few days, until the salt crystallises again. In town you can see these salted capers displayed in large blue-and-white bowls outside the fancier *alimentari,* but more usually they appear for sale in small plastic bags. You wash the salt off in several changes of water to remove the excess salt before you eat them.

'I love capers like that,' Rohan says. 'I saw some in the *alimentari* down the road a while ago. I asked the woman about them and she said she grew them herself. So I bought a bag.'

Nino's head snaps back as if he'd been shot.

'I went back a few days later and told her we'd used a few and they tasted wonderful. She's given me fabulous service ever since ...'

Apart from, 'Oh, I've just remembered. I *am* having my period after all,' this is obviously the worst thing to say. If word got out that the guests of Nino, the caper farmer, were so hard pressed for capers they had to buy them, like tourists ... well ...

'Didn't I tell you could have anything you wanted? Anything I grew?' He thrusts up his arms in disbelief. 'Why didn't you ask? It makes no sense to buy them from someone else ...'

'Well, eh, I didn't think. It was just that I was there at the time and ...' But the explanation catches in her throat as Nino begins ladling handfuls of capers into a plastic carrier bag, determined to give them to us. There are enough to last us at least a year, if we ate them with every meal.

'Nino, Nino, stop ... that's far too many,' I protest.

But he's having none of it. We couldn't have predicted from our cultural viewpoint that his sense of hospitality had been infringed. He is pretty limited in what he can give, and for us to go and buy capers from someone else takes away his opportunity to be generous.

'You won't have to go back to your *alimentari* in a hurry,' he says, still hurt, 'but when you do make sure you mention these ...' He pulls the lid off a small container and takes out a handful of withered, salty grey leaves. 'These are the tips of the caper bush. The very best. You only get to pick them once, in early April. It stops the plant producing capers for a while so you can't afford to do it to all your plants. Here take some ...'

He holds out a small handful.

'Let them sit in fresh water for a while and then eat them as an *antipasto* with a drenching of olive oil.'

He moves on to another container. 'And these are the caper fruits,' he says, dredging out a palm-full of wrinkled torpedoes. 'They sell for forty euros a kilo down in Lipari.' He turns to me. 'Which makes them twice as expensive as the shrimp you've been catching, *professore*.'

As the year progresses Nino will let more and more of his caper buds develop into flowers; delicate fairies, about the same size as a hibiscus bloom, but with a tassel of long violet stamens and snow white petals. When the time comes the evenings will be scented with their perfume, a buoyant smell, something like jasmine. The flowers live for just one night, like Cinderella at the ball, and by next morning they've collapsed. After this an olive-green caperberry forms. It grows quickly, and if left too long the seeds will harden inside and it becomes less palatable. In mid-July the final caper harvest will take place. The last flush of buds and the berries will fall prey to *vermi* — the dreaded moth maggots that lay their eggs inside them.

With Rohan getting more on top of things with Louis each day, and me being around much more often, there are far more opportunities to walk together in the countryside, holding hands sometimes. Our outings suit Nino too, and from time to time he knocks on our door, hands me a pouch, and makes me promise I'll pick the capers at various points along our way.

Unfortunately, it's tick season too. These blood-sucking parasites are waiting in the long grass and scented shrubs for any warm-blooded creature to come along.

We find the first one, a flat, ugly, tough little arachnid, creeping across Louis' face, looking for a spot to burrow its head and start feeding on his blood. We've been warned they can transmit pathogens in their saliva. In humans these can cause an incurable, debilitating illness called Lyme Disease. Dogs can die from *canine babesiosis*, which sees parasites infest and destroy their red blood cells.

When we check Tetley, we find several crawling around his neck. We scour the house, and find a tick making its way across our bed. Half an hour later I come across another one biting into my armpit. They soon get so bad that Immacolata bans Nino from wearing his field clothes in the house: he has to strip off in the shed at lunchtime and again when he returns home in the evening. He soon gives up doing this twice a day, and we find him taking his siesta in a shed, on a couple of coffee sacks, with his sickle by his side.

Each morning I take Tetley for his morning pee to the donkey field, and sometimes a pup from a house higher up the hill comes down to watch us. It's thin and bony and at first it skulks away when I get too close, but after days of coaxing it finally accepts a pat. When it wags its tail it almost loses its balance. I run my hand across its back and it's then I notice the ticks: dozens of them, fat and round, the size of sultanas. The pup's fur comes away in bloody lumps.

I pick off as many as I can, but I know it's hopeless. It's already incontinent and walks strangely: the signs of developing paralysis.

The state of the pup almost convinces us to give up our country walks, but after a couple of days at home we can't resist going out again. This time, instead of turning off to the *casetta*, we follow the laneway as it dips and curves downhill in the direction of the sea. The concrete soon gives way to a stone-paved donkey track and the rock walls begin drooping with wild caper plants. We're among skirtings of olive trees already covered with tiny green fruit and in the shadows of a few of these old twisted trees we find a perfect place for a picnic of semolina bread sprinkled with sesame seeds, sheep's-milk cheese, large salted anchovies rinsed beforehand, almond pastries and a small bottle of the island's golden sweet Malvasia wine.

Large volcanic rocks make perfect back rests, and when I inspect them more closely I become convinced that people have been leaning against them for centuries, and have moulded their rough surfaces with their slouching. When we find a couple of antique wine flagons nearby, half buried, with their exposed flanks frosted by time and plated in lichen, it's proof enough for me.

The picnic over, we follow the track as it continues downwards and crosses an access road to some Roman hot springs. We wander through more groves of olives and past a couple of houses with gardens lined with grape vines, until the country thickens with lavender-grey wormwood speckled with insignificant yellow flower heads.

When we finally reach the sea cliffs we make a point of standing high above the waves breaking on the boulders below, taking in the salty air and the cries of the gulls, and waving at boats as they pass close by. Sometimes, if they're close enough, we can see the fishermen onboard waving back at us.

Another of our favourite walks is to the top of a hill we call 'the mountain' because it's the highest thing around. Its slopes are etched with faint worn terraces; the walls that supported them have been carted away generations ago. On its summit, among swathes of thyme and sage, stands a gleaming white pole: a marker for something or other. We sit there sometimes, perched on a rock outcrop above a drop of hundreds of feet to the herring gulls wheeling across the sea, our souls transformed by the gentle wind through the grass, the bees working despite our loafing, the scent of hot, crushed herbs.

One day we meet the man who owns the hill. He's sitting beside his wife beneath the grapevine growing over the arbour in front of Nino's house. The weather is fine, and they're having coffee and cake with Nino and Immacolata. His name is Angelo, officially at least, and hers is Josefina.

He tells me they migrated to Australia in the 1950s, and settled in Melbourne, where so many Aeolian islanders ended up. Now they're back for an extended holiday. They're staying just around the corner from us in the family home, passed on to him and his brothers after their mother's death. The couple speak English, of sorts, but their accents are still strong after more than forty years. Apparently they sound odd to Nino when they're speaking the local dialect, something he ribs them about incessantly. 'What was that word ...?' he'll cry. 'What did you say? I haven't heard that word since I was a youngster. That expression you just came out with ... no one's used that here for decades ...'

Josefina is plump, but Angelo is lean and surprisingly muscular for his age, and soon after introducing himself he tells me he's got a black belt in karate. He stands up, puffs out his chest, and demands I punch him in the guts. 'Go on,' he says in his English, 'hit-a-me. Hit-a-me in the stomach.'

But seeing I'm not going to, he turns to Nino and instructs him to do the same.

'I'll kill you if I hit you,' Nino says, as he clenches both fists and curls up his bottom lip in mock determination.

'You kill-a-him, I kill-a-you,' Josefina screeches back, wagging her finger in front of her huge flowery bosom, before breaking out in a cackle of laughter.

The exchange christens our new friends with the names we continue to use: Hit-a-me and Hit-a-miss. We meet them regularly in the laneways, or while they're walking through the countryside, looking for various parcels of family land. She alone owns several houses, a few of them in ruins, and over a hundred separate pieces of earth scattered around the island. They track most of them down, but out of all the land they own between them, their favourite is Angelo's mountain.

Years ago a company wanted to build a hotel up there, he tells me. But his mother refused to sell. So the developers came back offering more money: she was going to be rich, they said. When she refused again they put on the screws: what did she want with the mountain anyway? It was just a big hill. She was far too old to even climb it. But she held out: every time she looked out of the window she knew it was hers, she said. Money meant nothing when compared to her mountain.

Hit-a-me can understand her decision, he says. Even today it's a remarkable feeling to sit up there and know the very earth belongs to you. It makes you feel whole, he says. Like it's reaching up from the ground and penetrating your insides. You feel full of it. Full of mountain. But he's convinced it won't be his for much longer — and most of the land belonging to his wife will be gone too. Under Italian law if you don't use a piece of ground for a certain amount of time the government will confiscate it and do with it what it likes. But even so, he could never sell it. It would be like setting him adrift from the island forever.

From its crown you can see almost every house in our village: a little oasis in a picture of scrub and fig trees. From here we can see Nino working on his tomato plants, and the donkey lady bent down beneath a load of grass, a falcon lazily hunting lizards, and out to sea the steam rising from the cone of Vulcano, and the chains of hills above the Sicilian coastline. It strikes me one time that it doesn't take too long to travel to Sicily from here, but it feels far enough away to make it virtually inaccessible.

Apart from looking pretty at night when it twinkles, its only role is to remind me of how hectic, how much more bruising life away from our island is, despite the problems we've had. I experienced a Sicilian port town en route to the island and, with the stink of car fumes and the veil of dust blown down from the hills, I feel it's remarkable that people live there at all, when they could be here, with the cries of gulls, kestrels tracing circles in the sky, the smell of crushed spearmint.

I come back often to contemplate the sea. Sometimes I'm alone, but at other times with my family or with Louis strapped in a pouch to my chest — just father and son.

It's on our way to set up a picnic rug one lunchtime that Rohan and I notice the pole on top of the mountain has been transformed. Now there's a saucer-like thing screwed onto its top, and wires leading to a box covered with a plastic sheet. We're tempted to examine it further, but we're lured away by the view out to sea. On the track leading homewards again we meet three men, dressed in jackets and ties and neat brown loafers. Among the volcanic scree slopes and the bushland they look completely out of place.

'Are you going up the mountain?' I ask.

'*Si*. It's our equipment up there,' says one.

He tells us they're vulcanologists. They're taking seismic readings, and the marker pole is part of their hardware. 'There's been a lot of movement,' he goes on gravely.

'*Si?*'

'*Si.*'

'Do you think there's a problem?'

'Maybe … *si.*'

We don't think much of it at first. After all, there's plenty of evidence of volcanic activity around here. But the following day another earthquake hits Lipari. It rattles our windows, and a cup falls off the table and smashes on the tiles. We rush into the laneway and find Nino already there, pointing in the direction of a thick cloud of dust rising along the coastline, where part of it has collapsed into the darkening sea.

'Are you frightened, *professore*?' Nino calls out, and his words hang in the air, conjuring up the fear we hadn't noticed before. 'Shame on you,' he cries, before starting to laugh. 'Go back inside, *professore*. It's just nature's way of tilling the soil.'

Thirteen

*To like and dislike the same things, that is
indeed true friendship.*

Kerri returns with her boyfriend in tow, a quiet, balding
man in his forties. She warns us he's independent and
solitary, and has strict rules and elaborate rituals of the
compulsive kind. But she tells us not to worry, because
they'll stay most of their time in town with Justine, and
plan to come up to the hills only in the evenings. Kevin's
not sure how long he'll stick around. He'd been seeing
Kerri for a few months before she came to Lipari, and
things hadn't been perfect. This time abroad would
determine whether they split up or not. It didn't bode well.

To try and make things up with Orlando, and to
welcome Kevin into our household, I seize the initiative
and suggest a meal on our terrace. I have some misgivings

about cooking a local dish for Orlando, knowing his mother and Justine have perfected things in that regard, and our attempt is likely to fall flat, so we're somewhat relieved when Justine hears of our plans and sends up word that she's desperate for something spicy — she knows we have a stash of curry powder put away for emergencies. Orlando has never eaten Indian food before, but Justine assures us he'll give it a go. In return, she promises to have another go at persuading Orlando to forgive me. It might help if we invite his best friend, Cesare. He's a swordfish fisherman, back in town after a ten-day stint at sea. He's married to the local vet: a French woman she's sure we'll get on well with.

We decide on a chicken curry, and drive down to Marina Lunga to visit the butcher.

We find the shop empty, but the butcher is just across the road, sipping coffee outside a café while making a call to one of his girlfriends on his mobile phone. We take the last remaining table and order drinks, sitting it out until he decides it's time to go back to work.

Ten minutes later he flicks the cover closed on his tiny phone, rests for a few moments with his legs stretched out wide apart, strokes his stubbly chin with a long thin hand, takes a final drag of his cigarette and, ignoring the ashtray, tosses the butt onto the floor. He slowly gets to his feet, stretches, throws a few coins on the table, twists the cigarette end dead with his foot, and lazily saunters back to his shop.

Most of the café tables are emptying around us now as people head indoors to pay. They've been waiting for the butcher too, it seems, and soon there's quite a procession of customers heading in his direction and rattling the beads of the fly curtain as they push through the doorway. We follow, knowing there's no need to rush.

The butcher works slowly. Every transaction requires a detailed rundown of an appropriate recipe, and he needs time to trim away fat and slice around bones with the precision of an artisan. Everyone waits patiently, even when his phone rings. Then he puts down his knife and takes a step back from the counter. 'Of course I love you,' he says, '*si, si, si* ... there's no one else ...'

When it's our turn we ask for the chicken — not cut up, we'll do that ourselves — just whole, *intero*.

'*Intero*,' he repeats. 'Are you sure?'

When we've twice confirmed we're certain, he disappears out the back, and soon returns carrying a monster of a bird by its feet. Its head swings forlornly on the end of its broken neck as the butcher holds it up for our inspection.

Rohan gulps. 'That's fine. But we don't need the head,' she says, aware her sensitivity will seem silly in his eyes.

But the butcher chops without missing a beat, then he raises his cleaver once more. 'I'd advise you to let me cut it into pieces,' he says, 'then with a little olive oil, some garlic ...'

We go our way, our bird safely *intero*, leaving him to answer his phone again.

I like cooking, and never better than when I have someone beside me who appreciates ingredients as much as I do. Rohan smells the garlic before I chop it, and I notice the curve of her waist as she pours the olive oil in the pan.

I move beside her and kiss her on the neck.

'You haven't done that for a while,' she says. She turns to face me and hugs me tightly. I can't believe that I risked all this. I know I've had a glass of red wine or two, but I know for sure that she's essential to me. We're two pieces that fit in a puzzle.

The meal goes well. Orlando is friendly and compliments the food. Cesare's never tasted curry before either, but they both go back for seconds. When the plates are scraped clean I join Orlando and Cesare at the far end of the balcony, where they've retired to smoke on the wall nearest the sea. Meanwhile, Kevin brings out a telescope and starts to set it up; and Rohan runs downstairs to fetch Louis, who's woken up crying.

Orlando's fuming about the evening before. He was riding his scooter through the town centre, he says, when suddenly a traffic policeman appeared out of nowhere. He pulled out his notepad and fined him for not wearing a helmet.

'I've been caught before,' he grumbles. 'I've paid thousands in fines. They've impounded my scooter three times, each time for a month. I had to pay them parking charges for the time they had it locked up, too! Every day people are breaking into shops and doing all sorts of things and getting away with it, and all the police can do is stop scooters and write tickets. They only write them because they have a quota to meet … I want to call them *bastardi* to their faces, but I know I can't. I have a bad temper, but if I spoke my mind they'd put the handcuffs on me. They do nothing all winter, just stand around smoking cigarettes and staring at the women walking down the street. Everyone treats them nicely, says hello, then just before summer — pow! — they're picking on everyone. Just so the place looks better for the tourists.'

'Then why don't you just wear a helmet?' I ask, trying to conceal my amusement. It reminds me of the seatbelt law recently imposed throughout Italy. The north buckled up, the south bought T-shirts with a diagonal black stripe printed across the front.

'Only tourists wear helmets,' Orlando continues scornfully. 'Look. I have respect for the law, but helmets are too hot, too heavy, and they restrict your view when you try to look to the side. They're dangerous. If you can't turn your head properly you can be killed by a car coming up from behind.'

'So it has nothing to do with spoiling your hairdo,' I almost say, but check myself, uncertain of how our relationship stands. 'I guess you'll have to get used to paying fines then,' I say instead.

Orlando ignores me. 'If that *bastardo* had been a hundred metres away I could have turned around and gone the other way. But he jumped out right in front of me. I had no chance.'

He lights another cigarette and I see it's my chance to ask him how the fishing's going, hoping he'd take it as a cue to ask me out to sea again.

'*Male*. We caught nothing. One or two shrimp in each basket. Just a few lobsters. Even they are scarce. We caught hundreds last year, but it's like a fruit tree, once they're picked they're gone.'

'Is it bad for you too?' I ask Cesare.

'Oh, you know, we've been lucky up to now,' he says. 'We're still going after swordfish. The police are trying to stop us, but now we leave and come back late in the evening when the cops are at home.'

I press him about what he does while he's out at sea.

'Most of the time we just play cards and eat bread and sardines,' he says. 'At night we spend two or three hours putting out the nets and marking them with lights, and then we have to make sure no ships run into them.' His teeth gleam whitely in his sunburnt face. 'It was more fun when we used to go long-line fishing for tuna,' he goes on, 'apart from when the hooks used to spear a thumb or finger. They're massive things, those hooks. They'd go right through. But you just pull them out. You don't feel the pain — not at first anyway ...' His teeth glint again, and then he's away, distracted by Louis as Rohan returns with our baby in her arms.

He insists on taking him, and coos softly into his ear. 'And then you're in agony,' he continues, 'with the salt and the fish guts in the wound. It takes twenty minutes until you can work again.'

Sometimes I'm still in awe when I think of the situation we've found ourselves in. We're on a terrace overlooking the sea, under the moon, with a swordfish fisherman kissing our child as he tells me about enormous bloody hooks he's had to wrench out of his fingers! And here beside me too is a shrimp fisherman, who's been trawling the seas since he was fourteen. Then there's Dominique, a Parisian vet who's thrown in her lot with a fisherman from a tiny island, and who I hear has just been treating a stranded dolphin over on Vulcano, which her husband could just as easily have drowned in his nets without a thought. I feel amazed to be here, and I'm sure I'll recall this evening as clearly as so many other times I've had on these islands. I'm sure you can extend your life, or at least your perception of its duration in hindsight, by living life differently whenever you can.

Cesare and Orlando wander away and soon I'm talking to Dominique. She's just returned from Paris, she tells me, and is already missing it badly. After she met her fisherman she'd spend six months at home and six months here. But now they have young kids, money is tight, and she's working for a practice in town, making house calls all over the archipelago.

Once she'd thought that Cesare might settle down in Paris with her, but now she's convinced he'll never leave. 'The sea is in his blood,' she says, before correcting herself. 'No, it's not *in* his blood, it *is* his blood. How can you lock someone like that up in a city, in an office? He'd be dwarfed by it all. He'd go mad. Every time he saw weather clouds coming in, bringing rain and thunder, he'd be thinking of his island and the sea … People might leave an island like this if they have no money, but if they have a livelihood they won't. That's why the government's attempt to stop them fishing for swordfish is so bad. It might drive them away and break their hearts. They have no idea what's out there, what it's really like. They have small horizons these fishermen.' She looks over at Cesare, who has returned from the bathroom and is entertaining Louis with '*na-na-na*' from a Kylie Minogue song. 'They drink coffee, work, talk of local things, like all the islanders of their age. Small world. Small island.'

'Small boats,' I put in.

'That's what worries me. One day some of them aren't going to come back. Just look at the graveyards around here. Almost everyone dies when they're in their nineties. The other ones are for the young who've been lost at sea.'

It's a maudlin point, and one neither of us wishes to dwell upon, and fortunately Orlando walks up again and shakes my hand with a smile. He's preparing to leave. But my hospitality seems to have done the trick. Orlando invites me to go fishing the next morning, and I can sense that as long as I don't criticise his mother-in-law our relationship should be fine.

Kerri has persuaded Raimondo to lend Kevin an old broken-down scooter in exchange for getting it fixed and insured. Our housemates leave on the bike early in the morning and most nights don't return until late. Justine rarely appears up in the hills, out of respect for Orlando, who's finally announced that he wants her and the children at home when he wakes up in the afternoon. In a way it's a shame, but I can't help thinking things would have been better if all along we'd met just occasionally, when we all felt like it, not because it was customary.

As for Kevin — it soon becomes obvious that he likes his routines too. We can time his departure in the morning to the second, and his arrival home just the same. At the coffee shop each morning he has a *café americano* and a *cornetto con crema* before heading off alone for his morning swim: two lengths of the beach, no more, no less, counting his strokes. He has a roll for lunch: same bread, same filling. He spends part of the afternoon on the usual beach, with the women, lying on his back staring up at the sky, never talking. As soon as he returns home he warms his mug to the correct temperature, scalds his teaspoon, and scoops out the honey he uses for sweetening. Kerri has warned us: we mustn't use his spoon, nor touch his honey (he's very particular). He goes on to consult his watch: counting down the seconds as the teabag steeps. He stirs four times, places two biscuits on a plate, then retires to the terrace to strum his guitar, so quietly I have to strain to listen. Sometimes his strict schedule is interrupted by a panic attack, or an argument with Kerri. Then he'll cordon himself off behind the closed door of their bedroom, restricting our access to the terrace overlooking the sea. When we knock he doesn't answer, and when we enter anyway we find him sprawled on his bed, either staring blankly at the ceiling, or with his eyes tightly closed, shutting us out. He wanders through the house like a shadow, and every day ends the same way: with a shower, the tap turned on at the stroke of midnight. If the weather gets in the way of things he is lost, agitated, unhappy; his mood only lightens once the clouds have cleared and things are back to normal. In a humorous frame of mind I could imagine him lying on the beach when the sun refused to come out, staring into the sky, with the raindrops falling into his eyes.

With such an all-encompassing routine how can there be room left for surprise? If life has to be planned down to the moment then there is little room for anything to interrupt. No emotional meaning or attachment. His behaviour is perplexing for someone as eager for variety as I am, but we can see that it's not a matter of choice. Not that that makes it any easier to live with.

While two largely separate camps have developed in our house, our one is getting tighter by the day. Louis is soon crawling, and we take it in turns to help him climb the steps in the kitchen. We take him out as often as we can and we always find there's something interesting to do, somewhere beautiful to see. By chance we discover *spiaggia bianca*, the white beach. The pumice dust from the nearby mine has settled beneath the sea in this secluded cove, and from the beach the sea looks like an exotic aqua sheet. Floating pebbles of pumice brush against our fingertips and collect around our chests and shoulders as we swim. Our favourite time is lunchtime, just as local mothers and their shiny, dripping children go back home to eat before their siesta. Then we find we've got the whole place to ourselves.

One day when I'm out on the boat, Rohan heads for the beach at Canneto. She's there with Kerri, Justine and the children, watching steam blow out of Stromboli's top, while Tetley and Luca play fetch on the shore. Rohan is happy. 'There's the indulgence you have with your children only other women in similar positions can understand,' she tells me later.

'Where was Kevin?' I asked above the crackle of shrimps in our frying pan.

'On another beach.'

After just two weeks together, it turns out that Kerri and Kevin are going their separate ways. Kevin thinks they've been living too much in each other's pocket, and Kerri wants to be alone with Justine.

'I want her all to myself,' she says, 'so it'll work out well if Kevin goes off by himself. He prefers it like that anyway.'

It sounds odd to me, especially because she rushed back to Australia to try to patch things up with him. But relationships can be strange things, as I well know.

I love these early summer days in the hills, when the green-backed ruin lizards are slumbering in the shadows, and you can catch the faintest of scents in the air. It's a familiar, slightly resinous odour, and your nose leads you towards the trees.

The culprits are Mediterranean stone pines, which you can spot by their chocolate trunks and their shady umbrellas of long glossy needles. On Lipari they line the laneways on the uppermost slopes, and you can also find them in the grounds of the citadel, overlooking Marina Corta, where their giant cones thud down onto the pumice covers of long-empty tombs.

Originally from the Iberian Peninsula, the stone pine's alleged aphrodisiac qualities make it the oyster of the tree world. The Roman celebrity chef, Apicius, whose creations were still being cooked up well into the Middle

Ages, recommends a mixture of pine nuts, cooked onions, white mustard and pepper to beef up your sex life. If you're interested in taking your research further, I refer you to the writings of the 2nd-century Greek physician Galenos. He proposes that eating a glassful of very thick honey followed by twenty almonds and one hundred pine nuts can enhance a man's sexual vigour. It's sage advice, and far less greasy than another of the book's offerings, which recommends rubbing 'the virile member and the vulva with gall from the jackal', or covering the offending part with fat melted from the hump of a camel. Thankfully, all we want is a few nuts to make some pesto.

We already have most of the ingredients. For weeks we've been stripping the bundled plaits of garlic hanging up to dry from the lowest branch of Nino's mulberry tree, and we're going through the bottles of olive oil he keeps in his barn. There's as much basil as we want too, care of Nino's nearest kitchen garden, which is bursting with the stuff.

Nino reckons November to January is the best time to collect pine nuts, but he's sure we won't have too much of a problem finding enough scattered around now. On one of my days off from fishing he tells us he'd come with us to collect some, but it's Immacolata's job. If he started taking over her tasks now, who knows where it might end.

So it's on a sunny afternoon that we find ourselves negotiating the rutted country lanes leading up to Lipari's second-highest peak. We park the car beside a forester's house set in a grove of conifers, unload Tetley and Louis, and set off towards our goal; a line of overhanging greenery a short hike up a thin concrete track. Tetley belts ahead, and we round a bend to find him waiting for us with a cone the size of a hand grenade in his mouth. He drops it as we approach, and it tumbles down the track towards us, clicking and clacking and spitting out nuts as it goes. Before long I've gathered an easy handful.

Further up the hill there are plenty more cones, and the path is covered in spilt nuts. I start banging the cones against the pathway to knock more seeds out. It's a messy business; each tan-coloured nutshell is covered with a dusting of black soot, and the cones exude thick globules of resin. But before long we have hundreds of nuts, and all we have to do now is drive back home and separate the shells from the kernels. I try hammering them with shoe heels, rocks and the bottoms of coffee cups, but the insides mostly end up crushed or splintered, and black with soot. I now understand why they're so expensive to buy back home.

There has to be a better way of doing it, though, and Nino is the man to advise us.

'Why not use a nut cracker?' he says, and lets us borrow his until we can buy our own.

Back out on the boat the catches are still small, but at least we're getting a regular feed of seafood. The brothers are fretting though, and there's talk about stopping for the summer and taking tourists out on sightseeing trips instead. But, while the younger brothers think it's a good idea, the older ones remind them of their allegiance to their father and their tradition, and refuse to contemplate it.

The beaches are dotted with a vanguard of tourists now, and entrepreneurs are bringing out umbrellas and sun chairs and lining them up along the pebbles. Everyone's marvelling at the water, which is so green and clear that fishing boats seem to float in midair.

In town the restaurants are serving the dish of the season — *scorfano*, or scorpion fish: ugly, poisonous creatures we've been bringing up from the bottom quite regularly. They're not at all like their beautiful feathery-spined cousins from warmer waters, so I'm not so sad to see the smaller ones added to soup, and the biggest baked and served whole to those who can afford it.

Up in the hills the figs are still small and hard on the trees, and the table grapes are hanging in unripened green bunches from their trellises. After years of bearing up, Immacolata has finally been admitted to hospital in Sicily for an operation to replace her worn-away hip. She'll be away for ten days, and has to take her own bedding and provide her own food, which Nino and Allegria take over every two days. When she finally returns home, she's still in terrible pain. It's healing nicely, but a surly hospital nurse has ripped the plaster bandages off, along with a layer of skin.

Hearing that Immacolata's back home, a stream of well-wishers turn up, not with cakes or get-well cards, but with new wooden pegs for her washing line, a chicken casserole, a second coffee pot. Practical things. Her brother, a builder, visits every day for three weeks, always with a parcel of biscuits under his arm, tied with a ribbon. He's a fearsome-looking man in his late fifties, with slicked-back hair, a heavy Roman nose, and a powerful frame. We often see him overseeing his construction sites in a white business shirt and sober tie. He nods his head in recognition when he sees us, but we feel it in our bones that it's not wise to cross him.

With Immacolata out of action, Allegria is run ragged with housework in both her homes, and when there's a threat of more bad weather, Arturo comes up too, and drives around with me to Nino's vineyards to pick stray zucchini and various other vegetables he's planted around his grape vines. We mostly talk about country topics when we're out together: plants and farming. He barely mentions the boat and the sea. He prefers it up here.

Over time I find we've drifted close together, and I think of him as a friend. I know I'm an outsider, but connections with people like Arturo can only help to deepen my sense that the risk we took moving here might pay off after all: this could be our home some day.

Fourteen

*What you seek in vain for half your life,
one day you come full upon — all the
family at dinner.*

HENRY DAVID THOREAU

It's June now, and the last of the apricots and mulberries are starting to shrivel on their branches. It hasn't rained for weeks and the tomato plants are brown and starting to buckle under the weight of their small red fruit. Eaten fresh, Nino's tomatoes taste dry and pulpy, but we soon discover their intense flavours when they're heated, so we raid the fields and fry them in olive oil for breakfast.

We've promised to help with the tomato harvest, and when it's time we spend hours in the fields filling up Nino's wicker baskets. Then, sometime after midnight, Nino gets out of bed, ready to make the *passata*, the tomato sauce the family adds to their meals. We join him before dawn down by the chicken coops, and find him inspecting his fruit and pulling off the remains of the stems, one by one in the moonlight.

Unlike commercial bottlers, who tend to use just one type when they're making sauce, Nino has a very mixed crop.

Altogether we have to press a couple of hundred kilos of San Marzano, a medium-sized, egg-shaped tomato, favoured for its pulp. Then there are a few rotund Santa Rosas, to add a bit of juice; and the Zeppelin-like Lampadina, a good all-rounder; and Nino's favourite, and our hamlet's speciality — various types of sweet *ciliegino*, the cherry tomato.

Nino lights a wood fire beneath a cauldron, pours in some water and waits for it to boil. When it's bubbling on the grate Nino rests the first basket of tomatoes on a wooden frame just inside its lip and leaves them until the skins begin to split. He pours the slurry of steaming, squashed fruit into the *Marta*, a flat wooden tray named after a woman whose story has been lost in time.

Just as we're removing the last of the baskets from the water, Allegria arrives to operate the pulping machine. It's only two years old, and runs off petrol, she tells me. It's just about the best invention she can think of. The days of crushing *a mano*, by hand, with a kind of mangle, are over. Good riddance. It used to take the best part of a day, with Immacolata and the Nonna helping too. Now it takes just a couple of hours, and Immacolata can take it easy indoors. Her hip is still playing up, and no one wants to push her beyond making pots of thick black coffee. As for the Nonna ... she can stay in bed. Her age has earned her the right to a lie-in until nine.

The machine chugs into life and Nino begins pouring the tomatoes into a funnel. Allegria pushes them into the machine with a plunger and a bright red slop gushes out of one end into a bucket, while the fibrous tomato pulp comes out of the other.

I'm roped in to carry crates of empty containers. Many of them are beer bottles, most of them our empties, while others are milk bottles, some more than twenty years old. Allegria points out the engraved logos of a company long since bankrupt. They've been appearing on the kitchen table each year for as long as she can remember, she says. But bottles get chipped and broken, and a growing family always demands more. It's fortunate there are massive recycling bins on the island now, and Nino is in charge of the recycling committee. To set an example, he takes as many old bottles as he wants.

Nino fills them ingeniously by sucking up the sauce through a rubber hose, stopping the end with his thumb, then placing it in the neck of each bottle and letting gravity take over. It's left for Allegria to give the tops a wipe with her fingers, and for Rohan to finish the cleaning with a rag. A mechanical capping machine seals them up, and soon I've counted two hundred bottles: a year's supply for the entire family.

The sun is coming up, the sea is gleaming, and the fire has gone out. Nino rekindles it with dried grass from the countryside, some prunings from one of the mulberry trees, and finally adds some thick logs of olive. He starts on a second grate beside it, as I manhandle the crates of filled bottles, and roll two enormous oil drums across the yard. When both drums are on the grates Allegria pours a bucket of water into each, and Nino layers the bottom of one with cardboard.

I hand him some bottles and he reaches down inside the drum and one by one he lies the bottles on their sides. Another layer of cardboard goes on top, and some of his old shirts and trousers too. It goes on, lasagne-style, until the drum is nearly full, and the contents are weighted down with chunks of concrete and iron. When both drums are packed I fill the containers with water. The bottles will boil for an hour, then be left to cool. Nino will unpack them in the afternoon, and store them in one of his barns. We get several bottles for our help, and buckets of hard black plums.

There's also a lunchtime run to our place whenever Immacolata has made something special. We get a plate of stuffed artichokes, and eggplants filled with tomatoes and capers.

To show our appreciation for the regular supply of food I bake some Welsh cakes; simple flat scone-like things made from flour, eggs, butter and currants. My grandmother taught me how to make them.

We present these simple cakes to Immacolata over coffee at her house one day. She brings out some biscuits of her own, and puts the Welsh cakes away in a cupboard for future guests. I'm a bit disappointed she doesn't want to eat them then and there. I'd like to see their reaction to this peasant food from the country of my birth. Later I hear she brought them out when Kerri and Kevin went over to visit. The Nonna loved them, Kerri reports back. She ate three in a row and had to be held back from going for a fourth.

In return for the Welsh cakes Nino appears with a rabbit he's trapped out in the fields. He meets us in the laneway and pulls the shocked animal from the pouch around his waist by its ears. The trap has shattered its back legs, and the bones are quite clearly poking out of the skin. Rohan puts a hand over her mouth to suppress a yelp. It was trapped yesterday, at dusk, as the crows were flying back to their nests. It struggled through the night, calling out mutely for deliverance, being driven mad by the pain. Then Nino found it, an hour or so ago, and carried it home, still alive. I raise my eyes to his. For heaven's sake, just kill it.

Nino regards us intensely for a moment, then gently lassoes a callused hand over the rabbit's head and pulls, breaking its neck. He holds the limp body towards us. 'You can have it for your lunch, if you want it,' he says. But we stand motionless, and Nino shakes his head and turns his back on us.

He appears again next morning, whistling loudly outside our house, waving a hand in the direction of the rabbit hutches. We follow him under the mulberry tree and he points out a plump coffee-patched female with a twitching nose and a dozen offspring of various sizes. 'She's the *mamma*,' he says. 'A good producer. All these are hers ...'

Nino pulls back the bolt, and all but one jerks towards the back of their cage. The stupidest comes closer to investigate Nino's open palm, and in an instant Nino grabs it by the ears and it's dangling in front of my face.

'This one will do,' he says. 'It'll taste lovely. Much finer than the wild one. Do you want to skin it or shall I? My wife will cook it. You probably don't have any idea how it's done.'

I know he finds it amusing that we're so squeamish when it comes to eating animals you have to kill yourself, but it occurs to me that Nino has treated those he keeps in the hutches almost like pets. From the day they were newborns he's fetched herbs from the fields to feed them, and brought home special treats from the countryside. He's changed their hay and water, and watched as his grandchildren poked carrot tops through the bars. So how can he then pull one out, break its neck, rip out its guts, pull off its fur, and hand it to his wife to put in the pot? If the rabbits were mine, and it was left up to me, I might be brave enough to get someone else to do them in, but I'm sure I'd be shining a torch into the hutch soon after dessert, desperately trying to see which rabbit was missing. Then, no doubt, the whole village would be shaken by my soulful screech: 'Oh, no. It was Fluffy! They went and killed Fluffy!'

Later that day Immacolata sends over some baked rabbit, which we pick at out of respect but end up giving to Tetley. Then, as the days pass, more meals arrive, along with a basket of beans and a late crop of lettuce. It develops into a game of shuttlecock: Rohan decides to pay them back with a chocolate cake. She fills the cake tin with a rich dark dough, and finds there's enough left over for a smaller cake too. When they are ready she leaves them to cool overnight on our only chopping board. The following morning she presents Immacolata with the largest. Rohan is proud of her offering. The cake turned out well. It is moist in the middle and crispy and dark on the top. Immacolata receives it graciously, puts it away in the cupboard, and brings out some biscuits her brother brought over.

We serve ourselves the smaller cake that afternoon on the terrace. It tastes strongly of garlic! I spit it out, perplexed. Then enlightenment dawns ... 'Did you wash the chopping board before you put the cakes on it?' I ask, insightfully for me.

'No. But it looked clean.'

'I cut garlic up on it for yesterday's pasta,' I confess, 'and, ummm, I forgot to wash it afterwards.'

Rohan laughs. I feel guilty for both of us. I'm always more sensitive to things like that, whereas she sees them as just part of the misadventures of life.

Anyway, I continue to wonder what they thought of that cake, which almost certainly tasted as strongly of garlic as ours did. I suspect that Immacolata probably served it to her guests with a flourish, telling everyone how thoughtful we were. There were only two conclusions they could have drawn when they tasted it; either combining garlic with chocolate was some odd speciality peculiar to our culture, or we were slighting them: sending a message, in no subtle way, that we thought the meals they were sending across were awful, unwanted, and that they must desist. Somehow we never get around to telling them the truth, and sadly it's a long time until we are sent anything more to eat. And when we offer Nino and Immacolata something from our own kitchen, they shake their heads vigorously and rush away, making their excuses.

The set-back doesn't stop us trying to impress our friends with our culinary expertise. It's probably unwise to prepare a pasta dish for an Italian, but when we hear Justine's been buying pesto from the supermarket we tell her we'll bring down some of our home-made sauce for them to try. Rohan makes a good pesto, and now she has harvested the ingredients from the countryside herself. Justine is encouraging, with a hint of self-interest. It'll be the first lunch she hasn't had to cook in years.

It's Sunday, and though the winds were up yesterday, conditions for fishing improved rapidly after dark. In the end the boys decided it was worth risking taking the boat out. It was the worst part of the job: leaving at midnight, motoring over to an island, emptying all the baskets and then transporting them to another one. I'd only done it once and found the extra hours so draining that I felt like collapsing from exhaustion before the coast of Lipari was even in sight. They were kind enough not to invite me.

We'd picked basil from Nino's garden and ground it up with some pine nuts from the hill. In went some of Nino's oil, some cloves of garlic from the plaits still hanging on the mulberry tree, plenty of Parmesan, and a pinch of salt. We'd even stopped off on the way to their house to pick up some pasta from the supermarket too. We knew how important it was that lunch was ready in time, especially on days like this when the fishermen end up shaking with tiredness and hunger, so we made sure we were at their house well before Orlando arrived.

But when we enter his house we find him already at the table. Eating pasta.

'I rang half an hour ago,' Justine whispers, embarrassed, 'but Immacolata told me you'd already left. He came home early. So I had to rush to it. You know fishermen. They can't wait. He was looking forward to it an' all, weren't you Orlando?'

'*Si.*'

We watch as he shovels spaghetti into his mouth, trying to fill his stomach as quickly as he can.

Rohan's crushed, and even more disappointed when he refuses to even taste her pesto.

'It just doesn't go with the tomato sauce,' Justine explains meekly.

She hasn't eaten yet though, she says as brightly as she can, and forks some into her bowl. 'It's gorgeous,' she announces, but later admits she can't get the taste of garlic out of her mouth. The jars from the supermarket don't use nearly as much.

It's a telling point. Apart from seafood when they're fishing, the fisherman and his wife rely on the shops in town for almost everything. It's not uncommon. Most young people do the same. The convenience society is beating down the old ways, and the sauces and preserves, the very basics, are the first to go. People like Nino and Immacolata could be among the last of a tradition of subsistence farming going back thousands of years. As for the Nonna, she's never been inside a supermarket in her life: she's never had a reason to.

But though many farming families are hanging on grimly to the old ways as much as they can, there are plenty of others in the hills who know the value of modern ways of working the fields, especially when it comes to making a profit. They eat crops that rely on nature for their success, but the stuff they sell to the shops in town, or boat across to Salina and Stromboli, is doused with artificial fertiliser, pesticides and herbicides. The family's crop is small and misshapen, and nibbled by slugs and insects. The vegetables they sell are unnaturally large and perfectly shaped. Anything that tries to eat them dies on the spot. So why should they feed them to the people they love?

Nino would never use chemicals, even on things he sells or swaps. This wholesome ideal has filtered down through his immediate family. When Allegria sees us carrying home some tinned tomatoes she is quick to warn us about the chemicals they use to line the tins. She would never buy a commercial bottle of wine either: she's heard about preservatives, and she has no idea about what they sprayed on the vines.

All of this makes no difference to Rohan, who's visibly upset by Justine and Orlando's reaction to her exquisite pesto. This, together with the fiasco of the chocolate cake, makes her vow never to cook for anyone again — at least until her pride is mended.

It's hotter today despite being early. It's windy too, and the harbour buoys are groaning as they're taken up on the swell and dropped again. The fishing's been cancelled again, but on land there's important work to do despite the heat.

Nino wants to tackle the tall dry grass around the olive trees on the way to the *casetta*. He'd like my help, but I'm not too keen at first. Hacking away with a sickle on such a hot day can't be fun, I surmise. When he tells me burning is easier, I'm even more sceptical. What with the heat and the rising winds, I would have thought it was probably the worst time to set a fire.

'Isn't it dangerous?' I ask.

'*Si, Si. È pericolosissimo*!'

'So it is dangerous.'

'*Si*. As I said. But my fireman friend is coming with us.'

He's lived here all his life, I reason, so he must know what he's doing. If he's got a fireman with him, what can go wrong?

The fireman turns out to be a charming man with orange overalls and a sporty moustache. He spends part of each summer on duty in Lipari, usually putting up at our house, but because we've taken over, he's sleeping on a couch in Nino's living room. In return for having a place to stay while on secondment from Sicily, he helps Nino around the fields whenever he can.

'Oh, and leave the dog behind, *professore*. Just in case ...' Nino says as I turn back into the house to put on my shoes.

Out in the countryside the grass beneath his olive trees is as high as our waists. Nino checks the wind with his thumb. The fireman does the same. When they're content all is well, and they see that I'm looking in the opposite direction, something happens ... I'm not blaming anyone: a cloud might have appeared out of nowhere and spat out a lightning bolt, or it might have been me who dropped a match in the grass, but however it started the result is the same — a dirty great fireball.

In a matter of moments, bushes are exploding all around us, and the flames are heading for the hills. I look at Nino, who looks at the fireman, who voices the thought we know we are all thinking.

'RUN!' the fireman suddenly screams, and he legs it back down the track with Nino hot on his heels. In my terror I overtake both of them and only slow down once to look over my shoulder. The fire is completely out of control. Prickly pear cacti are buckling and collapsing; huge flowering fennel plants are being overwhelmed; wormwood, wild oats and dead thistles are evaporating in balls of flame. In barely a minute, the fire has raged across the expanse of pasture and scrub almost as far as the feet of the cliffs leading up to the vineyards, and when we reach relative safety we turn to watch the flames hopping up the cliff faces like rabbits. Everything in front of us is ablaze, and all we can do is to shake our heads as the fire slams over the ridge and veers off towards the *casetta* and the caper bushes.

'I've got to ring someone,' announces the fireman, trying to catch his breath. He frantically jabs a finger at the keypad of his mobile phone, shouts down the line, and gives directions. 'It's out of our hands now,' he says finally, though I find it hard to believe it was ever *in* our hands in the first place. 'I've called the rest of the boys,' he continues, referring to his colleagues in town.

'Come on,' says Nino to me, as he turns tail and stomps off towards home. 'There's nothing else we can do.'

'But what the hell happened?' I ask.

'Who knows? But one thing's for sure, if the grasses were left like they were, some fool tourist would have come along in the middle of August and left a cigarette burning, and before we knew it everything would be ablaze. I know the winds. It's fortunate the fire came when it did. At least we know now that it'll run away from the houses.'

Plumes of thick black smoke are bowling up into the sky now, and, bravely, the fireman has agreed to stay behind to do his bit. He'll wait at the edge of the fields for his mates, who will arrive within the hour and stand about in the ashes, smoking their cigarettes, as the water-bombing plane from Naples busies itself dropping bucketloads of sea water over the ridge tops.

'It's a free service,' Nino will tell me later, safe on his terrace. 'It takes them just twenty minutes to get here from the time we call them. It's amazing, isn't it?'

That afternoon I take Tetley with me to explore the damage. The fields I'd waded through earlier in the year are black and levelled, and the paths that had started to become heavy going are clear of grasses and prickles. As I climb the long ridgeline that leads to the small plateau overlooking the *casetta* and the sea, I'm sure I'll find my favourite shack burnt to the ground. But as I reach the brow and cut across the blackened earth I see that by some miracle the flames have swept around its edges, burning down the reeds on one side of the last stretch of pathway to the hut, but sparing the rest. As I get closer I notice the caper plants are still green and healthy and the apricot trees nearest the building are untouched; the only real damage is a singed almond tree, which will recover in time. I'm elated. My little haven still exists, and I turn tail immediately, ready to burst in on Nino and tell him the good news.

I take the longer route back though, to see the spot where the fire started. I'm shocked when I arrive. The leaves on the smaller olive trees are brown and crispy, and smoke is still rising from the base of one large specimen's trunk. I push my way through charcoaled stalks that were once wormwood bushes and I find the roots of the tree still on fire, and there's a crater beneath it, where the earth has literally melted away.

'It'll probably burn for three or four days,' Nino tells me when I catch up with him. I'm not sure by the tone of his voice whether he's sad or resigned.

'Could we put it out with some water?' I say, with as much hope as I can muster.

'Yes, some water might help. Tomorrow perhaps. The firemen might come up for something to do. It gets boring sitting in their fire station.'

When Nino disappears in the direction of the rabbit huts, I spot the Nonna up above me, standing on the edge of the terrace. She's furious, and wants to get her message across to me so badly that she speaks to me for the first time in basic Italian, instead of her usual dialect.

'*Ogni anno …*' she says. Every year, it's the same. Someone sets fire to the grass and burns down my olive trees. '*Ogni anno … mamma mia!*'

The Nonna doesn't talk to Nino for a week and, although the olive trees eventually green up again, the year's crop of fruit is lost, and Nino will have to rely on trees elsewhere to provide the family with next year's oil.

On one of her now rare daytime visits to the hills, Justine is astonished by the blackened countryside visible from our house. She knows Nino well enough to guess he might be involved somehow, and when she overhears the Nonna still raging about her lost olive trees she's even more certain she knows who the culprit is. But she thinks the whole thing's hilarious, and laughs about it when she goes home to Orlando. Then Orlando asks Arturo if it's true, and suddenly everyone is on the defensive. When we meet Allegria in the street she looks me in the eyes and tells me sternly that Nino had nothing to do with it. I nod my head. Absolutely. But the Nonna won't have any of it, and is still raving on to anyone who'll listen.

Once someone, whoever it was, starts the first of the season's fires, it's the cue for all the island's peasant farmers to start burning off. For days a pall of smoke hangs over the island as the fires burn wild. Tourists down at Canneto watch from the beach as hillsides blaze and fire engines and helicopters try to keep things under control. From out at sea the whole island looks like it's one big smoking volcano.

Fifteen

*The little reed, bending to the force of the
wind, soon stood upright again when the storm
had passed over.*

AESOP

If you were to lay a bet on which was more dangerous, a wind strong enough to smash anchored vessels against their moorings, or a draught coming in through your kitchen window, you'd most likely go for the former. But then that would be the Anglo-Saxon response.

According to Aeolian logic, you can always move the boat to a safer harbour, and in any case you should have been forewarned of an incoming gale by the direction of the volcano smoke. The problem with a household breeze, or *la corrente* — a name so potent it can only be whispered — is that by the time you notice it prickling the back of your neck it's already too late; you might as well take to your bed, cross yourself repeatedly, ring all the relatives, and renew the order on the coffin. There's no doubt about it: you've contracted what all islanders around here fear most — the dreaded *influenza*.

It's curious, but on the Islands of the Winds you catch the flu in an entirely different manner from that endured anywhere else. For a start, the virus is never passed on by contact with an infected person. Instead, you usually catch it if someone leaves a window open (hence the common alleyway alert enacted when your neighbour's net curtains are spotted fluttering: 'SIGNORA, SIGNORA, QUICK, QUICK, THE TEMPERATURE'S DROPPING OUTSIDE. *MAMMA MIA* — *la corrente* — IT'S COMING. FOR GOD'S SAKE SOMEONE CLOSE THOSE SHUTTERS!').

Everyone knows the seriousness of avoiding contact with *la corrente*, not least the local infant-school teacher, a woman in her fifties who wears a thick woollen coat inside, even when the olives are withering from heat in the fields, and makes sure the windows in the schoolroom are nailed closed, just to set an example. At the end of the school day, which is just before lunch, you can find her sitting cross-legged on her desk, filing her nails and tut-tutting at mothers who seem a little too keen to divest their gasping, melting children of the jackets, scarfs and hats they are forced to put on at home time.

'Why are you so obsessed with making the children wrap up, especially when it's so hot?' Justine once asked in exasperation as she peeled off one of Luca's outer layers in sight of the blackboard.

The schoolteacher stared at her, dumbfounded, before waggling a half open hand level with her thickset chin. This gesture, which translates as 'Are you mad?' was replaced with another, made by closing the now upright hand to an all-fingered pinch and twirling it from side to side: 'Am I just supposed to stand by and watch?' it said. 'Outside is too fresh,' she concluded with a splutter. 'Why else do you think we have no playground?'

It wouldn't have done to argue. The flu is carried on a wind current and that's that. This is precisely why you should never stand in the middle of a busy local road, just in case you catch it from the tailwind of a passing car.

As for the cure — well, outsiders might well believe all you can do with a *virus* like the flu is just to let it run its course, and try to subdue the aches and sniffling with an aspirin or two. Here, though, the only remedy is a course of antibiotics, known elsewhere for their general effectiveness against *bacterial* infections. And you don't just pop a few piddly tablets of amoxicillin; you hit the virus with the strongest antibiotics known to man. These are injected, generally by yourself, in your own home, always in the buttocks, and preferably with all your friends and family close by to witness the true extent of your sufferings, and to notice the range of latest drug cartons and vials arranged on the kitchen table (or, better still, on top of a Bible to make them more prominent, and a touch more pertinent).

In my opinion this makes Immacolata, still recovering from her hip surgery, a saint. We barely hear a peep from her, despite a rather large incision, and the ball-end of her thighbone being sawn off and replaced with a metal component stuck in place with cement.

Most islanders are diagnosed with the flu several times a year, and are almost always either just starting a course of antibiotics or just finishing one. Some might say it's the doctors' fault for over-prescribing, but in fairness they really have no choice. Islanders expect a visit to the surgery will mean they'll be getting antibiotics, and most importantly *the needles*. If the doctor sends them away without a prescription for a five-day kit of syringes and drugs then word soon gets around that he or she is useless and the consultations dry up; not a good thing if you claim money from the government for every patient you see. So drug reps visit, doctors prescribe, and the patients are happy. Meanwhile the government pays for everything and the flu clears up naturally anyway.

No long-term visitor is immune to the ministrations of the local medical practitioner. You're going to catch something sometime, and at the slightest sign of a cold everyone you know will be imploring you to see the doctor immediately.

My first brush with one results from an ear infection that just gets worse. After several days of tenderness in my right ear, the pain spreads to the other, until both take turns itching madly and discharging a clear liquid, which I later find out are my white blood cells escaping.

Then, one morning, I awake to find that during the night someone's been pounding on my legs and spine with a mallet. Something else is not quite right either: it's quiet, eerily so.

'What's going on? Why is Louis crying like that?'
I try to say, when I notice he's miming his morning
tantrum.

'Wubbilubbub,' says Rohan.

'What?'

I pat my palm against my right ear and it erupts in
excruciating pain. In an instant I'm out of bed and
preparing to slice off both my ears with a kitchen knife.
Thinking better of it, despite the agony, I gulp down some
aspirins instead, and take to banging my head against the
tiling until the pain begins to subside.

I only manage to get out once that day, and meet Nino
in the alleyway on his way to weeding his tomatoes.

'*Professore*,' he drawls. '*Come stai?*'

'*Male, male*,' I say — bad, bad. And with these words I
have jumped a barrier that has kept me apart from many
of my fellow mountain dwellers and fishermen since the
day I arrived. On Lipari, you see, there is no misplaced
sense of duty to withhold the truth about how horrible
you might be feeling when confronted with the common
enquiry of 'How are you doing?'

In the more restrained, largely Anglo-Saxon nations, you
could be sucking oxygen through a respirator with a
colostomy bag strapped to your waist but still be expected
to come out with a cosmetic smile and a 'Mustn't grumble'
when someone asks after your health. But in southern Italy
the polite enquiry you would expect if you met someone
you knew in the street always results in a mutual and
sometimes very graphic dissection of both parties' physical
condition.

For months I'd fallen into the trap time and time again. *Come stai*? I would say automatically to people I knew quite well, or *come sta*? — the more formal form — when addressing a stranger or someone older than myself. Younger people would almost always answer with an enthusiastic *bene, bene* — fine, fine — but make the mistake of asking someone of middle age or older, and you were soon in trouble.

Sometimes you were hit with a *così così* — so-so — and a fluttering of a limp right hand like a broken wing, but more often than not you got the full *male, male* and a resigned shake of the head. Then you knew you were in for a half-hour rundown, with various groans and winces for effect.

If you were really unlucky you would get to see their aches and pains in the flesh. Shirts would be unbuttoned and bruises revealed, up would go skirts to flash a bad hip, and even — thankfully just the once — trousers and underpants were dropped to reveal a shrivelled penis that the old fisherman allowed his wife to flick to and fro with a stubby forefinger while bemoaning the fact her husband couldn't get it to work any more. But he was about to get *the needles* so at least there was some hope.

After a while you learn to avoid groups of people shaking their heads in unison; you know they are comparing their complaints. But the main thing to remember is you never, ever, start a conversation in the traditional manner, unless you have plenty of time and a cast-iron stomach.

But I'm not going to miss my own opportunity.

'Marrr-co, *come stai?*'

'*Male, male.* I have an infection. In my ears. I must have caught it when I was swimming.'

Nino looks blankly at me. 'Maybe you've just got some pumice in your ears,' he notes.

'Pumice. *Certo.*'

'Well, you can't get an infection from the sea, *stupido.* It's the wind.'

'What is?'

'The wind's caused it. You need to see a doctor.'

'For some antibiotics.'

'*Si.*'

'The needles.'

'*Si.*'

He smiles, and whispers something, then breaks out into a chuckle. He thinks it's hilarious. He can say anything he wants and I can't hear a thing. What fun!

'Thanks, Nino,' I respond glumly.

He raises both hands so I can see his leathery palms. 'My conscience is clean,' they say.

Things get even worse during the night. At around four I wake with a fever, and notice a hard pea-like swelling under the worst-affected ear. I spend a couple of frenzied hours rambling nonsensically to myself, and running to the shower every now and again in an attempt to stop the shivering. We've travelled a lot together over the years, and have had many fevers between us, so Rohan knows there's not much more she can do than bring me glasses of water and try and calm me when I start thrashing about. But by morning the pain in my lower back and legs has merged and is concentrated around my pelvis. When I try to walk I resemble a cowboy fresh off his horse.

The pain in my ears is almost unbearable now, but this isn't the end of it. I have an awful feeling. I put my hand down my shorts and grope around. Oh no, this can't be happening. But it most definitely is. Someone's been blowing up my testicles with a bicycle pump.

Because it is early summer, the *guardia medica touristica* is rotating doctors from Sicily to the island, presumably to guard the usual island medics from the rush of foreigners expected to overwhelm them with all sorts of exotic diseases. Specially trained in several languages and equipped with all the latest scientific knowledge and associated instruments — or something like that — these roving practitioners have been moved from the usual doctors' quarters in the main street (where most of the tourists are) to a room deep within the echoing bowels of the island's hospital (located in an outlying area of Lipari town, just about as far away as you can get from the tourist areas without actually being on another island).

The surgery is in the middle of a short, blank-ended corridor just past the morgue, with a hand-written sign advertising the doctor's presence behind the closed door. Fortunately, today there is no queue, or for that matter, no sign of life whatsoever.

After standing around for a minute or two waiting for something to happen, Rohan knocks gingerly on the door. There's no answer. She knocks again, more forcibly this time, but still there's no reply. She tries the door handle.

Through the widening crack she makes out a dark-haired man behind a desk with a green cardigan almost concealing his business shirt and tie.

'Excuse me. But are you the doctor?' Rohan asks.

'I am.'

'Do you speak English?'

He doesn't, but there's nothing for it now but to beckon us in.

'You might as well leave the door open while you're at it,' he says brusquely, defining his scientific prowess by defying the wind currents. 'It's a bit stuffy in here.'

I hobble in behind Rohan, who is soon busy organising chairs and taking Louis out of his buggy to sit on her lap.

'So, who is it?' the doctor growls, eyeing us all. 'You sir, you madam, or is it the baby?'

'It's him,' Rohan explains, pointing at me. 'He's got an ear infection, the glands under his ears are swollen, and his, um, *testicoli* hurt. We're not sure, but we think it might be mumps.'

We both have a vague recollection that mumps can be caught by adults, not just children, and can cause sterility in men. I don't care. I just want the pain to go away.

The doctor ignores Rohan's diagnosis, and begins moving papers and books around on his desk until at last he finds what he's after. He picks up a ballpoint pen with a chewed end.

'Name?' he asks.

Rohan tells him.

'Age?'

'Thirty-six.'

'Address in Lipari?'

Just then I notice we have visitors: a scruffy young man, his overweight wife and two young children, probably from another island and posing as tourists to avoid the queues at the more popular surgeries. They don't come in: while I'm in the middle of my consultation that would be rude. But, instead, they hang around the doorframe listening intently, and discussing my case in whispers.

'OK.' The doctor stands up, and walks past me to the far side of the room. He removes a thermometer from a dented-up medical trolley and starts wiping it clean on his cardigan. I nervously take note of the other medical equipment on display while he's at it: a scalpel stencilled in its own rust, a blood-pressure arm band with a leather strap so ancient it's as cracked as Nino's old donkey harness, and a few dusty test tubes with dried-out rubber stoppers.

'Put this under your arm,' the doctor orders. He looks at his watch and sits back down to continue scribbling.

After a while he gets up again, and checks my temperature.

'Normal,' he says, rather piqued that we have wasted his time.

'But what about my ears?' I whimper.

He pulls at an ear lobe from behind, then mutters something into my deaf ear.

I feel there's no point responding, as I don't know what he's said.

'Can't you understand Italian?' he asks, louder this time.

'*Si.*'

'Why did you not say *si* when I asked you if it hurt?'

He tugs at my ear again and I yell back in pain.

Satisfied, he writes out a script for antibiotics and an anti-inflammatory.

'What about a painkiller?' Rohan asks.

'*Si*. A painkiller.' He scribbles again.

'Paracetamol?'

He disregards the suggestion with a surly groan. 'No good. You need morphine. Take, um, twenty-five drops of this liquid orally,' he points at the prescription he hands over, 'whenever something hurts.'

'But do you think it's mumps?' Rohan pesters, concerned now that we're obviously being shown the door without a proper examination.

'Maybe, but it could be anything,' he concludes.

'Perhaps he should see a specialist,' Rohan says.

The doctor sighs loudly. 'Come with me then,' he announces with an irked shake of his head.

The family at the door looks me in the crotch as we follow him out of the surgery.

'Wait here in the corridor,' our doctor says, before disappearing down the connecting hallway.

I feel awful. It's muggy. Sweat is pouring down my face. I try the only window: dozens of layers of paint have sealed it closed. I'm exhausted. I need to sit down, but there are no chairs, and I can't squat with a couple of citrus fruit between my legs.

Eventually, after a good fifteen minutes, the doctor turns up again. 'Come with me,' he orders, and off we troop, back down the corridor; doctor, buggy, mother, and deaf crab-like human, until we reach the entrance hall, where we are told to wait, our doctor and all, along with a host of local outpatients.

I lower myself gently into a seat behind a young man with his leg in plaster, and watch the comings and goings of giant squat nurses clunking up and down a wooden staircase. I'm desperately hoping none of them are going to get involved with my testicles.

My worst fears seem to be confirmed a few minutes later when one of them stands at the top of the staircase with a clipboard and gets our tourist doctor's attention with a demand to know why he's waiting there and not in his office.

'TO SEE THE SPECIALIST,' he shouts back.

'WHAT FOR?'

'THE TOURIST —' all eyes turn towards me '— HE'S GOT PROBLEMS WITH HIS ...'

No. NO. DON'T SAY IT, I scream to myself. WHATEVER YOU DO, DON'T SHOUT —

'... *TESTICOLI.*'

The hall full of outpatients, squat nurses, doctors, and even baby Louis, who up until then has been struggling to remove himself from his buggy — all of them, without exception, stop what they are doing and proceed to stare at me.

'They're swollen,' my doctor adds, less loudly now that he has captured his audience. 'Swollen ... *testicoli.*'

As if on cue, a wooden door across the hallway opens and another nurse emerges. She looks in my direction and beckons me over with a curl of her finger. 'The specialist will see you now.'

I shuffle red-faced past the patients sitting beside the open door. Rohan and the tourist doctor follow me in, leaving the door ajar for all to see the room behind it.

The specialist's a dapper, middle-aged man with a jet-black military moustache, which bristles self-importantly. Two other doctors stand beside him, with arms behind their backs.

'What's the problem with you then?' the mouth below the moustache demands.

'He's got painful *testicoli*,' the tourist doctor announces almost gleefully.

'Get up on the bed then.'

I stand my ground for a moment, slightly perturbed by the crowd pushing around me.

'Can't he understand?' the moustache quivers. Perhaps it's delirium but I can't take my eyes off it.

'Yes, he can understand,' Rohan puts in. 'But he can't hear!'

'GET UP ON THE BED.'

I jump up as instructed, startled; the moustache grows larger as its host moves towards my trousers. But after much fumbling, he decides it's best if I get down again and expose myself, rather than him having to do it.

After his command gets the necessary response he comes closer, and looks me right in the eyes.

'Does this hurt?' he says slowly, as he squeezes.

'Yes,' I whimper.

'And *this*?'

'YES.'

'What about … *this*?'

'YES! YES! YES!'

He releases his grip, seemingly pleased with himself, yet not wanting to linger.

'Your doctor was right. Swollen *testicoli*. He has already prescribed some antibiotics has he not?'

'Yes.'

'Good. Who's next?'

All four doctors march out of the room, leaving me to hurriedly pull up my trousers.

'But what about my mumps?' I call out weakly.

'It's impossible,' one calls back. 'Only *children* get mumps.'

I check the prescription as we leave. Not surprisingly, the antibiotics need to be injected. But it's Monday, and thanks to the doctors who have returned from their weekends at home on Sicily, and are churning out the repeat prescriptions, it's the pharmacist's busiest day.

Fortunately, we find Justine at the tail end of the queue. She's after something to settle Orlando's stomach, which is playing up again. She agrees to translate for us if we have any trouble.

I stand there for what seems like ages, with a pinched expression on my face. When we eventually reach the front of the queue the pharmacist takes a brief glance at the prescription and produces a large cardboard box of vials. She takes out six and lines them up. 'Oh, and you'll need some needles,' she says. 'Or do you already have some?'

I shake my head.

'Then take these,' she continues, reaching down for another box. 'You can either inject them yourself or you can go to the *Pronto Soccorso*, the casualty department, at the hospital.'

Not likely, I think.

The till's rung up. The antibiotics alone come to more than our half of the weekly rent!

Now as it happens, both Britain and Australia have agreements with Italy to provide each other's holidaying population with the same medical services as their own citizens, which meant we were entitled to free healthcare on the island. The only problem is that it's a tortuous hour-long process to get your hands on the official documentation.

Rohan had already gone through the process soon after our arrival on the island, while I was out roaming the fields with Nino. Justine, who had accompanied her, had explained to an official at the hospital that *la signora* wanted her *bambino* to be covered by the national insurance agreement.

'And *la signora*? What about her? Does she want to be covered too?' he'd asked.

'Oh, yes, well, I guess for me too if I can,' Rohan replied.

An application form was duly filled out and stamped. Then came the *libretto*, or little book, a buff-coloured pamphlet containing dozens of pages of instructions and vouchers for medical treatment and prescriptions. Each page had to be signed, initialled and dated. An hour later, with the signing, initialling, stamping and dating still going on, Rohan turned to Justine and asked if she thought I should be put down on the forms too.

Justine translated. The officer put down his pen. 'You didn't tell me there was a *capo di famiglia*,' he wheezed. 'Where is he? The head of the family should have gone on the application form first, and it should be his signature here, not yours. Without him it's useless.'

In the end they decided it was better to leave me uncovered than for all of us to go through the whole ordeal again.

So now I have a choice: either pay up for *the needles*, which the pharmacist is making up into a nice gift-wrapped parcel, or waddle back to the hospital and put myself through the form-filling. By which time the pharmacist will be closed for lunch, which around here means it might open again at four, or maybe even seven.

I have one last hope though: the downgrade.

'Can't I just get antibiotic pills instead of the needles? I don't need anything strong, just something cheaper.'

But there's no way she can do it without another prescription. Besides, she says, diseases on the island were made resistant to the weaker forms of antibiotics long ago.

Then Justine has a brainwave. She remembers she might have a few vials left from when she had to inject baby Beatrice a few months ago when she had the flu. She can't remember how many there are, but there might be enough to see me through until I get the forms filled out at the hospital.

I agree and hobble behind the others as they head through the alleyways.

It turns out Justine has only two vials left, one of which I promptly drop on the floor and smash.

'Probably a good thing,' Justine says and reaches for a toothpick from the table. 'The needles I've got upstairs are as thick as this.'

Then Dominique the vet turns up.

'We think he's got mumps,' Justine explains, nodding her head in the direction of the sofa where I've collapsed with my legs well spread. She takes her through the story so far.

'But he should have prescribed something like amoxicillin,' Dominique concludes. 'If that doesn't work then you move up to something different, like we do with the dogs.'

We contemplate the idea of returning to the doctor and asking for a new prescription again. But somehow it has to be done without me offending him.

'I could tell him I'm off fishing every day and can't make the time to get down to the emergency department for the injections,' I say. 'Then he might give me pills.'

'That's no good,' says Justine. 'He'll know the fishermen can give you the needles on the boat. They've been injecting each other all their lives.'

'Wait. I have an idea,' Dominique suddenly announces. 'I'm just going home to get something. I'll be back in five minutes.'

She returns flourishing her veterinarian prescription book. 'The only way you can get normal antibiotics around here is if you're an animal,' she declares. 'Who shall you be? Tetley, yes. And your breed? German Shorthaired Pointer. And your age? Three? OK. There.' She pounds down her rubber stamp and hands me the prescription. 'Give it to the woman at the pharmacy.'

We troop off again and arrive just as the pharmacist is closing up.

'You want the needles after all?' she asks.

'No, the tablets.'

She looks dubiously at the prescription, then reaches for a packet of pills.

'You're a bit young to be taking these, Mr Tetley,' she says, handing it to me with a smile that says she is in on the conspiracy. 'But I don't think they can do you any harm.'

Sixteen

As Lucretius says, 'Thus each man
flees himself.' But to what end, if he
does not escape himself? He pursues and
dogs himself as his own most tedious
companion. And so we must realise that our
difficulty is not the fault of the places but
of ourselves.'

Seneca

Not much happens on an average island day when the
summer weather's unsettled and the fishing fleet is in
harbour. Nino's taking a siesta on an old potato sack on
the floor among the spuds, Immacolata's got her bad leg
up, and Allegria's cooking dinner, probably another of the
rabbits Nino trapped the other night. I'm over my illness,
and feeling good. But I need a haircut, which I hope to
tack onto a morning's shopping in town.

While Rohan pops in to see Justine I go looking for a barbershop. I find one not far from Marina Corta, a small place with just two chairs in front of a mirrored wall. One is free.

I explain cautiously in bad Italian how I want my hair: short back and sides, not too short though, and a little longer on top. I suppose I'm enough of a novelty to rouse the interest of the man sitting in the chair beside me.

'Good morning,' he says, in English. 'May I enquire your name?'

He introduces himself. His name is Massimo. He lives on Vulcano. He comes over to Lipari once a fortnight for a shave.

I take a look at his reflection in the mirror: he's thin and tanned and wears glasses. His barber is wiping the last spots of shaving cream off his face as mine starts snipping away.

Massimo gets up and stands to the rear of me, leaving just enough room for my barber to manoeuvre, but making sure I can still see his reflection.

He tells me that he lives on the far side of Vulcano, in a house he built himself from a ruin. I reply that I'm living up in the hills, with my wife and child, and that we plan to be there for some time.

We exchange details about our children and, as it happens, we discover our boys are roughly the same age.

He gets quite excited about this and informs me his son is at home right now, with his wife, Laura. She doesn't get out too much.

'My wife would love to meet you all,' says he, rather earnestly.

I find out more; he seems glad to talk. He's been married before. He has two other children in their twenties. Now he spends weekdays working on his farm on Sicily. He leaves Laura at home on Vulcano. She doesn't like it much, but someone has to go over to look after the olives and the prickly pears, and he likes being alone when he goes.

When my haircut is complete we adjourn outside, where he offers his hand and insists we must come over to Vulcano, after his shave in two weeks' time. We'll meet at noon, exactly where we're standing now.

When I tell Rohan of our meeting she's as enthusiastic as I am about the prospect of getting to know a couple of other people, especially ones with a child the same age as ours. It helps enormously that Massimo speaks very good English too. I'm looking forward to having conversations with locals that don't entail the usual stilted attempts at communication.

So we are both in a buoyant mood as we make our way back into town two weeks later.

We find Massimo waiting outside the barbershop as planned. He greets us courteously and takes a keen interest in Louis, who's strapped to my chest in his pouch.

We follow him through the last of the alleyways and into the piazza, where he nods to a fisherman busily sewing some bright red swordfish net onto a thick lead line. At the hydrofoil ticket office he says firmly that he's a *residente*.

Because he lives on the islands he's entitled to a discounted ticket, he tells us. It's a concession that on the face of it seems unfair, especially if you're outsiders like us and have to pay three times the price. But he explains that without the surcharge forked out by visitors the service might not be running at all. After all, it was the introduction of regular hydrofoils between the islands that brought the tourists here, and helped stop the great migrations to Australia.

'We refer to Australia as the eighth Aeolian Island,' he says.

He goes on to recount that emigrants from the Aeolian Islands settled in Australia in the 19th century. These were followed by many more before World War I, but the big exodus occurred from the 1940s to the 1970s, when the islands were dying and Australia desperately needed labour.

I'm intrigued by how he knows so much, and once we have got our own tickets and are sitting on a bench beside the water, I ask him what he does for a living. He tells us that the local tourist organisation sometimes rings him up, and he takes groups of visitors around the islands. He knows a lot about the general history of the place, but that's not really his profession. He's a maritime archaeologist.

I'm impressed. One hot afternoon when the air was as thick as honey we'd decided to seek solace in the cool interiors of the Aeolian Archaeological Museum, housed within Lipari's imposing hilltop citadel. Among the collections are grotesque Greek funeral masks and a few stone remnants of the King Aeolus cult, but what really stands out are the amphorae, or ancient pots, and their hoards of spilling coins. Many of them had been salvaged from looters, who'd plundered the wrecks that litter the bottom of the sea around here.

'You mean you're involved with all those sunken ships?'

'Sometimes.'

'That must be fascinating.'

'Of course. I have written many articles on them, for scholarly publications. I'll show them to you when we get to Vulcano.'

He'd presented himself as a farmer, but now I find out he's a bit of a generalist in local history and a professional maritime archaeologist as well. This is fantastic news! We're sure to have lots of stimulating discussions with this man, and a promised feast of freshly caught fish is ahead of us too. I can't help wondering if he might be our version of Dr Theodore Stephanides, the Greek poet, author, doctor and naturalist who made appearances in Lawrence Durrell's *Prospero's Cell* and Henry Miller's *The Colossus of Maroussi*. These were among some of my favourite travel books.

I'm hard put to keep from slapping him on the back and telling him how much I've been looking forward to meeting someone like him, but I'm worried about coming across as desperate, so I bite my lip. Until now we have gleaned very little about the islands from the people we usually hang around with. Even the farmers up in the hills have largely lost track of their heritage. Once I'd pointed out some tumbled walls on Nino's land and asked him who'd built them. I don't know what I'd expected him to say — probably his grandfather or something — but he pulled a face. He didn't know. 'They were here before I was born,' he said. 'Perhaps they're hundreds of years old. Maybe thousands. I build walls, they built walls. We're the same. When a bit falls down I build it up again. I build on what they built. It's the same with words is it not, *professore*?'

As for Hit-a-me, he didn't even know the origin of the name of the mountain his family had owned for generations. One day he'd scrawled the words on the laneway's concrete floor with a bit of charcoal he'd found around: *Mazzacaruso*. It was on all the maps, in dialect, and translates as 'slaughtered children'. But Angelo had no idea why it was called that, and I don't really think he cared to find out. But I did. Eventually I discovered that ancient Greek settlers once threw babies born with deformities off the summit and onto the rocks below.

By now the ferrymen are tying up the hydrofoil, and before long we are taking our seats.

'How many olive trees do you have in Sicily?' Rohan asks as she settles Louis down.

'A thousand. About eighty per cent of them are ten years old and the others are ancient, more than two thousand years old.'

He grows them in rows and between them he plants prickly pear. 'Have you ever eaten the fruit of the prickly pear?'

'Yes. They're starting to ripen on Lipari,' says Rohan.

'Do you like them?'

'They're fine if they're cold, straight out of the fridge. But the spines are horrible.'

'What about you?' he asks turning to me.

I think of Nino. He claims he eats up to a hundred a day when they're in season. 'They're nice,' I lie, remembering the dull warm flesh of these immigrants from the Americas, the *Fichi d'India*, or Indian figs. The taste is a little like under-ripe papaya. The best way to eat them is with a knife and fork, so you can get at the flesh without touching the spiny skin. 'But our friend in the hills told me it's not a good year for them,' I say. 'The lack of rain means they're full of seeds.'

'It's nothing to do with the rain. The ones you see squashed all over the roads are the fruits of the *primo fiori*, the first flowers. I don't like them much. The seeds get in between your teeth.'

He hires a company to cut off all the new growth in March, he tells us, and all the flowers too, and then after a while new flowers emerge. These produce bigger fruit with fewer seeds. Between September and December the company men turn up again. They pick the fruit, pack them up and send them all over the world.

'You have to irrigate to get the best fruit; and fertiliser helps too,' he says. 'They don't have enough water on the island to irrigate anything. They're called *Bastardoni*.' Then on reflection he adds: 'Big Bastards.'

It might not have been an exact translation, but it was as near as damn it, and it got the laugh he was after.

The trip to Vulcano takes less than ten minutes and we're soon skirting the chocolate coastline of Vulcanello, the 'little volcano', which Pliny the Elder saw rise from the sea in 182 BC. Way back then, the earth pumped just enough lava to create a tissue of land above the sea. Today it's connected to Vulcano proper by a neck of black volcanic sand, swamped here and there with shallow lakes the colour of tea, and topped with pine and eucalypt woods. In rough weather it's cut off from Vulcano entirely.

As we draw nearer to the landing pontoon I notice that the coastline is dominated by enormous sulphurous coagulations of rock squirming up from the ground like handfuls of squashed banana. The place stinks too, as if someone's lit a box of matches under your nose. It could do with a good breeze to clear the air, I think, which apparently happens from time to time if the windy names of the island's main harbour, Porto di Levante, and the black sand beach at Porto di Ponente, are anything to go by.

We'd already visited Vulcano earlier in the year and found the shops closed and boarded, with only a handful of tourists wandering around. All that's changed. As we make our way off the pier we pass clusters of visitors licking ice creams, and the shops are packed with T-shirts and sarongs.

With Massimo striding out in front we head around a bend of restaurants towards some mud baths: a muddy grey pool filled with overweight Italians and Germans. They're following a tradition dating back to the Romans, who came here to cure their arthritis and gynaecological complaints. The modern equivalent are paddling about up to their knees, stopping occasionally to stick out their rumps as they bend forward and slap handfuls of mud onto their potbellies or into their cleavages. Clayed up, they lumber out of the pool and across a gritty spit of volcanic sand to sink to their haunches in a radioactive stretch of sea, milky with flaky filaments of sulphur and bubbling with gas. Once they're back in their solidly respectable cities these tourists will find they'll lose friends easily. The stench of sulphur will stick with them for weeks. It will ooze from the pores of their skin and drizzle down the filaments of their hair, infecting everything they touch. They'll end up feeling like walking souvenirs.

'You'll have to excuse my car,' Massimo says as we approach a rusty Fiat. 'It's not my best one. I've left the four-wheel drive up in the hills. We'll drive back down in it later.'

'Don't worry about it,' I say.

'I'm not at all worried.'

'Oh good.'

I exchange a glance with Rohan, but the slightly awkward moment vanishes as we begin heading into the hills and the giant cone of the *Gran Cratere* appears on our left.

'According to legend it's linked by tunnels to Mount Etna,' Massimo says as he drives. 'The ancient Greeks believed every rumble meant the god they called Hephaestus was making jewellery, weapons and chariots down below. You know, he made the chains that clamped Prometheus to a rock —'

'That's right,' Rohan adds, remembering the ancient Greek story. 'The giant vulture kept on ripping out his insides —'

'— in revenge for passing on the secrets of fire to mankind. He was supposed to have created the first woman too, from clay,' he continues.

'Who was that? I can't remember her name,' I say.

'Pandora.'

'Ah, yes, Pandora, with her supernatural box.'

'*Si*. She released all the *hatred* and *disease* and *starvation* into the world,' he says, emphasising his points with such a surprising bitterness that I exchange glances with Rohan again. Perhaps it's just his way, I think; he seems harmless enough.

We're getting higher now, and the brown grizzled valley below us is running with goats. Further up it's surprisingly green, with mulberries, figs and acacia trees lining the road. We rattle through villages and past farms and a graveyard until we reach the crest of a hill. The road starts to wind downwards, in and out of view as it curls towards the sea. Massimo turns off the engine to save petrol, and we freewheel downhill for a quarter of an hour, swinging out towards the ocean and back into the windswept grass slope, time after time, in silence.

When we're nearing sea level, he turns the car sharply right, and we come to a halt at the steep uphill approach to his house. Above us is a small, white-washed building, which looks like it's been carved out of salt. It's dashed with the bright pink spots of a bougainvillea.

It's beautiful, but utterly lonely in its gully of rock and bare hillside, and I can imagine being here in the grim depths of winter, when the seas are wild and the mists are up, and there's no one to shout to; no allies at all. Just isolation.

The front door is open already: Laura's heard the car pull up. She's dark and pretty, and at least twenty years younger than Massimo. She's carrying seven-month-old Angelo in her arms. Massimo searches through his satchel and hands the child a small toy bear. He grasps it keenly and stuffs an ear in his mouth. Laura can't take her eyes off Louis.

Massimo guides us inside. We enter a spacious outbuilding, roofed with a scattering of rushes to shade the room from the summer sun. It's the only addition to this typical old Aeolian house, he tells us. He's rebuilt the rest to its original design.

Seeing I'm interested he announces he'll take us on a tour, and marches off, pointing out skinny internal doors with high arched tops, and the old thin logs blackened with age that beam their tiny living room. Thinner strips of wood run down the walls at regular intervals, and end, oddly, a couple of feet above the floor. Nudged up to some of these strips are bookshelves stacked with maritime hardbacks and historical pamphlets.

We follow as Massimo leads us into a strange beehive room made of lava blocks. It was a bread oven once, he says. It's perfect for the circular concrete bath he's built inside.

Next is the kitchen, which is largely uninteresting apart from a large hole in the ground just off to one side, and a curl of steps which head down to a small, box-like cellar.

'The peasants pressed their grapes down there,' he tells us, pressing his glasses to the bridge of his nose. 'It was a typical peasant's house. They would have grown everything they needed and traded any surplus for fish.'

The tour is now over, and Massimo informs me that Laura wants to spend some time alone with Rohan. So he ushers me off towards a terraced back garden to pick some figs.

There are only a few left on his trees, though. Apparently, the rats and birds have got the rest. 'But I've got some prickly pears,' Massimo says, pointing out a clump of misshapen cacti clinging doggedly to the rocky ground.

We return inside after just a few minutes, and I find the women sitting around the dining-room table set with bowls, spoons, and a half loaf of rough brown bread.

Rohan shoots me another odd look as I pull up a chair. Massimo heads to the kitchen with the figs and prickly pears and Laura follows him.

'Laura was asking me if Angelo was normal and if he was eating the right foods,' she whispers worriedly. 'And if he's sleeping like he should. And when he should sit up and crawl.'

'That's not so strange. We haven't really had a clue what to do either.'

'But Angelo's never seen another child! And the teddy bear Massimo gave him earlier, Laura says it's the only present he's ever had.'

Our whispering is curtailed as Laura and Massimo reappear. She's carrying a tureen full of spinach and lentil soup.

Laura serves Massimo first, and we watch as he pours some homemade olive oil on top, then sprinkles it with

Parmesan cheese. When he's finished pulling a chunk from the loaf of bread he tosses it back on the table between us. It lands with a thump. 'It's from Sicily,' he says. 'Not like the tasteless white excuse for bread they make on the islands.'

When I put some in my mouth I find it's as dry and tough as pumice, like Immacolata's loaves three weeks after she's baked them. The only way I can possibly eat it is to follow his lead and let it sit in the soup like a turtle in a swamp until it slowly starts to soften.

The next course is fish; palm-sized things, speared this morning as promised. Rohan chooses a disc-shaped *surago*, a white bream, and Massimo comments on her taste.

'It's the best fish you can eat,' he says, before going for a slim-line *cefalo*, a type of mullet. Both Laura and I have an *occhiata*: a saddled bream. Mine is fine and milky in texture, but when I try a little of Rohan's I find it's coarser and bitsy, and not as nice as mine at all.

Not much is said while we eat. We've come to respect that lunch is a serious business. But still, I can't stop feeling a little uncomfortable.

When we have finished we have the figs for dessert, and warm prickly pears. Massimo eats eight, despite the seeds; the rest of us settle for one each.

When the meal is over the conversation starts at last, but the talk doesn't turn to village matters, or anything so familiar. Massimo wants to stretch out further than the local gossip we've become used to. And his favourite topic appears to be travel.

'You must leave everything at home,' he announces. 'To travel well the maximum you must take is yourself, and then it's a pity you have to do that.'

'You've travelled a lot then,' I say, curious to know where he's been, and the same time keen to dodge the fact I've come loaded down myself, with a relationship, a baby, a dog, my attitude to life. I'd recently read some lines by Horace, the Roman poet:

Why do we aim so high, so bravely,
so briefly? Why hanker for countries scorched
by an alien sun? What exile from home
can avoid himself?

'I've been as far as Rome,' he says. 'But I travel all the time through the books I read. I travel all over the world with them, and back in time. And one thing I've learned is that you have to try to start to think in the same mentality as the people you are visiting. You must go there like a blank piece of paper on which things can be written. Every day should be long, and every night you should dream like a child. Then you should sleep, like a child, when you are tired, and eat when you are hungry, not just because it says lunchtime on the clock. Only *you* can be the measuring instrument. You should aim to live outside time.'

I'm enjoying this.

'Time is someone else's idea,' he continues solemnly, emphasising the point by waving a hand around the room. 'You see no clocks here. Nothing. I try to live by my senses.'

'But if you work ...'

'Then you do it in time with the seasons.'

'It sounds nice in principle,' I say, after pointing out that I don't wear a watch either, 'but it counts for nothing to the millions who are working in office blocks, factories and shops, and all those other places where things are governed by the clock.'

'We all make our choices, but even the savage knows only to work for what he can eat.'

'I had a job as a journalist once,' I say. 'I'd wanted to be one since I was a child.'

I told him how I had beaten thousands to the position. How I had started a cadetship, and how the management changed the day I was employed. From then on people started disappearing. First a handful, then dozens, then more than a hundred, sacked or made redundant in my first year. Those who were left shrunk into themselves. They barely left the office, afraid that if they returned their jobs would be gone. Work piled up, hours were stretched, imagination was crushed, and our union capitulated because it was largely powerless. I saw news-desk editors working with their heads bowed, to avoid the gaze of the editor-in-chief, who patrolled the aisles looking for slackers. Then a uniform was announced: short-cropped hair, blue shirts, a logo splashed across the chest pocket, to mark us out in the commercial war against our competitors. The shareholders were happy as the expenses tumbled. No one seemed to care about the falling circulation, caused by the marked downward pressure on quality. Eventually I had no choice but to leave. My dream was crushed by shifts running into the early morning, cancelled weekends and holidays, the dejected spirits I saw all around me. It was better to be free than a slave.

Massimo rubs his hand across his face. '*Quannu tira u ventu fatti canna*!' he says loudly, quoting a Sicilian proverb. 'Watch out when the wind blows!' he translates. 'It will come back on them,' he continues. 'They will be found out for what they are one day.'

'I hope so.'

'There are bad types of people in this world,' he goes on, before bringing the conversation back to the island. 'The worst types of people here are the ones who have no education but lots of money. Just look at them over on Lipari. They had nothing. Then the tourists came and suddenly they have more money than they know what to do with. There are too many people there now. *Italy* has too many people. The best thing for the world is for men to become extinct. Everything they think about is illusory — clocks, time, money, religion, everything.'

'Even happiness?'

'Especially happiness. I don't agree with happiness.'

'But you seem to have it nicely set up here.'

'Not everything is like it seems …' he responds, so intensely that I catch my breath. 'Things might look OK, but that doesn't mean that they are.'

He goes mute, and sits there, staring blankly.

I look across at Rohan. She has a worried glint in her eyes. Fear shoots between us like electricity. It might be paranoia that's making the hairs on the back of my neck stand up, but I can't help wondering if we've unwittingly wandered into a maniac's house. What did he mean by

'Things might look OK, but that doesn't mean that they are?'

Then it hits home: no one else knows we're here ...

It strikes me too that Laura hasn't said a word since we sat down. The beautiful young mouse is sitting beside me with her face turned down, resigned to the fate he has in store for us perhaps ...

I'm feeling light-headed with panic now. What could he want? Our baby? My God, I think he's poisoned our soup.

I'm frozen in my seat, and all I can do is gulp.

Suddenly his voice breaks the silence like a creaking door. 'It's just that I can never be happy with anything,' he continues darkly. 'I built this house but I just did it. I don't know why. Then I lose interest in it, and the farm, and everything. None of it ever makes me happy.'

'But your son ...' Rohan puts in.

'He's different. I never had any time for my last kids, I was too young, just twenty-two when I had the first. I'm too old for this one now.' He nods towards little Angelo, who is propped up on the concrete floor beside the table staring at Louis, who is playing with Angelo's new teddy bear.

'Do you know Petrarch?' he asks, and without waiting for an answer begins to quote from a poem Petrarch addressed to God following an unrequited infatuation with a woman from Avignon. Interestingly, she was also called Laura.

Father in heaven, lo! these wasted days
And all these nights in vain imaginings spent,
My thoughts enkindled to one maddening blaze,
On one alluring presence all intent!

He gets up, and I think he's going over to Angelo, but instead he walks straight past and into the other room. It's only when he's gone that I gain control of my wits. My mind is all too clear now. I suddenly realise he represents the worst of what I could become. Maybe that's what really scared me so much. He seems to have everything that should make him happy: a gorgeous house, a farm, a wife, a child, relative freedom, and he lives in a peaceful, beautiful part of the world. But he's obviously not in harmony with his surroundings. He's in limbo, suspended somewhere, unable to find happiness or home.

In the past, Rohan has hinted that the moodiness and restlessness I show at times was probably due to the fact that I often blame places for my unhappiness. I have always been seeking somewhere *different* and something more than I have. But what the hell *do* I want? I'd come to Lipari to escape. I'd talked about changing my skin, being a fisherman, but it's beginning to dawn on me that I will never be one. I'm not born to it. All it can be is a passing hobby. As it is, half the time the boat is in harbour because of bad weather, and the rest of the time I work hard for a measly bag of shrimp for the table. God, it's happening again! Had I made the wrong decision coming to this island? What about the farming? I'm enjoying that immensely. There were routines for sure, but they're based on vague ones, seasonal ones, and I can live with that.

But I know myself. I know that if I planted an apple tree I would be happy for an instant, visualising the apples to come. But once the task of planting was done then I'd need another project. I can't be happy with what I've got. Perhaps change itself makes me happy? Or perhaps I yearn to be still, finally, and to find a home I won't want to leave? AHHH! It feels like growing pains, like something's trying to poke up from the earth and announce itself. I feel like I'm going to burst. The logical extreme to all this is that I'm going to end up as unsettled as Massimo.

In a bid to put an end to the disquiet I'm feeling inside I go in search of the man who dredged everything up in the first place. I find him sitting on a plastic chair on the balcony, looking out to sea. Somewhat reluctantly, he offers me a seat beside him. He doesn't want to speak about the islands or the islanders, he says. He's developed a lack of faith in his fellow man. Apart from the British, that is. They're different. 'Everyone sails over there,' he says. 'They have such a connection with the sea.'

'Not everyone,' I correct him, glad to be back to some semblance of normality. 'It's a big place with a huge population. Most people live inland.'

'No. It's a small place. They all go to sea.' He grinds his cigarette into the side of a rusty can. 'It's the height of civilisation. Nowhere else compares with it. I would live there at once if I had the chance. The Americans are barbarians by comparison. It's like comparing the Roman Empire to the savages that lived outside its borders.'

I think of the slums in Coventry, the violence in the North East, and the thugs in the town I once called home, but left so long ago. I remembered the poverty, and the aggression just below the surface in a London pub on a Friday night ...

Though England had plenty of good points in my eyes too, it was easy to knock it, especially from afar.

'Have you ever been to England?' I ask.

'No. But I have a friend who lives there.'

'Where?'

'I don't know exactly. He works in Greenwich, at the maritime museum. So I guess somewhere around there. He writes for the journals.'

'You've never met him?'

'No.' He suddenly rises from his chair. 'It's time to leave. But first we must go to the beach. Angelo must have a swim in the sea. He swims twice a day. Laura will drive. We'll take the good car and drive back to the port straight afterwards.'

The beach is a slip of black gravel, and a concrete jetty has the task of helping in the evacuation of the island should the volcano explode. Massimo, unabashed, strips to his baggy white Y-fronts as Laura undresses their son. She hands him over, and he squeals as he's dunked into the clear water. I stand there for a while listening to Laura's pleas for more baby advice: she's never met another mother of a newborn before, she repeats time and again, and she only has Massimo's experiences with his other children to go by.

I overhear Rohan asking her if she's ever worked. Laura lowers her voice and tells her, somewhat flustered, that she once had a job as a graphic designer over on Lipari. She loved it, she says, and would like to go back when Angelo is old enough. But Massimo will have none of it.

'A woman's place is to look after the children,' he calls out. 'Pass me the towel.'

After this jarring comment I wander off towards a fisherman casting a seine net into the water at the end of the jetty. I stand there, watching him bring up dozens of tiny, flickering silver fish and pour them into a bucket. He'll fry them up at home, he tells me when I ask. He'll add olive oil and pepper, and eat them whole. When he's not looking I reach into the bucket and rescue one. It flaps weakly in my hand. I throw it back into the water. It lies beneath the surface on its side and flaps its tail. But it's weak, and goes nowhere, and I watch it slowly sink.

The weather is turning. Soon it starts to rain quite hard. As we head back to the port the downpour has settled the dust and darkened the scree slopes. The goats stand out brighter than before, and the trees hang heavier alongside the road.

We say our farewells, and I tell Massimo that I hope we meet again. Though, in my heart, I feel doubtful. And, even if he's taught me more about myself today, I don't think I can return the favour.

Back on the hydrofoil Rohan tells me about her own reading of Petrarch. 'The Laura in his poetry was an object of desire,' she says, 'placed on a pedestal, loved for what she represents, rather than who she really is. She had no life or personality of her own except for what Petrarch made for her.'

I stretch out a hand and take one of hers in mine. I was tolerably content just to make it out of there in one piece.

I've seen Massimo's self-absorption, and noticed his refusal to take responsibility for his restlessness. I've recognised my own tendency to blame external factors for my feelings of dissatisfaction too. And I've seen the difference between Rohan and Laura, as well as more proof of the rigidity of the roles of men and women on the Islands of the Winds. There's a lot to think about. But one thing I know for sure: I need to take a closer look at myself, and how I am in my relationship. I need to find out what I really want from this life. Otherwise I will never change, and I'll always be discontented.

Seventeen

Be wise, decant the wine, prune back your
long-term hopes. Life ebbs as I speak:
so seize each day, and grant the next
no credit.

HORACE

A searing *Scirocco* wind arrives from the plains of Africa. Everything is covered in a thick red dirt. We soon find out that the design of our house is just as hopeless in the heat as it was in the cold. Our little whitewashed box traps hot air like a balloon, and if you stay inside for too long you start to melt. We try migrating to the beach, but the wind is so harsh and dusty that it quickly becomes unpleasant, even with just our faces out of the cooling water. Ice creams drip down our hands on the promenade, bare-chested children jump into the shallow water, desperate to cool off, and at Marina Corta there are reports that giant café umbrellas have been ripped from their concrete bases by violent blasts of air.

In the late afternoon the air sucks in its breath. Now it's just hot, and while Rohan fans Louis to sleep with a book of fairy tales, I take Tetley out into the hills in search of a hint of breeze. The best I can get is on top of the mountain, but even then I'm drenched in sweat and itching from the heat. As usual Tetley brings me a stone to throw, and I toss it down a slope. He brings it back again and again. For an hour or more we carry on like this, until it's time to make our way home. Back on the track I throw the stone again. Each time Tetley sprints after it, sniffs around, finds his quarry, and then searches for cover under overhanging clumps of wormwood. He lies in the shadows, panting heavily, until I catch up. Then he pulls himself up and drops the stone at my feet once more.

Back home I find Rohan splayed out on the floor tiles in the kitchen, barely dressed, trying not to move. The book she's been reading is discarded beside her. Louis is naked apart from his nappy, his hair has been dampened with a cloth, and he's sucking on a plastic teething ring in the shape of a fish. It's been cooled in the refrigerator's freezer compartment until the water inside has turned to ice.

Next morning I walk across the laneway, slide back the bolt on Nino's barn door and unchain Tetley from his place in the corner. He emerges unusually slowly, shakes himself, and stops to pee against the rock wall. He sniffs at his bowl but only picks at a few biscuits, and spends the rest of the morning stretched out on our bed.

By lunchtime the heat is just as intense as the previous day and we retreat to the shade of the terrace. Tetley struggles up the stairs, looking unlucky, and slumps down on the tiles. It's then that I notice he's labouring to breathe, and the light's gone out of his eyes.

'I think he might be ill,' I say.

'It's probably just the heat,' Rohan says.

The afternoon wears on. Rohan brings out a plastic paddling pool for Louis to splash in. We read, and doze, and swelter.

By the time evening comes Tetley is lying on his side, his tongue lolling and pale. He refuses to eat and when I drag him by his collar to his water bowl he recoils, cranes his neck upwards and away, and gasps for breath.

Suddenly the previous afternoon comes back to haunt me; the heat, the running. Once someone told me about a couple who'd agreed to look after their neighbour's collie for a weekend. They were handed a tennis ball and a racquet. 'He likes you to hit a ball for him down the park,' they were told. It was a hot day, so they took him out. They hit the ball. The dog retrieved it. Two hours later he was still fetching the ball. 'This dog never tires,' the couple thought, and whacked the ball around some more. Once back home again the dog collapsed. He had literally run himself into the ground. They rushed him to a vet, who put him on a drip for two days. The dog only just survived.

So maybe Tetley's suffering from heat stroke; and it's all my fault.

He's trembling now, and his eyes are half closed.

'Perhaps you should call Dominique?' Rohan says. 'I think he needs to see a vet. Now.'

I rush downstairs, across the laneway, and into Immacolata's kitchen to borrow the phone. I ring Justine to get Dominique's number. When I get on to her she tells me she's busy at the surgery, and that I should ring back in half an hour.

Back at the house there's no improvement. I offer Tetley some water, cupped in my hand, but he refuses to open his mouth. In desperation, I half fill a plastic water bottle from the tap, prise open his jaws with one hand and pour the liquid as best I can down his throat. He desperately tries to pull away, coughing and spluttering, and the water flows out between his teeth and onto the tiles.

Half an hour later I'm back on the phone relaying the symptoms. Could it be heat stroke? I ask. Dominique thinks it's unlikely. 'It sounds more like a tick bite,' she says. 'Meet me in, what, twenty minutes? At the veterinary clinic.'

Tetley lies limply on my lap in the passenger seat. The air-conditioning is on full, and I'm desperately worried. I snap at Rohan to drive faster as we swing at speed around the tight corners heading down into town, and when we're finally there I can hardly bear to wait as Rohan unbuckles Louis from his child seat and clicks him into his buggy.

We storm through the main street, me carrying Tetley and Rohan pushing Louis. The barriers are up to block the traffic for the duration of the evening's *passeggiata*. Small groups of youths amble up and down the street, tourists peer into shop windows, and fishermen emerge from the street cafés after knocking back their espressos. It's even hotter and stickier down here than in the hills, even though the sun has set. A temperature gauge fixed to a nearby wall indicates 38° Celsius.

At the clinic I haul our dog onto a table. It takes all his effort to stand now.

Dominique feels his stomach, checks his eyes and the colour of his gums. 'He's in very bad shape,' she concludes. 'We must get some fluid into him, and then I'll take a blood sample.'

She finds a vein in his leg, inserts a needle and in no time at all he's attached to a drip line and a bag of saline. We take our stations by his side, and watch him closely as the fluid drains in. A quarter of an hour later there's a noticeable improvement, and I'm elated when he licks my hand and raises his trustful eyes to mine.

'Don't get your hopes up,' Dominique warns, her words turning like a knife in my ribs. 'It's only a temporary solution. We have to get to the bottom of the problem. From the look of him it's definitely not heat exhaustion. If it's a tick bite then we'll only know when the blood test results come back from the laboratory on Sicily. That could take a few days. There's another possibility too: he may have eaten rat poison.'

She's heard a couple of dogs have died recently up in the hills. If that's the case then he'll need an injection of Vitamin K to try and counteract it. It'll be up to us to inject him, and keep him re-hydrated with saline. We can collect the stuff we need from the pharmacy: a needle, some bags of saline, some tubing, a couple of catheters.

Back in the hills I inject Tetley with the vitamin, and following Dominique's instructions we rig up the re-hydration kit on the terrace. It sounded easy enough to do, but we fumble over it for half an hour. I take four attempts to insert a new catheter into the vein, and attach the tubing. I stand there, holding the bag in my hand, as another litre of saline solution drips into Tetley's poor worn-out body.

I stay up with him throughout the night, stroking his back as he stands on our bed, his throat rattling noisily as he struggles for breath. I feel helpless. Oddly the situation reminds me of Rohan and Louis, and that dreadful anxiety that Rohan must have felt when she couldn't get him to settle, not knowing what to do. Since the day I got Tetley, as a little puppy, he's been my baby. And now it's clear in my mind that there's little chance for him. I'm convinced he's going to die.

At some point I'm overtaken by the urge to sleep, and when I wake it's with a start. It's morning, and he's made it through the night.

It's hot again. I make an emergency treatment room up on the terrace with curtains from our bedroom window hung over the kitchen chairs to shade Tetley from the sun. I reattach the drip every few hours, but the second night passes as the first, and there's no real improvement. Then, sometime early in the morning, I doze off again, and when I awake I find his breathing is easier. He eats a single biscuit, a chocolate one, for a treat. He laps a few drops of water from my hand.

Late in the afternoon he finally falls asleep himself,

just as a cool change in the weather arrives on a breeze from the sea. He's left skinny and ragged; his fur's lacklustre; and his eyes are still dull. But he's made it through alive.

A few days later we come across a sign on a telegraph pole in the laneway. It's half hidden by the arms of a blackberry bush, and someone's had a go at peeling it off, but it's obviously a warning. The local authorities have announced they're placing rat baits along the roadsides. There's no date for when they plan to start, or if they have already, or when it's safe to let your pet out again. It's just kind of informal, an aside, of no real importance, but the authorities feel it's their duty, no, an act of friendship, of community spirit, to inform their subjects, though vaguely, of the likelihood of a drawn-out, painful death for their dog should it happen to be released from its chains in its owner's front yard.

Our next-door neighbours know about the rat baits, and they know how to keep their dogs from eating them too.

One afternoon we see the son leading the youngest of their two mutts up the driveway, seemingly set on taking him for a walk. It's the first time I've ever seen him do this, and I call Rohan over for a look. We're even more surprised though when he ties the dog to a rope and then hitches it up to the back bumper of a car. He gets in, starts the engine and heads up the laneway with the dog padding along behind. A second spent sniffing at poisoned rat bait on the ground results in the dog being dragged along the concrete on its nose.

I have another day fishing ahead of me, but after my time on Vulcano with Massimo I'm not quite sure why I'm doing this any more. It's three in the morning. I'm tired. I could be in bed.

I check on Tetley in the barn before I make the drive down to town. He jumps up to lick my hand. He looks well. He's putting on weight and the brightness is back in his eyes again.

Back onboard the boat there's disappointment at the amount of seafood we're bringing in. All our exertion through a moonless night and the sweat of a morning has brought us just seven small bags of prawns and a handful of fish. Even the seagulls have abandoned us.

The boys are despondent and silent as they cart the next day's bait onboard. Orlando blames it on the heat wave, then on the Sicilians who are trying to cut in on the catch.

Once the final jobs are done we wander across the blinding flagstones towards the tourists sweltering over their mussels in wine and their frosted glasses of lemon *granita*. They're silent too, and sit there with their faces bulging and dripping from the exertion of lifting a fork, while the overdressed waiters sway on their feet to make their own breeze.

It's almost midday and we need pasta and sleep, but we stay knotted together for a while beneath a shop awning, the boys smoking last cigarettes and muttering about the day's misfortune.

At first we ignore the cries from the far end of the piazza, but as they grow nearer the boys pick out angry shouts thrown at them in dense dialect. We turn as one and see a thickset man in his mid-thirties pacing towards us. His face is contorted and red, and he's spitting out accusations: 'You bastards pulled up my anchor and let the boat drift!' he's yelling. 'What are you playing at?'

The boys around me jump to the defence, their arms waving madly.

'You madman!' screams Raimondo in his face when he comes too near. 'We haven't touched your anchor. We've just come in!'

'You moved it. I saw you come in and throw yours out. Your line crossed mine.'

'So what are you accusing us of?' roars Rocco.

'You pulled up my anchor to free your rope. Then you just threw it back in the water with the line slack. My boat could have drifted. It could have been smashed to pieces on the seawall. I saw you.'

'I'm not standing for this,' Rocco shouts, craning forward as if he's threatening to strike, his fists clenched. Abuse belts from his mouth, followed by an equally angry stream of insults from his sizable opponent. One brother lunges at the accuser to push him away, but the disgruntled fisherman rolls back just in time.

'We didn't touch your anchor,' Rocco rages on. 'You're seeing things. We're honest men. If we had to pull up anchors we'd put yours back in the same place. You don't believe me?'

The fisherman throws up both his hands.

'Well then, there's nothing more to say,' Rocco spits, 'we have a problem between us.'

'Between all of us! Remember I've got brothers too.'

'We'll see.'

'Yeah, we'll see.'

The heat that appeared with the *Scirocco* wind is fraying everyone's nerves, and that same week there's more trouble. I'm with Rohan and Louis outside *Il Gabbiano* when a lanky, unkempt, bespectacled drunk rampages through the string of cafés, flailing his arms and screaming abuse at his victims. A couple of waiters try to step in as he crashes into tables and chairs, and tourists dive to save cappuccinos and children. The man's father, a former jailbird and famous drunk in his own right, tries to calm him down with his own tirade. But what strikes me most is how everyone stands off: the accused, the waiters, everybody. Anywhere else in the world and someone would have thrown him out, or knocked him to the ground.

But not here. Because you never quite know what trouble you can land yourself in. Knives are part of a fisherman's toolbox, and in the heat of the moment, especially when someone is drunk, who knows if one will come out or not. Then there are all those relatives to deal with. Even the drunk seems to have this ingrained somewhere, because when he's faced with a clear punch at one of his victims, he turns at the last moment and thumps his father instead.

But there's a problem. He misjudges a second swing, and it catches a bystander flush in the face. It isn't a hard hit, more of an open-fisted tap really, but in an instant, black clouds roll over the faces of the locals and a waiter runs wailing into our café's interior, with tears streaming down his face.

Within minutes dozens of scooters and three-wheelers are pouring into the piazza, and the whole place is in uproar, as brothers, uncles, fathers and grandfathers from several clans turn up to protect the honour of the various families involved.

The drunk is gone by now though. His glasses were broken in the earlier mêlée, and he's skulked off home to find another pair. He leaves the piazza echoing with a barrage of shouts and denunciations, windmilling arms, and not a policeman to be seen.

It goes on for hours, until gradually the last of the would-be combatants have wandered away, shaking their heads. It's always like this at this time of the year, they tell each other, it's the heat, and the African wind.

As for the dispute between the boys and the fisherman who accused them of pulling up his anchor, I hear only that the brothers are not talking to him now, and that he and his family are ignoring them too; which, in the end, brings their relationship back to the status quo. After all, no one's forgotten the disputes of earlier years.

Thanks to the *Scirocco* dust that's settled at the bottom of our rainwater tank, our water is bright red too. Even Tetley's white drinking bowl is stained. The locals are turning to chlorinated water, brought over by ship from Sicily, and transported around town by a tanker lorry. It's expensive, and Nino hates the taste and price of it, but that's the way it is on an island with no natural watercourses of its own.

Then suddenly it rains. It starts with thick black thunderclouds rolling in from the mainland, and by the morning it's pouring down. On days like this in Sydney, if we weren't forced to go to work, we might have stayed in bed for longer than usual, and maybe watched a video later on, and the day would have passed with nothing much achieved. Here we spend the morning under the eaves of our terrace, watching the rain drenching the olives and the fruit trees.

Rainy days in summer. Nino sits in his shed and weaves wicker baskets to place around his demijohns of wine. Immacolata's still resting her hip, and is watching soap operas on the television upstairs. Allegria is making the second round of coffee for the morning.

Rohan has discovered that she's run out of disposable nappies for Louis. She has a towelling one as a backup, but no safety pin to hold it in place. She walks across the laneway, hoping Immacolata might be able to help. When the Nonna hears about it she pulls up her dress and fumbles through layers of threadbare cotton. Although Rohan pleads with her not to go to the trouble, the Nonna insists, and stands there, holding her skirts up with one hand and a safety pin with the other.

Down the road, in a stable smelling intensely of hay and animals, Maria is struggling to brush the knots out of her donkey's hair with a comb she's made out of three-inch nails. Hit-a-me and Hit-a-miss are fighting their way through the storm, intent on completing their usual morning's walk, stopping along the way to talk to old friends. Arturo is sorting through seeds on his windowsill; Orlando is down at *Il Gabbiano*, keeping an eye on the boat as the swell gets up; and his mother is choking to death on a fishbone.

We arrive moments before, knowing Justine's routine and the rain ensure she'll be home with Kerri and the kids. We're just sitting down when there's a loud, frantic rapping at the glass kitchen door. Justine opens it in a hurry and finds the family matriarch, the fisherman's wife, gasping like a landed mullet and clinging onto the wall as if she's about to fall. '*Una spina* ...' she croaks, before turning out of sight. We hear her retching violently. 'I'm dying, I'm dying,' she gasps.

She bundles through the door and makes the kitchen table, where she steadies herself with both arms outstretched and her short stockinged legs splayed like a deckhand's. We try to calm her and urge her to try swallowing some bread to dislodge the bone. But she refuses with a tragic wave of a hand and bleats for Orlando. He's a fisherman. He knows about such things.

'Quick, Luca,' Justine cries. 'Go and fetch him!'

A little while later Orlando bursts through the door, with two of his brothers in tow.

His mother is supporting her head in her hands and is inhaling more loudly than ever. 'Luca came down shouting *morta, morta* — she's dead, she's dead,' Orlando puffs. 'What is it? A heart attack or what?'

'She's got a fish bone stuck in her throat,' Justine says.

'Then get her some bread!' Orlando orders, and now that her son is suggesting it, the matriarch obliges and, with her eyes tightly closed, she wrenches a piece from the loaf in front of her. She stuffs it in her mouth and chews frantically. She swallows, then grabs for the rest of the bread, tearing a chunk off, and then another, and another. By the time she's demolished half the loaf she declares there's been no movement: *la spina* is still there. So she continues eating until the whole loaf is gone, and Justine is just about to ask her if she wants a cake too, when the matriarch calls for water.

When a couple of neighbours arrive, brought by the commotion, she begins slapping at the side of her throat, showing them exactly where the problem is. The water's failed to shift the bone, so she demands Justine brings her the telephone. She calls Allegria, and tells her in a strained, husky voice to meet her at the hospital at once.

'Look, it'll probably come free if you cough hard a few times,' Kerri says.

But in the matriarch's mind, only a doctor can help now.

When we meet Allegria later we ask her if she has heard how things went. She rolls her eyes in response. The matriarch arrived at the hospital, she tells us, but the queue in the emergency waiting room was so long that she had to sit there for half an hour, time enough to ring everyone in her family on her mobile phone, while trying desperately not to cough in case she dislodged the bone before the doctor got to see her. But it was no use. She couldn't help it. At last she spluttered, and up it came.

Back in the hills late that afternoon Rohan returns the Nonna's safety pin. She looks quite relieved. She's been sitting in a chair all day, she admits, embarrassed to move in case her skirts fell down around her ankles.

The matriarch has been married to her husband since they were teenagers. But it was a different time back then. Things have changed. Most of the young men on the island are marrying later, and playing the field with the foreign tourists in the meantime. Some, *mamma mia*, are even tying the knot with them. There's Orlando and Justine of course, and Raimondo and his Polish wife, and Cesare the swordfish fisherman and his French wife Dominique. But interestingly, there are no local women married to foreign men that I know of, though men of Liparian descent who have lived most of their life abroad, usually in Australia, have been known to come back and marry a local.

On the whole, most islanders tend to be sceptical about the success of relationships with foreigners. The time will come, they say, when the woman will miss her mother too much and will run away, taking the kids with her.

Most don't make it as far as marriage though. Several women from colder climes have turned up here on holiday over the last few years and exchanged the pale insecure youths of home for a suntanned local. They'd been seduced by the romantic idea of living on an island in the Tyrrhenian Sea with a bronze-skinned man who, as soon as he sets eyes on her, and her alone, is astonished at her beauty, or so he says. If the man isn't already married, she has a chance to stay there, to live out a dream …

Many of these women have ended up in Justine's kitchen, crying their eyes out. They feel like slaves, they weep, all they do is wash up and clean, and are shouted at if the coffee isn't ready on time or the pasta over-boiled.

The latest casualty is a thin ginger-haired New Zealand girl, who's been living with a fisherman for the past eighteen months. Now she thinks he's a bastard. He's always shouting at her, she says. She can no longer stand living here with an island man. He's told her to move out for a while, to think things over. But where can she go? It's nearing the height of summer, and everywhere will be full. She certainly can't stay with his family, and apart from Justine she has no friends.

Like the others before her she has started smuggling her possessions back home, piece by piece, by post. It's the only way. She can't just tell him she's leaving forever: you can never tell with an island man what he might do, and what he might think. Perhaps he'll accuse her of having another man. No, it's too much of a risk. But soon the day will come when she'll just pack the last suitcase and head out on the hydrofoil. When her husband is out fishing. She'll never come back.

There've been times when Justine has almost gone too: as far as the citadel on top of the hill, where she can look the furthest out to sea. She's had her bags packed and her children dressed for a journey, and it was only a last-minute phone call to her mother far away that persuaded her to return to the alleyways.

But it's Kerri who's in trouble now.

It started with a decision to climb Stromboli's volcano, something difficult enough if you're fit. It's a tough four-hour climb, and with pastries for breakfast and pasta every lunchtime Kerri has put on weight. She and Kevin set out at five on a hot afternoon, and the track got steeper, thinner and dustier as they climbed. Kerri started tiring, and soon began to feel the effects of the heat, still considerable despite the setting sun. Kevin became frustrated at the pace, and thrust ahead. It's a dangerous track, alone and in the dark, but it's better than trying to go back down. So she pressed on, and after what seemed like a lifetime, she reached the top.

They don't speak to each other for three days. Kevin spends much of the time locked in their room, while Kerri is down at Justine's house. Then Kerri finally announces that she's going back to Australia on the earliest flight. Their relationship is over. Kevin is staying on, maybe for another month.

We feel this extended intrusion is unfair. He's already been here for three months, and we were led to believe that he was only staying for a brief holiday.

Rohan grabs Kerri first thing next morning. 'You can't do this to us,' she pleads. 'We don't feel comfortable with Kevin staying after you leave. You brought him over, he should go back with you, or find somewhere else to live. The house is small enough as it is. We've got a family and we have no relationship with Kevin at all. He barely even speaks to me. Sorry to put the pressure on you, but he's kind of your responsibility.'

That evening Kevin confronts us on the terrace.

'What's this I've been hearing? You don't want me around after Kerri's left? I'm staying. If you don't like it *you* leave.'

Stupidly, we hadn't given much thought to the implications of Kerri actually telling him about our concerns. We just hoped things would sort themselves out, one way or the other. It didn't help that apparently the news had been passed on to Kevin rather bluntly. Now there's no choice but to confront the situation head-on.

'But Kevin, we heard you were coming here for three or four weeks, for a holiday,' Rohan says. 'We were quite happy with that. It's nothing personal, but the house is small, and you guys are splitting up.'

I add: 'Look, we're really sorry about it, but if you can't patch things up then, well, it just makes things *difficult* for us.'

'We aren't a couple,' he spits.

'Yes, I've heard that … but you were.'

'I came over here alone and I'll leave here alone.'

I don't know what to say.

'I didn't come over here to make friends, I came here for a holiday,' he continues angrily. 'You guys aren't my cup of tea either.'

With that he turns on his heel, slams the front door, starts up his motor scooter, and roars off down the laneway.

There's only one road that rings the island, and gossip travels its length in a flash. Countless times we say something to somebody and hear it from someone else later that day, the message having passed through six or seven people. We soon find that simple messages are often passed on by this circuitous route too.

One day, a while ago, we heard from Kerri that Nino didn't like us leaving Tetley in the house when we go out, something we've been doing occasionally in the hot weather when the barn heats up to suffocation point. Instead of telling us directly, Nino informed his wife, who told Allegria, who passed on the message to Arturo down in Lipari, who told Orlando out at sea, who rang Justine back at home, who informed Kerri while they're doing the housework, who brought the message back to the hills when she returned that evening. Our affable landlord, whom we'd both seen several times that day, would never have dreamed of telling us himself, in case we got embarrassed or took offence.

There's a trap related to this message-passing though, and one day we fall right into it. It happens when I mention, off hand, that Kerri is leaving a little earlier than she'd planned. Nino doesn't ask me why, and I'm not about to tell him, instead he just nods his head. I'm taken by surprise later in the day when Kerri appears and tells me that Nino and Immacolata are terribly upset. Apparently, they believe they must have offended her in some way. In their minds there could be no other explanation, otherwise why hadn't she told them she was leaving herself, rather than pass the message on through me.

It turns out that Kerri had heard about their concern down in Lipari that afternoon, via the usual route of daughter, husband, brothers and wives. Now my loose tongue has meant she's had to spend the last hour in damage control. The politics of living in paradise are daunting.

It's only much later that we realise that since we arrived on the island we've been at the centre of plenty of conflicting cultural situations. One incident that comes to mind concerns the mulberry tree. The day after we'd arrived on the island Nino had insisted we park our car in the short stretch of driveway that fronted the shed where he wove his baskets when it rained. The mulberry tree would help keep it cool in summer, he said, and because the parking spot was off the laneway, there was no chance our immaculate car would be scratched by a passing vehicle.

This worked fine for a while, but soon after the mulberry tree started to fruit we found the car was being heavily splattered with half-eaten berries and the droppings of the birds that dined on them. Instead of washing the windscreen with a bucket of soapy water every time we wanted to drive anywhere, we decided it was best to move it down the lane to another parking spot.

On one of Justine's visits I remember her asking me why we'd decided to move the car. In hindsight it's obvious Justine was the go-between, and by a route that back-pedalled to town and up to the hills again (via the sea) Nino found out the reason. The next day we found Immacolata's brother had parked his car in our new spot, so there was nothing else for it but to park under the mulberry tree again. The next morning the car was covered in droppings and fruit as usual, and there was Nino, with a bucket of water from the rainwater tank washing the car for us. He apologised profusely, saying the mulberry tree would continue to fruit for another month, and that he'd gladly wash the car every morning for us. We laughed and told him he didn't have to worry, that it wasn't such a big deal, and we'd wash it ourselves if we needed to. He nodded. When we arrived back home later that afternoon after a drive to town we found Nino had removed part of the stone retaining wall opposite our house, and had spent the afternoon digging out a new parking spot from the hillside with his mattock.

Now, according to Kerri, when Kevin heard we wanted the house to ourselves, he appeared at Justine's and broke down in tears. Allegria was there to witness the entire thing. He accused us of attempting to throw him out. He didn't mention the split-up.

Allegria, her heart ever open, invited him to stay with her. We are mortified. What will Allegria think of us? And Arturo? And Nino and Immacolata, they're sure to know by now. They must think we're heartless. What a mess! What a complete, utter, shambles.

In bed that night Rohan voices something I'd been afraid to contemplate, but which I knew was a real possibility.

'They're going to throw us out, aren't they?' she whispers.

'But what have we done wrong?'

'You know what family's like here. Blood's thicker than water.'

Kevin was Kerri's boyfriend, and Kerri was Orlando's mother-in-law, and he was the brother of Arturo, and Arturo was married to Allegria, and Allegria was Nino and Immacolata's daughter. And we were nobodies.

The following day we apologise to Kevin. We should have approached things differently; we didn't want to hurt him. He takes it graciously, then departs for the beach alone. Later, Kerri appears to pack up her things and take them down to Justine's house. Kevin will be staying with us for the present, she tells us, but as a compromise she will stay another two weeks and he will cut his holiday by the same amount of time, so that they can travel home together.

We're still worried about what our landlords must think of us, though, and we tell her we are worried they will throw us out because of the dispute.

'Don't be silly,' she says. 'They like you. They wouldn't do anything like that. They don't want to become involved.'

'Are you sure?'

'Nino told Allegria, and Allegria told Arturo, and he told Orlando, and Orlando told Justine and she told me. Now I'm telling you guys. How much more certain do you want it?'

Eighteen

*Bear in mind that you should conduct yourself
in life as at a feast.*

EPICTETUS

We've been invited to the joint christening of Justine's youngest, Raimondo's baby daughter and Rocco's twins. The service is long, the children cry when their heads are forced under water, and Arturo turns up late to show his respects. He doesn't bother to shave or dress up, and stays outside, smoking, with his back towards the sea. He's religious, he tells Rohan when she steps outside with Justine, only for Christmas and Easter.

The christening dresses, the *bombonieri* — this time ceramic cherubs for the guests — the function afterwards: it's costing the brothers a fortune. Those silly little cherubs are expensive, useless things, Justine says. I remind her of Christmas crackers, and how Christmas wouldn't be the same without them. She admits that *bombonieri* might have some symbolic meaning to these people, but she's still furious about it all. After all, there's Orlando, complaining about her asking for a little more money for housekeeping and now he's squandering thousands, just because they all expect things to be so *grandioso*. It's all about impressing people: fishermen and their families, who are all struggling with money too.

The restaurant for the reception is halfway up the hill on the way to our place. It's a barn with trestle tables. We take our seats opposite Orlando and Justine. On one side of us is the latest broken-hearted female refugee. She's about to decamp in the morning. On the other is a group of teenage girls.

The noise is overwhelming. When they're grouped together, the locals are content to talk over one another in that particularly Italian way, until the loudest, and most insistent, wins. The clamour keeps up until the first course arrives, a dish of fried aubergines. Then there's only the sound of scraping and chopping.

We're halfway through our plates when I notice the teenage girls are already onto their second, and finishing that too. A few gulps later and they're mopping up the olive oil on the serving dishes with extra servings of bread rolls.

'Don't look now but the Bullfrog has already finished hers,' Justine whispers and motions towards one of the girls, who is eating with her mouth open and slapping her lips together like she's catching flies. 'She's thirteen,' she continues impishly, 'and look at her friend over there, the one walking towards the door. She's always had problems with her weight.' She stops to take stock of the girl for a moment, then pronounces, 'But she's not looking too bad now. I guess she's on the lookout for a husband. She'll stack it all on again once she's married, they all do.'

I exchange a sly smile with Rohan, but then I realise that Justine's not the only one passing judgement. When the aubergine is finished, and voices are raised again, we have no trouble eavesdropping on a group of women at the table behind us, who are commenting on others sitting across the room. One is wondering aloud where her opposite bought her tacky white shoes. Another comments on the style of someone else's hair. 'It looks like it's growing up rather than down,' she says.

The women on the far table are huddled into conspiratorial groups too, and are throwing looks back in our direction. As the gossip swirls around us, and clings to us too, I notice Bullfrog and her mates have scored another cache of bread rolls, donated by their parents, who are concerned they're not eating enough.

The next course is prawns: huge ironclad whiskery things, bigger than we've ever caught. There are several large platters of them on each table. I go for one, but it's so hot that I burn my fingers when I try to peel off its shell. Unperturbed, the teenage girls quickly demolish a platter-load and move on to another. The prawns are delicious, but in the end I manage only two before the table is stripped clean by Bullfrog and friends, who've gone through dozens between them, and have even managed to blackmail some young boys to skid between the tables and beg for more, which they bring back to the girls in return for promises to keep quiet about secrets they're in on.

And so the meal continues, with volleys of noise in between courses, until it's time for the speeches and the *bombonieri*, and flashing cameras, and toasts, and a christening cake topped by a fairy. Rocco's wife pulls the dainty little plastic doll clear of the icing, which is blue to represent the sea, and tosses it judiciously across the room towards someone who wants to get pregnant, and who's been trying for months, but can't seem to manage it … as everyone knows.

Back in our village, we all decide to spend the last two weeks sharing the house as pleasantly as we can. This means days in the countryside for us, with the occasional visit to town, and days in town for Kevin and Kerri, with a ride up to the hills late at night.

We were out when they packed up their belongings and left the house, but we met them by chance in the alleyway. Kevin was driving Justine's car. They were catching the late afternoon ferry.

We shake hands and exchange kisses, all a little uncomfortably. And then they are gone.

Back home we hug each other and dance around in childlike glee. I carry books, bedding and clothes upstairs while Rohan sweeps our new bedroom floor. At last, Louis has a room to himself and we've gained enough experience to know when we need to respond to his cries and when we should leave him to sort it out for himself and go back to sleep again.

I open the terrace doors, hoping for an onshore breeze. But there's not even the slightest current of air. The rain has come and gone, and the land has dried in an instant, leaving the island struck dumb by the heat. Dogs pant and seek out the angled shadows of the walls. After lunch we can't hold off the afternoon siesta if we try, and find as soon as the last of the pasta is gone our eyes are droopy. Louis has the same idea and is soon in his cot downstairs. I close the door on the drowsy chirp of the songbirds outside as they search for water and we settle down with our heads on our pillows. It's totally extravagant, this siesta; it means you don't have to work, or have finished for the while anyway, and better still, you have enough time on your hands to let some slip away. There's no one around to disturb us this afternoon. We make love. The balance has come back into our lives.

As I drift into sleep I have an emerging sense of what home truly is: being here, with my partner and child, together.

I've not been to the *casetta* for several days now, and I can feel it calling me. When I finally give in to its pull and struggle out of bed I find the country is subdued and blurred, and the sea itself seems to be evaporating. The islands are floating on a cushion of soft blue vapour that thickens and creeps upwards as the afternoon wears on, until it's encircling Salina in bands like smoke rings. Even though the others seem to be suspended above the sea, the island I'm on appears heavier. The stones, my legs, the cliffs, the almond trees: everything around me is bearing the full weight of the sun.

The water is calm and the sky is blue and the sun is warm and the smell of salt is crisp in the air. There's a boat coming towards us. We're moored off Salina, and the boat is carrying some fishermen: Orlando's old school friends again. They pull up beside us and Arturo sets the engine to idle. We've been looking for the baskets for a while now; the boys are becoming upset with it all, and once again I'm wondering what I'm doing with this fishing hobby of mine. By now, I know I should have decided whether to continue with it or focus on farming — or even reconsider our plans to live on the island at all — but it always takes me time to understand where my daily activities are taking me.

According to the school friends there's word out that a boat came over from Sicily last night. It was spotted hauling up the brothers' baskets and stealing the catch. Presumably they cut the ropes and sent the baskets to the bottom of the sea.

It's a disaster. It's not just a day's catch: it'll take weeks to make new baskets, and it'll cost the boys a lot of money. Suddenly, cigarette lighters are flashing, and brothers are storming about stamping their feet and yelling at each other, at the sea, at the island, at everything. Before things have calmed Arturo has turned the boat around and is pointing the bow across the deep water towards Lipari, against the wishes of some of the others who want to rush over to Sicily and get even. Whoever saw the boat stealing the catch had managed to relay its size and shape, and the brothers think they know who it belongs to. Orlando tells me they've had trouble with them before, these Sicilians. They're known to be thieves and have no scruples when it comes to ruining the livelihoods of others struggling to survive as fishermen.

Back on the island word gets around fast, and I hear visitors are pouring into the brothers' houses offering support. When I meet Nino later that afternoon he tells me he's heard the news too, and we can't help turning our heads towards the Sicilian coastline. He's been meaning to warn me for a while, he says; he's convinced the Sicilians will steal our dog some day. The Mafiosi never make it this far, they get thrown into the sea between the islands if they try to, but common thieves are everywhere. Tetley will be in the boot of a car and on the ferry before we realise it's gone. It's a nice dog, he comments, a *bello bracco*, a beautiful hound, a bird dog, and soon it'll be the hunting season and a dog like that could fetch a lot of money. He's seen how people look at it, and he knows the ironmonger wants to breed his bitch with it. It's better if we get it castrated as soon as possible, then it'll be less attractive and can't be stolen and put into stud. He has a special knife. It's a bit rusty, but he'd used it on his own dogs when he was younger.

He likes it when I wince.

Meanwhile, over in Sicily, someone's been selling kilos of shrimp to the local restaurants. Word travels across the sea and reaches the brothers. Now they're sure who the culprits are and to save their honour the brothers have no choice but to sort them out. Orlando grabs me by the shoulder as I board the boat the next day and tells me I should stay onboard and not get involved in the confrontation they know is coming.

I grin, stupidly. 'Of course, of course I'll come with you just for the fun of it,' I say — or something equally garbled.

A puzzled look stretches out across his face. 'It won't be fun,' he says, pumping my hand. 'It's serious. People might get hurt.'

I might have thought of Rohan — will she be a widow before the day is out — and Louis, who stands to lose his father. But I can't know how grave the situation is. After all, I'm just a blow-in fisherman, and this is just another adventure of many.

We're skirting the Sicilian coastline at lunchtime. The brothers had expected to find the wanted boat out at sea, but there's no sign of it, and they're more edgy than ever. If the boat's not around here then it must be out among the islands, or worse, it could be stuck in port. Their worst fears are confirmed as we draw closer to the wharves, and Rocco spots it. Now the conflict looks likely to take place on land, where the enemy has friends. Arturo is for turning back, but the younger brothers will have none of it. They've come all this way, they face weeks of making new baskets, they've got children who need to eat and wives who need to buy clothes, and now they're expected to go home like dogs! No. There must be revenge.

Giacomo is immediately ordered below decks to fetch the wooden clubs we use to kill the eels. To my horror the boys check their knives and their supply of cigarettes. As I'm handed a knife too, just in case, a sickening feeling of dread rushes up from my stomach.

Arturo noses the boat into port towards our target: a boat as large as the MSS *Levante*, snug among a pod of others. There are people onboard; rough-looking sorts. But we're rough-looking too, unshaven and windswept, and there are six of us to their three.

We nudge up to their stern, taking them unawares, and four of the brothers are onboard in a flash, like pirates, with clubs and knives leading the charge. One man shouts and another bolts towards the cabin, but a brother is behind him, and in an instant has him pinned to the wheel. The boat pitches violently as two brothers dash to hold another man down. The third manages to escape by vaulting over the bow, and we see him running towards the cafés on the other side of a busy road.

The brothers are screaming at the captured men now, and you don't have to understand dialect to know their threats are meant to be terrifying. Then, just as quickly as it started, the brothers are back in our boat, leaving a victim splayed on the ground, and another on his knees in his cabin, still in shock. They haven't seriously injured anyone, just put the wind up them with ideas of what will happen next time, but there's still no time to lose. My heart is pounding as I try clumsily to cast off. We have to get out of there before reinforcements arrive, and by the look of the crowd that's emerging from one of the cafés, and the waving arms of the escapee as he directs them towards us, there might be a chase out of the harbour.

The engine is galloping now and pouring out thick black diesel smoke. We lash out at the tight-knit hulls around us, trying to free ourselves, but the prow of the boat has somehow dipped and got itself caught in a mooring rope. Orlando darts across the deck and lunges at the thick cord that's denying our escape. He slices with his knife, the MSS *Levante* bucks like a pony, and we begin to turn towards the open sea.

We're away and out in deep water before any pursuer has a chance to get a crew aboard. Cafés, houses and whizzing cars and scooters are growing smaller as we motor at full speed back to the relative safety of our island. The boys are slapping each other on the backs, but I notice their hands are shaking like mine as they light up their cigarettes.

Orlando tries to put me at ease with a wink. 'I thought we were done for then,' he says, 'when we couldn't get the boat out. For a moment I thought we might have trapped ourselves.' He has a huge smile on his face, and Raimondo is bellowing with laughter and slapping his legs at their audacity.

Arturo is guiding us homewards, so I can't see his reaction, but Rocco's is plain. He's staring back towards the receding coast with ice-cold eyes, watching for the sign of boats heading our way. It's only when we're sure there aren't any that Giacomo peels off his fingerless, yellow rubber dishwashing gloves. He hates getting blood on his hands.

I'd arranged to go out on another boat the following afternoon, just for the experience. We'd be fishing for *totani*, a type of squid, but bigger and inkier. A friend of one of the brothers owns the vessel, one of those typically colourful, long, thin boats you see lined up on beaches all across the southern Mediterranean. He was a loner, I'd heard.

I saw Bartolo one day down at the wharf as we were unloading the catch. He was filleting some sardines for *totani* bait and tossing the heads and skeletons into the harbour. It was Orlando who introduced us. Bartolo shook hands and rattled on in dialect. He spoke little Italian.

I'd often expressed an interest in going out on one of the small fishing boats, so I asked him then and there if I could go with him on the boat one day. Orlando translated, and the answer came back that he would send a message when the time was right.

Orlando doesn't like it one bit.

'The boat is so small,' he says, shaking his head. 'He goes out at night, in the dark, far out, in the middle of the sea. The engine is tiny, and old. Marco. It's dangerous. Boats like that sink all the time, they get hit by another boat, a ferry or a container ship, and then … *morto…*'

He recounts the story of an old school friend, who went out one dark night with his mother and father on just such a boat, fishing for *totani* even though they didn't have a licence to catch them. Out at sea, between Lipari and Salina, they'd spotted the lights of a larger boat heading their way. They were sure it was the police, coming to check if they had a licence. Not wanting to be caught fishing illegally they turned off their lantern, the only light they had on board. But the father misread the boat lights coming their way, and instead of passing to starboard as he'd thought it would, the larger vessel ploughed straight towards them. It ran them down. They were drowned: mother, father and son. It turned out it wasn't even a police launch. It was only a hydrofoil, with a few evening passengers onboard.

Rohan doesn't like the idea either at first, but she has a highly sensible approach to life, and after weighing things up she concedes that the odds of anything happening to me at sea are remote. Bartolo had been out thousands of times, and she suspects Orlando is a bit of a worrier. 'Perhaps it's because he feels he has some responsibility for you,' she says.

I'm less sure, but I don't let on. When you're far out in that sea you can feel so small, so vulnerable, and so alone. The Mediterranean always looks sleepy on the tourist brochures, but I'd seen how it could quarrel with itself. What can I do, though, now that the message has tracked me down? It has come up from a bar on the waterfront, over to Arturo's house, up the hill, and passed on by Nino who comes knocking at our door: '4 pm. Marina Corta. Bring a jumper.'

The story of the capsized boat apart, there is also the possibility of a flow-on from the battle in the harbour over on Sicily. Who knows what the victims might be planning? Presumably they know who the brothers are, and who their friends might be. Though I'm not sure they'd recognise me in the street, I suspect I might have stood out as a foreigner when we attacked, and if they came across me in the middle of the night, they might put two and two together and I'd be done for. I don't tell Rohan of my fears. Still, I suspect that the best thing to do is not meet with Bartolo right now. The problem is, I don't know if I'll get another chance. The weather could turn bad again, or he might change his mind, or just disappear, as Orlando says he had a habit of doing.

So it is that I find myself at a little after four in the afternoon, sitting in a rowing boat, alongside a man who speaks only dialect.

The trip starts as it'll mostly go on: in silence. We slip below the weather-beaten cliffs, and skirt Canneto and its line of beach umbrellas set up for the tourist rush. Then we pull out to sea.

Two hours later and Lipari still looks large enough to swim to, but as the early evening progresses the island gets smaller and less distinct. The boat dips gently up and down. We motor further into the deepest, darkest of water. I feel, frankly, nervous. If the engine fails, all we have left to get us back home is a set of skinny oars, and who knows what the currents are like out here. There are no flares onboard, no spare motor, no lifejackets; and as far as I know we haven't got any lights to warn away boats coming towards us either, only the smoky lantern that Bartolo's just put a match to.

There's gushing and burning, and the shadows darken around us. The faint glow of the light picks out the ribs of the boat and spills out over the sides to bring the liquorish water into more frightening relief. I take a nervous bite of a sandwich and try to pull my mind away from thoughts about what it would feel like to plummet into the blackness. Then Bartolo cuts the engine.

As the boat slows to a stop, the waves — which have been largely unnoticeable — start slapping harder: thump, thump, thump. The air smells like gasoline, and we begin to pitch like a queasy stomach. Then, insanely, Bartolo the loner stands up. The rowing boat sways dramatically as he turns and crouches and pulls out a straggle of hooks and weighted plastic balls knotted to a nylon fishing line. When he sits down again with a clump, I notice one end of the line is strapped to a string. This joins up to a thicker rope weighted with lead. The other end is also attached to a rope, which he hands over, before motioning to me to hang on tight.

He drops the weighted end over the side, and it tumbles through the faint liquid glow of the hurricane lamp and into the blackness. He checks the line as it runs, and stops it when he comes to the first plastic ball. With a flick of his thumb it lights up, powered by a battery. He reaches into a bucket and pulls out a sardine, hooks it up beneath the ball-light, and lets the line out again. The bait slides into the depths.

I have to row now, and I'm glad at last for something to do. I gather up the oars with a clatter, position them over the sides, and start to work the boat backwards, leaving behind a trail of ghostly green fluorescence. The oars are thin and inefficient, so the progress is slow, even though I only row for a few moments before I'm signalled to stop and another bait goes overboard.

When Bartolo's ready he pulls the line towards himself again, and slowly the first light appears. It clunks over the side and into the boat. The bait is still intact.

A while later I spot another light wobbling below the surface, and an ominous shape coming up from below. Bartolo traps the line beneath his foot, reaches for a net and leans over the edge. The *totano* has grabbed the light with its arms, and its huge spellbound eyes are clearly visible in the glow from the boat's lamp. With a swish of his net, Bartolo scoops up the hapless creature, brings it aboard in a spray of water, and drops it onto the decking between our feet. The *totano* is larger than any squid I've seen, and coloured a splendid off-white and shimmering purple. It wriggles uselessly, beating its wings faintly, trying to fly.

I put my back to the oars again and soon we land another *totano*, and so we go on, until we have all the floats back on board, and some thirty flickering creatures spread between the ribs of our boat. It's a good haul, Bartolo seems to say, as he nods at me, lights up a cigarette, and lies back, contented, with his shoulders resting on the painted woodwork. All that's left to do now is to make the run back to port, with the tide against us.

The homeward journey takes much longer than the one that got us out into the middle of nowhere, and I'm forever vigilant, looking in the direction of Sicily, trying to pick out any changes in the lights that might mark an approaching boat. But there's nothing.

The waves have risen with the wind, and although Bartolo pays no attention to it, as we slap through the water I'm doused in spray. Luckily, the night is warm and, even though I'm quickly wet through, after all those hot days the coolness of the sea comes as a relief.

It seems strange to be thinking of the land when you are far out at sea, but I find myself, in a sense, doing just that as we putter slowly homewards. I think back to Massimo, and how I was so disturbed that day over on Vulcano, and how I'd felt something was changing inside me. Then it hits me that I'm experiencing a fallow period in my life. For years I've been rushing around, caught up, sometimes thinking things were more important than they were, with nights and days coming and going like the wind. But after a while it became obvious I was stale and unproductive. I was in a drought: losing energy for things. Everything about the city I was living in seemed worn out. Even my relationships were losing their crispness. Now, unconsciously, under the surface, things are breaking up. The weeds are being destroyed; the soil is mellowing. I don't know quite where I'm heading yet, but I'm sure I'm being reinvigorated, deep down.

I'm realising though that there's no need to worry too much, no hurry to see where things lead, no necessity to question myself too deeply. I'll just take my hand from the helm and see where I end up. Wherever it is, I'm sure it will be to my benefit in the end. And to my family's benefit too. If we'd stayed in Sydney perhaps we might have split up by now, but here, stripped of the trappings of our city life, with all its conveniences and luxuries, we've been forced to look at the bare bones of our relationship, the negatives and the positives, to explore what each of us wants, and to reinvigorate each other.

We arrive home as the sun is coming up. I walk up to Bartolo's namesake, the island saint and one of the twelve apostles, standing at the edge of the piazza at Marina Corta. He's holding a tanner's knife and staring blankly towards the sea. Bartolo leaves me with a quick wave of his hand and I stay there for a while, looking up at the saint above me. Known to us as Bartholomew, they say he once washed up on Lipari after his coffin fell off a Roman galley. One of his fingers is kept up at the Cattedrale di San Bartolomeo, in the heart of Lipari's citadel. He's celebrated on Lipari in late August, during the Festa di San Bartolo.

I walk back to my car, with Bartolo the fisherman still on my mind. Bartolo had the saint to protect him, but the risks of life out at sea, isolated in that vastness, have increased in my mind. Still, I plan to stick with Orlando and the boys just for a while longer, mainly because it's sharpening my idea of my identity.

A few days after the events at sea there's the annual Blessing of the Fleet. The boys usually take the day off to join in the celebrations on board their boat, but this year they're so upset by the loss of their baskets they decide to leave the MSS *Levante* resting instead.

We drive down from the hills and explore the street fair beforehand. As usual at events like this, the stalls are bursting with novelty lighters, bracelets and brooches, blow-up balloon dogs, and fairy-floss. There are shooting alleys too, and Asians — the only ones we've seen in months — and gypsies with barrels of sweets and dodgy brass scales to weigh them on.

We bump into Allegria and Arturo, Justine and Orlando, and Hit-a-me and Hit-a-miss, and Raimondo and his wife, and the fishmonger and his family, and the woman who sells us bread, and we see so many other familiar faces. Arturo has bought fairy-floss, Allegria has snagged a pair of jeans, the delighted fishmonger has secured a cigarette lighter that looks like a child's scooter and throws out a flame when you pull back the handlebars, and Justine has succumbed to Luca's pleas for a slinky coil of metal that walks down stairs, which he manages to tangle up immediately.

At the far end of the street, outside the church, we find a stage and a local rock band setting up. The musicians are all in their late teens. They have long hair and ripped jeans. Their audience is mostly old ladies who are babysitting their grandkids and making use of the chairs in front of the stage.

The church doors are open the following day and we see a statue of the Madonna, pinned with bank notes, and a priest readying his microphone. Milling around outside is a raggedy brass band, dressed in red, with feathers in their hats. Their leader, a man in his fifties with a thick grey growth on his chin and pudding-basin hair dyed jet black, is lighting a cigarette off the one he's just finished. When he's ready, he rallies his troops into some semblance of order, just in time for the pronouncement of the priest. Then the church bells start up, ringing insistently, and the band ambles off, trying to march in step but failing badly.

The statue of the Madonna, hastily stripped of its dressing of euros, follows on a platform held up by four island notables. Among them is Nino, dressed in a red cassock, his finger in every pie.

We latch onto the end of the trail, ambling behind cymbals, trumpets, drums and trombones, and troop through the alleyway of fairground stalls towards the Madonna's boat. We part with the crowd beside the water's edge and find ourselves on the quayside. The Madonna is hauled aboard, and the nuns, the *carabinieri*, the officials flashing their gold braid and everyone else on the surrounding vessels start cheering and clapping. When the Madonna is secure someone pulls up the anchor, and the boat slowly drifts away.

Soon there's a flotilla of boats moving across the bay and around the headland. They pass beneath the citadel and beside the breakwater at Marina Corta, and then out to sea, just a little way, until the priest feels he's ready to utter the Madonna's blessings over a crackly sound system and anoint the boats that have made it this far with his cask of Holy Water.

The festivities are still going on at two in the morning, and our little family is there among the crowds, and the streets and cafés are bursting with the squeals of children, still going strong after their afternoon siesta. We are relaxed and happy, and the sense of possibility that I felt on Bartolo's boat is still coursing through me. I'm just taking things as they come, and it all feels right.

Nineteen

Happiness belongs to the self-sufficient.

ARISTOTLE

We snake down the laneway, newly dug up and filled in by workers laying cable to a new house on the hill. The dog has already nabbed a pine cone for us to throw, an alternative to the rocks he usually drops at our feet. Louis is sitting upright in his buggy, leaning over the side to watch the wheels turn.

We walk alongside the little timber yard and the country ironmongers, with their blackened, heavy gates stacked up outside against a rock wall. Then around the bend and past the little track where we pick our blackberries. Up the slope, with Nino's vegetable patches and the last of the tomatoes drying on their stalks in the burning sun. Everything is brown. Gone are the mats of yellow ragwort and wild garlic flowers, and all the other speckles in the grass. It's high summer and only the bravest and strongest survive in the fields: prickly pear, olives, pumpkin, squash and brambles.

Just past the house on the hill the road turns to cobbles. Around the bend the sea opens up, an expanse of blue stretching from Vulcano to Filicudi. A boat with a white sail appears frozen between the yellowing grasses of the land and the outline of an island out at sea. A farmer tilling soil around his trees utters a *buongiorno*, and we reply with the same.

Off the path to the right, just past the pines, is a narrow track sheltered by dense olive trees. This is a favourite of mine: a secret path leading to hidden treasures, a dusty pathway opening out onto grass under the olive trees. We must have another picnic here, maybe tomorrow. Something simple, some bread, cheese, fresh ripe figs.

Back at our house we think of dinner. We have a few of Nino's tomatoes, pungent, luscious creatures grown in the deep, volcanic earth. There is crisp, peppery *arugula* salad, fresh from Nino's kitchen garden. The capers are his too, the olive oil comes from his trees, and we've picked the wild herbs from his land. We've had feasts like these so many times, and each one serves to deepen my understanding of Nino's love of the land and his family. In my old life I'd think nothing of buying in everything for a meal, but I know now that there is no act more gratifying or more liberating than to coax food from the earth. The rhythms of nature are the ultimate template by which Nino and his family lives, and it feels right that we should follow them.

Out in the fields I'm helping Nino pick thin, green black-eyed bean pods. Immacolata serves them steamed, with pasta, and olive oil flavoured with garlic. One time we shell *borlotti* pods to reveal the speckled red-and-white beans inside. Immacolata makes a *borlotti*, fennel and sardine soup. She chops an onion and a fennel bulb, and fries them until soft in her olive oil. She adds a vegetable stock she's prepared herself, four gutted sardines chopped into chunks, and two cups of beans. The food simmers until the beans are soft, then she adds four more sardines, and cooks the lot for a few minutes more. A garnish of roughly chopped fennel tops and a splash of olive oil and we're all mopping it up with some crusty bread under their grapevine.

On another afternoon Immacolata brings over a bowl of early green olives. She's crushed them to reveal the pip, soaked them in fresh water for five days, and a saline solution for three, changing the water daily. When they're cured she drains them, and adds some olive oil, chopped raw garlic, oregano, and chilli.

August is watermelon season, and trucks ply the towns and villages offering whole and half-cut ones for sale. We watch as the kilo price drops from day to day as more competition arrives on the ferries from Sicily. In Lipari town the trucks use their pavement placards to announce the cost by the kilo. The locals understand they'll pay half the advertised price.

The height of summer calls for cooling food; double scoops of gelato from a beachside café, watermelon by the slice, summer plums, long silver ribbon fish or slices of swordfish marinated in white-wine vinegar, cold whole sardines in a thin coat of breadcrumbs and sea salt, and refrigerated prickly pears, which we've seen turn green and orange then red, like traffic lights. Arturo comes up to see us regularly and, to avoid getting caught on the niggly little spines that grow out from the fruit's wrinkled skin, he picks them with a metal tube fixed at right angles to a long pole. He places the tube over the fruit, twists, and off it comes, ready to be dropped into a basket.

That way's fine for delicate fishermen, Nino contends, but to do it right you knock off a paddle-leaf of thorns with a rock, rub it on the ground with your boot to remove the largest spines, then bend it in two to form a kind of glove. You use this to pick the fruit. All you've got to do now, he tells me, is to roll the fruit on the concrete to break off the prickles.

In one last flush thousands of prickly pear fruit ripen at once beside the laneways. But by then even the pigs have eaten their fill, so much of the fruit is left to fall on the roads, where it's eaten by the ruin lizards and rats, and squashed into a vibrantly coloured slick by the passing three-wheelers. By the time we take our afternoon walk the whole village smells sweetly of fermenting fruit.

August is also the month when the island half-empties, then fills to overflowing just as quickly. On the first day of the month Siremar puts on their largest ferry, a boat as big as an office building. Lines of cars blockade most of the roads around the town centre. Hundreds of local families are leaving. They'll stay with friends or relatives somewhere else: the rent they get from letting out parts of their houses to tourists will more than cover the cost of their holiday.

After this exodus, the island's population dramatically swells overnight. Car number plates change, and with a bit of guesswork you can tell by the letters where the drivers come from. Most are from Sicily, but there's a smattering from everywhere. Tourists cram into restaurants and cafés; Marina Corta is given over to rock bands and fashion shows. Bad *gelato* sells as rapidly as the good stuff. Women from the north wear scandalous bikinis in the main street. Romans and Neapolitans sway their hips languorously on the evening *passeggiata*.

During the day the touts roam the streets, and congregate in Marina Corta, where they try to sell cruises around the archipelago. They're mostly men in their twenties, and all are friends of Orlando. Each of them wears a straw hat with the name of their boat, and their nicknames, one and the same thing, written across the front. I run into *Confuso*, *Intrepido*, and *Situation* whenever we pull in at Marina Corta after a night's fishing; and again on evenings when we come down to listen to bands or for takeaway *panini* and a couple of beers from the sandwich shop. I meet *Confuso* more often than the others and we're soon on backslapping terms. He tells me he makes plenty of money from the tourists, and has wisely invested the money the European Union gave him for changing the size of his fishing nets. Along with some fishermen friends, he holidays in Cuba, away from prying eyes. The women there are so poor, he says, that they throw themselves at you. All they want in return is a present, a cheap pair of shoes, perhaps.

Cesare's taking tourists out too, on a boat he's gone halves in with a friend. Every morning they take their foreign catch across to Panarea, and in the evening to see the volcanic eruptions on Stromboli. They're raking in over 2,000 euros a day; a small fortune for people who'd until recently relied entirely on the diminishing catch they brought up from the sea. Cesare tells me he's saving up for a bigger, faster boat, to take tourists all the way to Filicudi and Alicudi. They'll be just about the only boat going out there. They're sure to clean up.

The signs that other fishermen are doing better than they are is angering the crew of the MSS *Levante*. After the loss of their fishing baskets some of them are on the edge of giving up, but in the end the loyalty they feel to their tradition, their father, and even the wholesalers and fishmongers, turns their minds back to the task in hand. As fortune has it, the season means a change in fishing techniques, and the boys had already planned to supplement most of their shrimp baskets with bigger ones they made last winter. These are far better for catching the larger fish that come to feed in the warmer waters.

Now, after teaching me how to weave baskets out of green plastic fencing, and all of us working together to replace as many of the stolen ones as we need, we're back in business. The problem is, just when demand has driven up the price of seafood, we find we're still barely catching enough to survive. The great schools of fish the boys caught last year just haven't turned up.

'We try, we try,' repeats Orlando in what's turning out to be his mantra, 'but they're just not there. It could be the water. It could be *too* warm. But the weather is hot like last year, I don't understand. We're going to starve if things keep going on like this.'

The brothers have another gripe too. Since the tourists arrived the service in the cafés has been awful. Those waiters from Palermo have no idea who they are and have even tried to charge them the tourist price.

The streets are always full too. Last year some bright spark in government decided in a misguided fit of civic pride that if they banned cars coming over from Sicily for the entire month of August then it would free up the town centre and make it more attractive. The idea was enforced, but before too long the authorities began to realise how much money they were losing by not being able to fine people for parking on the pavements, and across the fire station's driveway, and in the middle of the road. So, to make some of the money back that they lost last year, the authorities have come up with a cunning new plan. They've decided to get rid of almost all the island's parking spots. Now everyone is parked illegally, including the locals who've stayed on the island. Last year the car parked across the entrance to an alleyway would most likely be gone by the time you'd finished your shopping. Now, because a traffic policeman will only issue a fine once, for a car being in one spot, people are wearing the fine, and staying put wherever they are, sometimes for weeks.

Fortunately, we've found a place way back from the main street, down a laneway lined with enormous potholes.

Because half the island's cars have left for the month, and drivers from elsewhere wouldn't dare to put their cars at risk in such a place, on an island where they don't know the mechanics at the garage, they tend to avoid it.

I tell Nino about our special parking spot, but he cuts me off. He knows the place exactly, he says, and the owners of the potholes. They go to work with their shovels, digging deep into the dirt and piling it up behind a wall. Then they refill the hole when they want to park there, and dig the track up again when they're about to leave.

A downpour of sunlight falls across our bed. A bird sings. Someone starts pounding our bedroom wall with a jackhammer. The family next door is gobbling away at each other as they rip up their concrete driveway, which has become a bit discoloured over the years, what with the dog food being thrown across it each evening and the tyre marks and oil spills from their cars. Being Saturday they can rely on some boys from town to work a bit of overtime to help them. Being summer it's best to start at five in the morning. This way you can put in a good day's work and still get home in time for a siesta. The quicker they get it over with the better.

When I'm not at sea we start the day with breakfast together. At first, in early August, it's bread and some blackberry jam we've made ourselves. But by the middle of the month we're eating almonds straight from the tree, and soft yellow figs that have ripened along the laneway. These we peel with our fingers and suck out the sweet caramel-coloured insides.

The season for figs is remarkably short, and though it's always wonderful to eat things as they appear and look forward to them coming back, we try to preserve the memory by making our own fig jam.

We give some to Nino and he thanks us kindly before ushering us onto his terrace to show us *his* figs. They are drying in the sun on a raffia tray. He's cut them in half, leaving just a hinge of skin to hold them together. He'll leave them here until the sugars have intensified, then he'll wrap each fruit around an almond and Immacolata will put them in the oven. A short blast of heat kills any worms or insects that might be in the flesh, and when they're ready he'll skewer them onto spikes of dried Spanish broom, and hang them up in a shed, ready for Christmas.

At this time of the year Nino's well-worn fig jokes come out of storage too. He tests us repeatedly, trying to force us to slip up and use the feminine *fica*. *Fico* means fig; *fica* is slang for vagina. '*Ucelli*,' he says one time, pointing at a fig with beak marks in it. It translates to 'birds', which in Italian is slang for women, as it is in English. 'What do you think about birds eating the *fica*, eh? What do you think, *professore*?' Nudge, nudge. 'I know. It depends on the bird, eh?'

'*Si*, Nino.'

Twenty

The bird a nest, the spider a web, man friendship.

WILLIAM BLAKE

Our little boy is crawling around everywhere now, even up the stairs. He pulls himself up on furniture and does a little bouncy dance. He's into everything (except his own toys) — fans, chairs, the radio, earphones. He has a fascination with feet and shoes, pulls Tetley's ears, and tries to suck on paws and claws. Rohan is so much more confident with him. She's devised a new method of putting him back to sleep at night. Instead of a feed she picks him up, gives him a cuddle, makes sure he doesn't have wind, then puts him back in his cot. He screams. She strokes him and talks gently to him, lying him down again when he tries to stand up. Then the sobs die down and he's finally asleep. She stays with him for a while, in case he wakes up and feels abandoned. Last night he went to bed at eight, woke at 1.30 am, cried for twenty minutes, and woke again at 7 am. We mark it down as his first full night's sleep.

It's the middle of August, and it's time to prune the vines in the vineyard at the top of the cliffs. Nino will pick me up early, as usual.

The following morning I find myself in the trailer behind the three-wheeler's cab, with Tetley tied up beside me. We freewheel past our house and down the slope towards the donkey field. Nino swings the *Ape* around the corner and starts up the engine to take on the rise. We zoom down the laneway, narrowly avoid Hit-a-me and Hit-a-miss, who've just stepped out of their house, and snarl past walls and vegetable gardens, picking up speed all the time. I hang on to Tetley's collar with one hand and some iron fencing behind the cab with the other, and watch goggle-eyed as people flatten themselves against walls and buildings and we scatter chickens and dogs. Nino slams on the brakes and crashes through potholes, flinging us against the metal of the cab with a thud. He accelerates around hairpin bends and jolts through the gears as we sweep off the concrete and onto the bitumen.

Almost immediately we encounter the first steep rise. The engine tone shifts up a notch and I hold even tighter on to Tetley and the fencing as another *Ape* flashes past with a pitiful parp of its horn. It makes me wonder who people think I am, squatting there in the back of a peasant vehicle with a hunting dog. In my mind's eye I see myself here, with the wind rushing through my hair and the bruises developing on my arms and knees, not so much Nino's right-hand man as a simple labourer. It makes me feel more alive than I've ever felt.

The hill crests, then flattens, and Nino cuts the engine. We coast until we swing around a corner and onto the dirt, then the engine *ppwwopps* into life again. We trundle down a laneway edged with brambles, where we're jolted back and sideways by the uneven ground. I see Nino raise a hand and slam it down just in time, and instinctively I duck, just before a sizeable overhanging blackberry branch belts across the hood and narrowly misses the top of my head.

Nino slows at last, and we turn again onto another track. Through the brambles and fencing I can see neat rows of grapevines. It's the communal vineyard I'd seen so many months ago on my climb up the cliffs. This time though we're on the other side of the trellises, pulling up on a grassy verge next to a large white house.

It belongs to two German men, Nino says. Doctors, he thinks. Maybe gay. But who cares. They spend most of the year in Germany, and he barely sees them. Some of the vines are theirs, but they hire a local to look after them. Nino's are these ones, just nearby.

I untie the dog and he tears off down one of the rows as Nino leads me towards the first vine. He bends down and nips off a few leaves with a miniature sickle he keeps in his back pocket. Revealed is a bunch of small black grapes. He pulls a couple off, hands one to me, and slowly brings the other up to his mouth. The sharpness of the fruit makes me wince, and Nino flicks his away into the dirt untasted.

'Horrible, eh?'

'*Si*.'

'You don't know anything,' he mocks good-heartedly. 'It's August and you're eating grapes, *professore*?'

'When will they be ripe then?'

'A lot depends on the sun in September. Here, take this. Snip that branch away, and pull off those leaves. We need to get as much sun on these grapes as we can. What was I saying ...?'

'The grape harvest, when will it be?'

'The *vendemmia*? Sometime. Probably the tenth of October,' he averts his eyes from me and starts clipping himself, 'but will you be here?'

'Of course — well, I hope so. Why do you ask?'

'Well. I've been thinking. I know you like the *casetta*. And I know that sometime soon you'll probably go back home. There's no real reason for you to stay ...'

'Well, except that we love the place. Anyway, we haven't decided on anything yet. I mean, that's all right with you isn't it? If we stay on the island we can still live in the house?'

'Of course. For as long as you want. But maybe one day you will want a place of your own. Some land. Somewhere to plant your olive trees ... and you like the *casetta* ...'

'*Si*. I've told you before. I can't think of a better place.'

'You can have it then.'

'You're joking. The *casetta*?'

'*Si*, and some land. You can have the capers and the almond trees and the apricots. It's good land. You can grow a lot of things there.'

I look at him carefully, but he's avoiding my gaze. I know he's serious. If he were kidding he'd want to see my reaction. But I'm still not sure exactly what he means. Is he saying we can have the little shack and the land to keep forever, or just for as long as we want to stay? Then it comes back to me that the land isn't his to give anyway. It still belongs to the Nonna. She's told us before she'll never sell any of her land before she dies. New buildings are restricted on the island in any case, but there may be a chance we could do something with the old place, depending on how much swing Nino really has, and how much it costs to line some pockets. But then there's the cliff. Louis would be over that in an instant. We'd have to fence it off. Then I remember the mist in winter, pouring up over the edges of the bluff and streaming past; and then the spring flowers come into my mind — the poppies, the earth covered in ragwort; the sun setting between the islands; lying almost naked between the sea and the sun, with the sweat running down my chest; and the rabbit traps and caper flowers, the wine, my mind emancipated, invigorated, racing away. Wine is a bridge between modest, everyday reality and soaring imagination. '*L'acqua fa mali e lu vinu fa cantari*,' I say to myself, remembering one of Nino's most-quoted proverbs. *Water does harm but wine makes you sing*.

The rest of the day passes in a blur. We cut back and snip, me with a small knife. I remember coming across golden *malvasia* grapes speckled with red, and a straggly cherry tomato plant in the grass at one point, and a few clumps of garlic, and the odd tomato, and, when I ask Nino why they're here, he responds: 'Why not? I like surprises. Don't you, *professore*?'

Black grapes, green grapes, yellow ones, pink and purples: twenty varieties in all, some for wine and others for the table.

'I was never content to grow just one type,' he says, and reels out the names on request, demanding that I write them down. The blacks, for wine: *merlotto*, *shirazella*, *catariatti* and *occhio rosso*. And the whites: *la creme di Maria*, *Trebbiano* and the famous *malvasia*, the sweet apricot-flavoured nectar of the islands. Then there are the blacks for the table: *cardinale*, *muscato*, *perricone nero*, *barbarossa* (sweet but fleshy, he says, though a little tough, just like Barbarossa, the murdering swine) and *fragola nera* (the black strawberry; you can suck out the insides, and smell this, what a perfume!). And white grapes to eat: *uve italia*, *zibibbo* (perhaps brought to the islands from Tunisia during the Arab occupation), *malica*, *insolia* (a native of Sicily) and, finally, *maddalena*. As I make note of them with a pen on the back of a ferry ticket I find in my pocket, Nino checks the spelling over my shoulder, and corrects me when he thinks I've got it wrong. I suspect some of the words are spelled in dialect, and others in Italian, and some perhaps a mixture of both.

If I'm going to grow my own grapes then it's best to know as much about them as I can, he tells me. That goes for what they taste like when they're made into wine.

With that he produces a flagon and fills a glass to share. I produce a few blackberry jam tarts, made from the fruit picked on our walks. They are small things, like the mass-produced replicas I had in my childhood. But unlike the products of our bland convenience society, these are intensely flavoured — and so easy to make. I can hardly believe I have lived all these years without ever tasting home-made jam tarts! Easily the most important thing we have learned in our short time on this island is that any considerable step towards self-sufficiency is a tonic for your soul.

We head back home, but halfway there he pulls off the road and up a driveway. We're visiting his eldest daughter, he tells me. I've only seen her a few times since she made the bread at Nino's house, terrorising the entire family and me as well. But under Paolina's rough hard-hewn exterior there is a rough hard-hewn centre. She's never really paid me much attention before, apart from throwing menacing looks in my general direction, but this time she seems quite pleased to see me, and though there's no table set with victuals under a grape vine, she does offer me the chance to scratch her pig.

The sow is squatting in a filthy pen at the end of a grass garden. We make our way through a dusting of chicken feathers and half burned rubbish, skirt the hens pecking in a chicken-wire coop wrapped around a couple of citrus trees, and there it is, the home of a domesticated, even-toed ungulate being fattened for sausages.

Paolina picks up a trowel and pokes the end through the pigpen mesh. She scratches the metal tip against the sow's side, and the animal sinks to its knees, shuts its eyes, and utters a pleasurable grunt. It's obviously a favourite of Nino's too, because after I've had a go, he smashes a yellow gourd against the metal gate and throws it into the pen, followed by handfuls of prickly pear. The sow hauls itself up, and starts snuffling at the food in the mud. Paolina cackles with laughter, and Nino smiles.

The tour concludes with some skinny cats, two tied-up dogs, and a Sicilian pheasant: a male, with an impressive large red blotch across its heart. Paolina's bred them for many years, for both the flesh and the eggs. But due to a bit of a miscalculation, and the recent death of the breeding female, they only have this single male left. Now she has to work out how to get another one over from Sicily, a difficult job it seems as most of them have been shot by hunters.

We don't stay long, and I'm not really sure why Nino has brought me here at all, unless it was just to say hello because he was passing. I have a funny feeling that he wants to show me what I could have if I stayed here. Not just the fowls and rabbits, but a pig too, and some pheasants, if I can find any. And some cats to kill the mice in my barns, and maybe even a donkey like Maria's.

He nods towards the old lady, who's leading her beast back from the fields as we stand, back home in our laneway at last. 'She's got lots of land,' Nino continues nodding as Maria draws nearer. 'And lots of olive trees. All abandoned though. She's got three daughters and one son. He runs the fancy restaurant in town. But she's only got the donkey for company. You see. The old ways are dying.'

The sun is bleeding on the edge of the sea and the sea cliffs are forming a wall of bronze. I have a glass of Pinot Nero in my hand. Suddenly I realise the real meaning of being here. It's living like this, right now, in this time and place, on our terrace overlooking the sea, with the smell of grass being burned off somewhere, a casserole of rabbit, potatoes and black-eyed beans in the oven, knowing we've been accepted up in the hills ... if all this can't keep us here then what could?

Over the next few days I put my heart into getting to know as much as I can about the life I might be setting myself up for. I learn how to graft plums and pears, and olives to the wild rootstock that springs up direct from the pips. I plant carob seeds, help cut away the dead wood from the olive trees burned by the fire, and watch the new flush of green leaves appear. All the time I can't believe how joyful it is to work with my hands instead of with words. Nino teaches me to sex young cockerels by the shape of their neck feathers and to choose what tomatoes are best for various pasta dishes. We spend a windy night sitting around in the darkness by the *casetta*, whispering and laughing quietly to ourselves, swigging from wine flagons, talking about how anyone can have a place like this if they seek it out: an escape from the kids, the partner, the work, the worries. A place that invigorates you, that puts you on an even keel.

'Have you seen those fishermen down at Marina Corta sitting in their boats in winter, even when the boats are on the cobblestones?' he asks. 'They know what I mean.'

And while we speak he holds a shotgun ready for the rabbits; and finally I tell him how I've learned to stab an octopus.

The boys had been laughing about my reluctance to do it for so long that they'd set it for me as a test. So I did it. I grabbed hold of the squirming creature. I pulled its muscular tentacles free from Giacomo's arm and pressed the point of my knife between its energetic eyes. I hesitated for a moment, then braced myself and plunged the blade into the creature's brow. Someone cheered out loud, but I felt like I'd lost my innocence.

'Do you mind if I take it?' Orlando said, reaching for the corpse. He held onto one long arm and slapped it hard against the side of the boat. One thump, two, three … After every few strokes he gripped a different arm, and kept up the tenderising until he'd worked his way through all eight, until the poor grey body was stretched and slack. He sliced out the beak, removed the eyes, cleaned the body cavity, then handed it back to me.

'You're a fisherman now,' Orlando said. 'You've grown your teeth.' I'd been transformed from a deskman to a man of the sea.

'But have you?' asks Nino, almost in a whisper.

Twenty-one

In time the wind sags, and we hoist new sails.

PINDAR

Once you've marvelled at the blueness of the ocean, the occasional pod of dolphins, and the various kinds of aquatic life pulled up gasping from the depths, the hours on a fishing boat can drag. As each basket is pulled up, emptied and stowed away, then thrown overboard again, you begin to feel like you're working on a production line. The boisterous camaraderie and the gossip of earlier months have receded into lengthy bouts of silence, a quiet that causes the same old thoughts to run through your head until they drive you crazy.

Perhaps it's the long sessions out at sea, or the lingering fatigue brought on by the odd hours we keep, but after a while I find I'm losing any regard for the suffering of the creatures we are pulling up: the doomed eels squirming and gasping uselessly on the deck, the hermit crabs slowly broiling in the sun. They might just as well be dog biscuits on a conveyor belt for all the emotions they stir up.

But fortunately there's a break coming up. For two whole weeks the European Union will pay the boys to stay at home with their families while scientists try to determine how the sea life is bearing up under the relentless pillaging. The money isn't as good as they'd get if the fishing were going well, but because catches are bad the boys are happy enough to take the cash. What's more there are violent south-east squalls around. The exposed harbour at Marina Corta is no place for a fishing boat to rest between outings in times of shifting gusts. Several times in recent weeks Arturo has been forced to bolt for Vulcano. More than once he has tied up at the island's Porto di Levante, the east harbour, only to be expelled by the wind several hours later and pushed to leeward, to the Porto di Ponente. Back and forth, from island to island, all day and night, trying to escape the squalls. It's exhausting enough, without having to think about fishing for a living too.

The promised break offers the opportunity for me to get away. As part of our discussions that followed Rohan going to Germany earlier in the year, we'd agreed that I might have some time out too, if the chance arose. Now I have the opportunity to go to London, to stay with my old mate Daniel for his fortieth birthday.

I'm half-hearted about leaving, because I know I'll miss the island, my family, the continuation of the seasons up in the hills; but I realise too that it'll do me good to get some perspective on our stay, from a place far away.

It's the last day in August. I'm sitting on our terrace, watching our next-door neighbours setting up a barbecue in front of pillowslips and shirts drying on the line and blocking their view of the sea. I ponder whether they're just so used to the incredible vista that they don't see it any more.

When evening falls they gather around the coals with a fluorescent torch set on the concrete. Wrapped as I am in a growing nostalgia for the place I'm leaving in the morning, I begin to question my attitude towards them. It's true they're noisy, with their cars, their building work and their bickering, but I'm chiding myself for thinking the less of them for it. At least, like us, they can see the romance of eating under the stars.

I watch them with interest, visualising the calamari on the hotplate and the skin crisping on the fish. I find myself thinking fondly of Georgio, the overweight son. In the months we've been here I've only once seen him with children his own age, when his school decided to take the class on a field trip up the laneway so the kids could raid Nino's mulberry tree. It was Georgio's territory. He was king for an hour. I've never seen him so happy. Usually he's confined to the family driveway, where he plays tag with his youngest dog, or rides his bike around in circles, or kicks his football against the wall for hours. He reminds me so much of myself, in my teenage years in a small town, when I was bored, and powerless, and wanted more than anything to escape.

The food is ready. Someone turns around. But there's no fish. No calamari. Just sausages. And suddenly they're rushing to squeeze through the doorframe, heading towards the kitchen where they plan to eat. I hear the television blaring, the family fighting over the tomato sauce, trying to crush each other under the weight of their voices.

Evenings like this, especially when they're your last for a while, are meant for being outdoors. We've planned a trip to town to celebrate my last evening on the island for a while. But before we go Nino insists we join them for a cooling drink. They've heard that Louis is standing. They want to see it for themselves.

Louis performs admirably, swaying on the spot for a minute or more: proud of himself, before collapsing on his backside.

'My son, my son,' the Nonna cries. Tears run from her eyes and pool in the furrows on her cheeks.

'He's eating *pastina* now too,' Rohan says, showing her a box of tiny star-shaped pasta she boils up with milk.

'*Tutt'aposto!*' Immacolata exclaims delightedly. 'He's eating pasta. Everything is in its place.'

In Lipari town we discover the restaurants and bars around Marina Corta are crowded with Italian tourists. We find the last table in the piazza and order drinks. There's a TV set out here too, and the cameras are zooming in on pearly-white smiles, high-topped briefs and breast-hugging tops. The local beauty pageants have given way to regional finals, and soon there will be the big one: *Miss Italia*.

Italian television has taken commercialism to extremes. Companies have even paid for the right to have their names associated with talented girls on the catwalks. There's *Miss Wella*, for instance, the hair-product girl; *Miss Rocchetta Belezza*, who carries the hopes of a bottled water firm; and *Miss Bio Etyc Smile*, who Rohan believes has something to do with yoghurt.

Their official titles may have missed something in their translation, but we have a particular affection for some of them, like *Miss Delta of Po* and *Miss Hollywood Goats*.

'I think *Beautiful Miss of Lagos* has a chance of winning something, if only for her name,' Rohan says.

'I thought Lagos was the capital of Nigeria.'

'That and a company that sells underwear or make-up, who knows?'

'I'm putting money on *Miss Triumph Moda Mare*,' I say. 'She's got everything. A nice figure, pretty face, likes motorbikes, looks good wrapped in seaweed.'

The fashion pageant phenomenon has even reached these remote parts, and just before it's dismantled, we find ourselves drawn to a temporary summer stage set up below the walls of the citadel.

We stand on the edge of the crowd as prim young island women in one-piece costumes do ungainly twirls in high heels, then pose with a hand on a bony hip while attempting to hold up a quivering smile. The judges are old ladies and middle-aged men: a line of them, perched on a second-storey balcony, so far away from the stage that they need binoculars. But there's only one pair, and just three pencils to go around, so by the time they've all had a good look and have passed on their pencils to mark up their scores, the poor girl on stage has been reduced to a grimace and a backache.

I find myself disoriented in Waterloo train station. I'm in the middle of a stampede of commuters of extraordinary height and unnatural paleness. They're moving so fast, rushing like insects, following scent trails to stop them colliding, thinking of their slippers; just three hours until sleep, until they are obliged to catch the train again.

I buy a ticket for the Tube and make the mistake of thanking the clerk in Italian. He's too bored to notice, but I'm embarrassed by my slip and turn away, feeling like a bumpkin, with mud and potato skins stuck to my shoes.

There are delays as usual on the underground. The station is four-deep with faraway looks, clenched mouths, silent facades hiding their screams. They look so dissimilar to the people I'm used to now; hairpins instead of handkerchiefs, nice suits instead of holed shirts, stiff collars instead of sun-reddened necks. It occurs to me that they must spend much of their spare time bent over ironing boards, polishing their shoes, or trying to recuperate. I wonder how many among them would consider packing away their work clothes and living more simply.

The train is hot and claustrophobic. Sweat and electricity. The seats are all taken and I'm forced to stand, with buttocks against my spine and armpits in my face. I spot a man with a hamburger behind his newspaper. Another is cramming in a sandwich left over from lunch. I recoil when I see them. Suddenly I'm aware I'm suffering culture shock in the country I was brought up in and thought I knew so well. You'd never see an Italian eating like that, in a place like this. The boys won't even eat breakfast on the boat. It's just not the right situation.

I close my eyes and see soil instead of metal beneath my feet. I need a drink. Thankfully, Daniel has several planned.

We end up in a pub with baskets of summer flowers hanging outside. Several acquaintances turn up. The conversation flits from politics, to love, to history. No one mentions the price of watermelons, or gives advice on how to feed a donkey that's losing its teeth.

It's expansive talk and I struggle to keep up until they ask me what I've learned from my time away. I don't know how to answer at first, without thinking hard, but with all eyes on me, expecting an answer, I let loose my tongue. I've learned about community, I say, and the value of family. I had forgotten what it was like to have one before I went to the Islands of the Winds. I've learned that I like the relationship Nino has with his wife and daughters, and his freedom to be away from them when he needs to. I'd like to emulate that one day. I realise too that I want space, and country walks with my dog. I'm learning the basics of shade, and small places carved out of larger ones. I'm learning about the great pleasure of being self-sufficient when it comes to food, I say, and I mention that Nino is teaching me so much, about how I really want to live my life. I talk about the olive grove where we have picnics from time to time, the place where we can see the storms coming in from the sea. They nod wisely. The olive grove strikes them as a mythical symbol; something bequeathed to them through history, through the Roman invasion: a whisper of a homeland. One wants to know why I went there in the first place. I strain to think again; I've almost forgotten. Then someone brings another round of drinks and the question hangs in the air, and disappears without being answered. But it refuses to lie down. My mind is fuddled by beer but it's been set on a course I can't shake off, and when there's a break in the talk I take them back to the conversation before.

'I thought it was to get away from everything, to sail free, in a way,' I say. 'But now I realise it was to anchor myself. You know how it is. I was faced with life — a tide of it — work, getting a mortgage, children … I wanted to jump out and shout: "Halt! Let me think!"'

Sometimes in life you just need a place to dock, to consider your course for a while.

Daniel's flat is cool inside despite the summer heat wave. I stay up late, long after my friend has gone to bed, with a beer in my hand and the television on, catching up on news and events that have passed me by, slipping back into the old world I'd so much wanted to leave behind.

Towards the end of my stay a few of us make our way through the traffic and out into the country, for a couple of nights in a cottage to celebrate Daniel's birthday. It's an enchanting place with a hump-backed bridge over a brook swimming with trout. We laugh at the straw ducks and pigeons on top of thatched roofs. My island seems so far away now, not quite real.

That night I have a peculiar dream. I'm ten years older, and still in England. I never returned to the Islands of the Winds. I'd abandoned my wife, my baby and dog.

I look back at Louis, sitting in his little paddling pool on our terrace, sucking on his teething ring. His blue eyes, a mirror of the Mediterranean, are fixed on my movement, waiting until they catch mine so he can smile. But he's gone now, and Rohan has too, gone forever. And Tetley? He's old now, maybe dead. I'm so saddened by it all that my sigh of grief wakes me up well before the alarm clock. The relief at knowing my little family is out there, waiting for me, leaves me thunderstruck. I realise many of our relationship problems are a reflection of our struggles to reinvent ourselves. We are no longer individuals struggling to work as a couple. We are a mother and father, with new roles to play that we hadn't rehearsed. For the first time in our lives someone else has to come first. We could no longer be selfish. We had no choice in the matter. It was the nature of things. The thought of my child guides me back through the decades, to my own infancy. In some ways it seems so long ago: in others so near I can almost hear the lullabies. I see my innocence, my trustfulness, my gullibility. I feel myself growing, being clipped and pruned, shaped by people, institutions and events, until I arrive here in this time, a man coming to terms with fatherhood, and with all that swirls around it.

On Lipari I find I'm disoriented again. I hardly recognise Louis. He's less than two weeks older but he's totally different. His body is longer, his face is wider, and there's something else odd about him, which I can't put my finger on until it's pointed out to me — his hair has turned from dark to blond, making him look more Anglo-Saxon than ever. It shocks me that I've missed out on its changing colour, but it makes me realise how lucky I am to have spent so much time with him since he was born.

Our house in the hills seems smaller too, and I'm aware of the lack of comforts. When I mention this to Rohan she nods her head. It's strange, but she misses simple things, she says, like floorboards and carpets instead of tiles you have to mop twice a day; a comfortable bed instead of lumpy old mattresses; the feeling that it would be warm and cosy inside when winter came. She doesn't think she can take another winter here on the island. Besides, she's had enough of being a sitting tenant, perched among other people's belongings. 'I'm sure the Lawrence Durrells and the Bruce Chatwins of this world would say all you need is a bench to sleep on and a bunch of grapes, but I've got a family now,' she says. 'The three of us: you, me, and Louis. I want a family home. I want our children to grow up with the door bell, you know, so that it's higher than they can reach when they're small, and down to their chests when they're older — a permanent place, somewhere they'll remember.'

'I'm not sure we can rely on it ever happening here and, really, we're running out of money. The fishing thing didn't really work out. We've got to make a decision.'

'I don't want to go back to all those cars, and that lack of greenery,' she says. 'It scares me, especially after seeing all this. I've been thinking a lot about it recently, you

know, about what I want. I really don't want to go back
to work, but at least I have that option at the end of my
maternity leave.'

She goes on to tell me that she'll miss the walks if we
leave. She'll miss the relative smallness of the island too,
and she'll miss Immacolata, and Allegria and her family.
She likes the way they are so tight-knit, even though she
realises they're held that way by a kind of duty to each
other. But it's positive: non-reproachful.

'This island has given me a lot,' she says, 'when I think
about it.'

The most important thing is that it's allowed her to
become a mother on her own terms and in her own time,
she says. So in a way it's served its purpose — but that
doesn't make a decision to leave any easier.

There have been other changes on the island since I went
away. The morning after my departure the summer
cracked up in a storm and large drops of rain began
falling on the island at last. Now the countryside is green
again and there's an almost imperceptible chill in the
evening air; and, as the week progresses, I notice the sun
is inching back along the horizon, towards its winter
setting point.

Out in the fields Nino is already starting to prepare for
the cold, burning off the last tufts of long grass, and chain-
sawing olive logs to store away in his barn beneath sprigs of
oregano and clusters of tomatoes hanging from the rafters.
It's joyous, autonomous work that frequently changes. In his
cupboards are jars of preserves: jams, chillies, tomatoes,

dried fruits, smoked meats. He saws and stacks branches and cuts hay, making ready for the cold months ahead. I'd love to be able to prepare for winter like that.

When I meet Nino one morning he jerks his thumb backwards to indicate his wife. She's sweeping the terrace with a broom above us, one-handed, with the rest of her weight on a crutch jammed into her armpit. 'She's obstinate,' he says loudly enough for her to hear. 'She should just lie down and feel sorry for herself, but she keeps seeing things on the news. Now it's those people who died of heart attacks in Palermo, because of the shock of the earthquake.'

'*Male fortuna*,' she calls out, shaking her head. Bad luck. She's grateful she's only had a hip replacement. There's so much to do before winter comes.

Nino mutters to himself, before brightening up.

'I've got some things for you,' he says. 'Just help me with these cabbages and cauliflowers and I'll get them for you.'

We work together planting and watering under the mulberry tree. We are both experiencing an emotional connection to the things we put in the ground. For him each plant means a meal in the future, a feast perhaps, and provisions for his family and friends. As for me, I'm experiencing a feeling of completeness, of deep satisfaction, to be working here with my friend beside me, with our hands in the earth and the slightest of breezes playing through our hair.

When we've finished he shows me some cuttings he's taken from his herbs and rooted in plastic milk containers he's rescued from the recycling bins. He's planted some seeds for me too, he says, and collected some wild mint from the base of Hit-a-me's mountain. Arturo's supplied a rosemary plant, dug up from his garden. There's some thyme from a crevice in the laneway. I can grow them around the *casetta* if I want.

I'm touched, and every couple of days I make a pilgrimage to water them, and bring back leaves for our evening meal. It's a half-hour walk each way, which is not really practical. Herbs are usually best when they're on your doorstep and you can step out in your slippers to pluck a little when the meal is on the stove. But, as Nino reminds us, if we choose to live in the *casetta* one day, then our herbs couldn't be handier.

Later in the week we go hunting rabbits, Nino with the gun and me with the wine. We sit together in the moonlight, looking out across the cliff tops to the lights on Salina.

The bare, dry slopes remind me of Australia, and I can't help mentioning it.

Says Nino: 'It's like here you say, *professore*? Go on, tell me more.'

I paint a picture of the tinder-dry grasses, the eucalypts dropping their branches in thirst: the countryside looking ready to self-combust at any moment.

'There are olive trees there,' Nino says. 'People have told me.'

'There are. They're not old and huge like the ones around here though. There was one in the garden of the house I was renting before I came here. It was quite a few years old, but it only just reached the top of my head.'

'Did you water it?'

'No.'

Nino laughs out loud. 'Olive trees are tough. But they need water when they're young, like children need a little taste of wine, it sets them up good and strong for later. *If you want to live to be old you need to start early*,' he says, quoting a Sicilian proverb.

'I'll remember.'

'And grape vines? Do you have grape vines in Australia?'

'Yep. They make lots of wine.'

'When do they plant grapes in Australia?'

'When? You mean what season?'

'*Si*.'

'In spring, I suppose.'

He shakes his head. 'They have to be in the ground in autumn, *stupido*. They need to put their roots down before the hot weather comes. Haven't you learned anything, *professore*?'

I grin, but secretly I feel a tinge of longing inside. Even though I love these islands, just talking about Australia makes me think fondly of the place. It had never occurred before but, just maybe, after all those years living there I'd put roots down too.

A few days later I probe Hit-a-me and Hit-a-miss for their feelings about their imminent return home.

'Will you miss the islands?' I ask.

'He will,' Hit-a-miss replies, jutting her nose towards her husband. 'But I can't wait to get back. I miss my family, my friends. He's different. He's spent forty years wandering around his garden, every morning, checking his plants and trees with a coffee in his hand. You should see our garden. It's got a lemon tree, and wormwood bushes, olives, capers, tomatoes, mint — everything from here. They're his memories. He'd live on Lipari again in an instant.

'But me,' she goes on, 'I'm upset. I don't get on with so many of the locals here now. They're trying to move in on my land, always asking me if they can have it because I'm not using it any more. They don't understand that it's *my* land. It's part of me, even if I'm not here.

'I'm different from them now. They think I'm a foreigner. I can't fit in here, not any more. I've seen so much. My mind's outgrown the place.'

Nonetheless, all the years she'd lived in Australia the island had been in the back of her mind. The memories of the old place constantly tormented her, and she never felt entirely whole in her adopted land. Now she's found that the place she remembers from her younger years doesn't exist any more. Even the language is different.

'I guess I go where she goes,' Hit-a-me adds sadly, before punching her softly on the arm.

'It's hard to be stuck between two places,' Hit-a-miss says, turning to kiss him affectionately on the cheek.

'I know what you mean,' I say. 'I really do.'

Twenty-two

*If we are always arriving and departing, it is
also true that we are eternally anchored. One's
destination is never a place, but a new way of
seeing things.*

HENRY MILLER

The decision to leave is one of the most difficult we've
ever had to make, but the reasons have mounted up and
we finally settle on going. Now that it's done it feels like a
weight has been lifted off our shoulders, but we want to
keep our resolve to ourselves for a while. We have a lot
still to do and see, and long goodbyes would just make
things harder.

Rohan's year of maternity leave ends in November, and
although she can't even face the prospect of going back to
work as yet, it seems a good date to aim for, especially as
it will be the start of winter here by then.

It's the beginning of October now, and we'll have to get the car back to Germany and then sell it. And Tetley will need to be checked over by vets, crated up, and sent on his way to Australian quarantine.

So that gives us about four weeks to fit in as much as we can. We start by visiting Panarea, where we stroll among the whitewashed houses and spend a while sorting through pebbles on a beach for broken pieces of worn old pottery: the cups and plates of generations past. Then it's over to Salina, where we spend much of the time in a café, eating *gelati* above a rack of squid boats with pointy sterns. Finally, I take on a project I'd set myself months before: to climb Stromboli.

Rohan volunteers to stay on Lipari with Louis and Tetley. She's sorry she won't be coming with me, but she knows too there'll be another chance, when we come back to these islands one day.

I don't want to do it alone, and although I know I can do it with a group, I'd far prefer to attempt the climb with someone I know. So I approach both Arturo and Orlando, and try to persuade them to accompany me, but both give a vigorous shake of their heads.

'Impossible,' says Arturo.

'Why?'

'It's madness.'

'Tourists do it all the time. There are even professional guides who will take you up.'

'They're all crazy. I'd rather be out at sea in a bad storm.'

'What about you, Orlando? You're fit enough. Surely you've wanted to climb it sometime in your life?'

'No. It's unnatural. A monster.'

'It's very natural.'

'Like death.'

I laugh. 'We won't die! I'm sure it's safe. Thousands of people have climbed it and come back alive.'

'It's a volcano. It's unpredictable.'

'The sea is too, and so are the winds.'

But whatever argument I try to use I still strike the deep vein of fear running through them. No end of reasoning will shake their resolve to keep well away. They've fished around the volcano since they were children, they say, they've seen what it can do.

Disappointed with their reactions, but unperturbed, I book a tour boat across to the island, where I meet our guide.

It's late afternoon by the time our little group starts off through the village, with hard white helmets on our heads, torches at the ready. We tramp past shabby houses and shops and out into a country laneway, eventually turning onto an unmarked rocky track.

We begin to climb. At first the trail curls around the steeper inclines, and we vie for the lead, optimistic that we won't have much trouble. But before too long the gradients increase and our progress slows. Every few hundred metres we collapse as a group on our backsides, gulp from our water bottles, and wearily take in the views out to sea.

The Tyrrhenian looks smooth and empty, apart from the tiniest boat, twisting as it changes course. My heart leaps, but then I realise it's not the MSS *Levante*; she won't be out until early morning. My shoulders slump as I think back to my days on board, and the moods and currents I've witnessed in the sea and among its crew. I'd like to call out and wave, but with these strangers beside me it doesn't seem right. So I remain there mute and overcast by the realisation that I'd not be a fisherman again. The gulf between earth and sea is too distinct. I'd stretched myself thin between both, but I'd been washed back to land in the end. You can't be a fisherman and a farmer. You have to choose. I know that now.

People are jostling past me. They're off again, just as the sun is sinking behind a ledge. Soon it'll be nightfall, and we'll be crawling on our hands and knees up shelves of rock studded with boulders. When we stop for another rest we'll notice how cold we are. The sweat on our backs is freezing.

The vegetation thins, before disappearing completely as we inch forever upwards. On the bare slopes above we can clearly see the torches belonging to snaking lines of tourists further up. The sight of them spurs us on just when many of us are thinking we can't make it.

After an arduous four hours we near the summit, and soon we're sitting on a lip of dirt and clinker, hanging our legs over the crater's edge. We pull on layers of spare clothing, adjust our helmets, and watch for an hour or more, entranced by the significance of what's happening in front of us. Every few minutes we're rocked by explosions and propulsions of fiery lava that turn the night sky into a blaze of oranges, yellows and reds. The ground trembles as rocks and cinders catapult into the air with each fusillade, and moments later a soft rain of ash drifts down. We can hear it skittering on our helmets and feel the smell of acrid sulphur burning in our nostrils.

After each thunderous eruption the volcano rests and sucks in its breath, and we see bright red corals of molten rock crusting over as the night pulls in again. Tourists are murmuring around me, too in awe of the cataclysmic scenes we're witnessing to raise their voices.

Suddenly, a deep, throaty grumbling arises from the volcano's core and we instinctively huddle back as three vents go off at once. Now everything's ablaze and bleeding in front of us; spitting red, fiery cannonades of lava, blotting out the moon and the stars and leaving an afterglow that burns in my eyes for minutes afterwards. People call out in wonder and fear, and cameras click in shaking hands. No one has seen anything quite like this, and we're reminded of our own insignificance on this planet, our powerlessness compared to something as awful and phenomenal as this.

As the night wears on the shadows are punctuated by more bombardments, as intense and terrifying as those before, each wave of fire creating new land that pours unseen by us down a far slope and into the sea.

The experience is a momentous one, and it brings about a two-fold revelation. First: to be happy I had to change. Second: I suddenly realise what I've been searching for all this time. Home.

I already had some sort of inkling of what home was, mostly gleaned from my experiences on these islands. For me, it was being with Rohan and Louis, my family. In general, it probably also related to your ability to externalise your interior world, through your furniture (perhaps a sack on the floor and a mattock in the corner), your choice of plants in the garden (or the varieties of tomatoes in your fields), the shelves full of the books you've chosen to read (or the garlic and potatoes in your barn), the friends you've chosen to invite, the people you've chosen to live with. You could take home with you, wherever you went. It helped if you weren't at the mercy of a landlord, unless it was someone like Nino.

Talking of Nino, a couple of days later I'm walking beside him in the fields and he's listening intently to the conclusions I've drawn about home and happiness.

'It's like the olive or the grape vine,' he says. 'First you plant the tree. Then you get the little grapes or olives. Then comes the most difficult bit — the waiting, the contemplating, protecting the crop from birds and hoping the wind won't blow your efforts back to the beginning again. But it's miraculous when it comes — that wine and olive oil!'

The days are rushing away. I can hardly believe we'll be leaving soon. I've got so used to this place: the smells of the sun on the pine trees, the salt in the air, the crow of the cockerels. But as I look outside at the mist enveloping our little house in the hills again, cutting the island off from the rest of the world, I comfort myself that at least we've come almost full circle.

The nights are drawing in, and wisps of cloud skate into the walls and telegraph poles around us by day. On our walks we see the lemons yellowing on the trees, the last black figs being eaten by flies, the land ploughed up, ready for the winter crops. The mists come and go in the hills like woollen hats on Nino's head. Each bout lasts a little longer. As the month rolls on, the island will close in on itself again and the fishing boats will be pulled out of the sea.

One day, when there's a break in the cloud, we make a dash up to the vineyards in Nino's three-wheeler and meet Arturo's battered white Fiat beside the grapes. We work down the rows, slicing off bunches with our sickles, picking out patches of dried, shrunken husks that the songbirds had feasted upon. There's plenty of laughter as we labour together, and Tetley races between the alleyways of vines, rummaging in the soft black earth like a truffle hound, thrilled at the heady, dizzying scent of fallen grapes, which he gulps down without tasting.

When the last clusters are snipped away we stock the back of the *Ape* with wicker baskets full to the brim with green and black fruit and head back together to the barn beneath Nino's house. Once there, our landlord pours the grapes into a concrete bath as high as our waists, while Arturo takes off his shoes and socks and climbs in. Nino urges me to do the same, and brushes Rohan away before she even asks.

'Don't take offence,' Nino says. 'You know how it is. We can't have them ruined.'

'I'll just watch then,' she says, taking it in her stride. 'For a while. Then maybe I'll go to Canneto and leave you men alone with each other.'

He chuckles. 'Are you going to the beach to wash your *fiorlino*?' he responds with a roguish grin.

Immacolata whoops and slaps at his shoulder and joins in with Allegria's blushes.

'Your *fiorlino*?' he repeats, indicating her crotch with his chin. 'Your little flower?'

Rohan just rolls her eyes. She's become used to him.

It takes over an hour to mush and crush by foot. By the time we've finished our legs are aching and stained bright red.

We quench our thirst with cups of grape juice ladled from the gallons of deep pink liquid waiting to be siphoned into barrels. Nino shovels the remaining skins and un-squashed pulp into a wooden crusher and we all take turns pushing our weight against the wheel cranks which turn the rollers. The last drops of juice trickle out into a bucket. Stalks, skins and pips will end up as fertiliser on Nino's onions.

Later that day we meet Nino again, just as we're about to go down to Lipari to book our tickets for the overnight car ferry to Naples.

'*State partendo, professore*?' he asks, though he says it with a hand in front of his mouth, so we're not entirely sure. Are you leaving?

I'm taken aback. We haven't told him about our plans to return to Australia yet: we've been trying to pick our moment. How could he have guessed?

He chuckles mischievously.

'*Si*,' Rohan responds, glum-faced.

'*State part-u-rendo*?' he repeats, emphasising the syllables so we can read his lips.

I turn to Rohan, and see her mouth arch into a smile.

'No, Nino,' she says. 'I'm not *giving birth.*'

He's fooled us again with his word play, but we have something to counter this time. It's just such a pity that it has to be so serious.

'Actually Nino, we are leaving,' I say quietly.

He looks at me with his soft but serious eyes. 'When?'

'After the olive harvest. The middle of November.'

'*Ma ci siamo abituati a voi,*' he says, crestfallen. But we've got used to you.

He doesn't ask why we're going; it's almost as if he knew we always would.

It's morning. There's a storm predicted. Rohan is making pancakes and Louis is emptying spaghetti from the cupboard onto the kitchen tiles. Nino wants more help before the rain comes. He's already ploughed the land beneath his olive trees with a mechanical digger he shares with his extended family: the cousins, uncles and remote relatives who tie in from marriages generations back. Arturo and Allegria have offered to put in some time too. After all, they'll be getting half the supply of oil.

Nino drives the *Ape,* while the rest of us walk into the countryside together, armed with sticks to beat the trees with. We whack the branches to loosen the olives and scrabble about on our hands and knees to collect them. Baskets fill up quickly and within a couple of hours the three-wheeler is loaded up and on its way to the barn.

All thoughts of siestas are abandoned, and the harvest continues after some pasta, until all the trees have been stripped of their fruit. In a few days Nino will take the softening black fruit to Sicily to be pressed, and will return later with flagons of golden oil. The fire and the heavy winds that blew through his trees earlier in the year have made for a small crop, so they'll have to use it more sparingly over the coming year. There's a bottle for us though, and one for the fireman as a thank you for calling the water-bombing plane.

The fireman turns up again a few days later with two long-eared lambs from his farm in Sicily. They're thin, bandy-legged creatures with doleful eyes. Nino locks them up in a small concrete enclosure down near the chicken coops. The children will pat them and ride on their backs, and the lambs will eat last spring's dried flowers and hay, and basins of rock-hard beans.

'Forty days and then we'll have them with potatoes and carrots,' Nino announces as I tickle their noses between the bars of their cage. 'Delicious.'

'And will they stay here until then?' I ask.

'No. I'll take them out on a lead to the fields every day, like dogs.'

'They're so beautiful,' says Rohan sadly. They wag their long tails when she approaches.

The storm comes later, when it's dark and cold. We sit it out under the awning of the balcony, dressed in heavy jackets. Thunder rolls across the sky. A swarm of midges shelters beneath the rusty hood of the street lamp tacked to one of our outside walls. There's a powerful scent of wet earth and plants, and the sharp electrical smell of lightning.

The following day the clouds gather out at sea again.

'Don't forget to bring in the sheets when it starts to rain,' says Rohan as she goes downstairs to put Louis to sleep.

'It's not going to rain,' I call out as she disappears through the doorway. 'Not judging from the way those clouds are looking, at least. It's heading towards Vulcano.'

I'm right. The downpour misses us entirely and my successful prediction delights me. The riddles of the winds and clouds, which had for the most part been unintelligible to me before I'd come here, had been partly solved by the knowledge I'd accumulated over the months. I felt like the king of the island just then, a modern day Aeolus: the Lord of the Winds.

I'm sitting in a shaft of sun in front of my *casetta*, probably for the last time. The clouds are blown up against the horizon like sea foam. The apricot and nut trees are losing their leaves.

Nino turns up as planned. He uncorks a flagon of wine, and sits down beside me.

I've been thinking. For as long as we've known each other I've been using the formal form of address when I talk to him in Italian, in deference to his age.

'Now we've become friends can we be informal with each other?' I ask.

'I'm always informal.'

'Well, yes, you are, when you talk to me. But can I be informal to you too? You know I always address you as *lei*. Can't I use *tu* instead?'

He turns his head towards me. I notice his eyes are twinkling again.

'Were we born together?' he asks.

'No.'

'Are we part of the same family?'

'Well … no.'

He nods his head. That's settled then, it seems to say.

Later I ask Allegria to clarify the situation. 'Put it this way,' she says. 'I'm thirty-two, and I still use the formal *lei* when I speak to him. I've only just started to call my mamma *tu*.

'I was only joking with you before, *professore*,' Nino whispers seriously when we meet up again. 'We *are* good friends are we not? So why be so formal? Call me *tu* whenever you like. But only in private, just between us, and only when we're drinking wine. If you're drunk then I can put it down to you forgetting your place.'

Twenty-three

*The next best thing to being wise oneself is to
live in a circle of those who are.*

C S Lewis

We do the rounds, say goodbye to almost everyone we
know and have one last coffee with Orlando and Justine.
When the house is cleaned and the car is full, we wander
up to Nino's house. We pose for last pictures together.
Nino clenches my hand in his behind our backs as we
look towards the camera. I'd never seen a hard man cry
until then. He kisses me on my cheeks, with tears
streaming down his face, and the women and children let
loose their sobs at the sight of him.

I mutter something glib to Nino, wishing my Italian
were good enough to really tell him how much I feel he's
influenced my life. The old goat has taught me about the
land, the olives, the grapes, the vegetables of everyday,

and how to live in harmony with the land — except when it comes to snakes, of course. If you'd had a son I wish it were me, I say in English, knowing he doesn't understand. I'll remember you with great affection, I think, and I'll miss your smile, your laughter, and your silly jokes. You're like family to me now.

I turn to Immacolata and kiss her gently, tasting the saltiness of her tears on her cheek. Thanks for your smile, your laughter, your hospitality, your love for Louis; you've seeped into our hearts. My thoughts flicker back to watching her work over the stove, cooking food as unspoiled as she is; the delight in her eyes when she saw Louis take his first steps; and with Allegria, stoking the flames of the bread oven like the servants of some fire god.

Out of the corner of my eye I see Rohan hugging Immacolata, as Arturo's hand cups mine. His grip still surprises me with its delicacy. He promises to write. Then Allegria grabs me around the shoulders, pins me to her chest, and kisses me hard on both cheeks before rubbing her eyes. The Nonna hugs Louis one last time. Inevitably, we'll never see her again.

'Remember my offer,' Nino whispers as I climb into the passenger seat. 'Come back someday soon, before I'm old and my mind no longer works so well ...'

'I promise I will,' I say, as I look one last time into his liquid eyes.

'Sail while you have a good wind, *professore*,' he says, and he holds my hand through the window as the engine starts, his fingers slipping as we roll gently forward, and away.

We drive down the laneway, our eyes glazed with tears and a swell of emotions threatening to burst out in howls of regret to be leaving. We only manage to compose ourselves when we're well on board the ferry. All that's left now is to stand on the foredeck, and watch our island slowly slip away.

As if to prolong the emotions of leaving, the ferry runs achingly slowly below our village. I see our house on the hill, a speck of white. I think we can make out someone standing on our terrace, waving a red bobble hat. He's so far away, but I wave back nonetheless.

Soon we're passing the cliffs below Hit-a-me's mountain, and there's the white seismic marker pole on its summit. I've watched so many boats and ships pass by from up there, and now it's we who are leaving. I scan the slopes for the *casetta*, but in vain: the angle's wrong and the ferry's heading out to sea now, towards Naples. It'll seem like a lifetime until I sit beside it again.

Epilogue

*A man travels the world over in search of what
he needs and returns home to find it.*

GEORGE MOORE

Back in Australia we return to renting in the suburb we'd
left a lifetime ago, just as a stopgap until we find somewhere
more fitting. It seems unreal at first. The streets and shops
are somehow familiar, but strange all the same, as though
someone had rubbed out the map in our minds, and it's
being reinvented in front of us as we drive around.

We spend weeks looking in newspapers and visiting
real estate agents, getting more and more depressed when
we find house prices have climbed steeply during our time
away. Then, just as we're about to resign ourselves to
renting forever, I walk into the living room to find Rohan
standing in shock, holding a plastic lollypop-stick with
two crimson stripes on it.

She's pregnant again; but our pilgrimage, in search of a home, still isn't over.

But then the key turns in the lock at last.

'Have you found a place to live yet?' a friend asks one morning on the phone. 'Because if you haven't I think I've come across the perfect place for you.'

Her husband, a builder, is renovating a house in a seaside village south of Sydney. It's cut off from the city by national park and water and, just like an island, you have to make a special effort to get there.

We'd been there before, years ago, but it gave no clue then to our future life. How could it? Living in a place like that would have been unfathomable back then, when the pull of the city lights was so strong. But now we're older, and very much changed — and we've had Lipari to show us what we wanted from a place.

Some days later we find ourselves sitting on a little ferry boat sailing towards a saddle of land and a net of trees strung out above a beach. As we draw closer a flurry of bare-chested children leap from the jetty into the sparkling green water. It looks idyllic, and remarkably familiar, and memories of Lipari come flooding back.

We find an agent with houses to show. The first one we look at is dark and dreary, its architecture soured by a lack of imagination.

We've an hour to wait until the next house is open for inspection, so we buy some chips and sit on the beach with Tetley and Louis, watching the waves and the seagulls. We say little to each other, scared of putting what we're thinking into words in case they jinx the magic we're feeling. It feels like a homecoming.

The second house is simple: a one-level fisherman's shack with a pot-bellied fireplace for cold winter nights. It is a good house. A good place to live. It has warped wooden floorboards, with a couple of joins from one wall to another. They show where new sections of building were added on, over the years, as a family grew. Home-cut skirting boards meet at odd angles. Internal doors are too short, and leave great airy gaps beneath them. Four bedrooms line one side, one for us, another for Louis, a third for the baby to come, and the other for an office.

A large-enough garden runs back from a deck topped with corrugated iron, perfect for listening to the rain when it beats overhead. From the front steps we can just glimpse the sea. If I stand on tiptoes I can see the storms rolling in, and can judge the direction of the winds from the swell.

We know it's ours before we make an offer.

In the first few days after we move in, I plant some olive saplings, some lemon trees, herbs and vegetables. And we buy some chickens, to keep in a run out the back. We are as excited as children when they lay their first eggs. I search out some stone pine seeds too, which germinate quickly, and end up growing alongside a couple of grape vines, planted in autumn, just as Nino advised. Hit-a-me sends up a caper plant and some tomato seeds; the progeny of others smuggled in from Lipari decades ago. Every morning I'll wander through our garden, with a coffee in my hand, just like him, checking how much they've grown.

We soon make friends: like-minded souls, refugees from the city just like us, and we come to realise there's an island mentality here too. Young mothers team up to talk babies, the men group together in the local pub — just one night a week, so as not to rock the boat. And one day I find my new *casetta*: a place beneath a wiry bush, with sand for a seat, and views across a bay. It feels right: a place where I can think and write, where no one comes to disturb me.

Meanwhile, the seeds that had germinated deep inside me on the Islands of the Winds spring out into a new career as a writer and freelance travel journalist. I promise myself that I'll never work in someone else's office again, instead I can work from the place I'm starting to call home. I relish the variety that my frequent trips bring. And Rohan sets up her own business too, and soon she's earning twice as much for half the time. We've bounded ahead after going away, while most of those who had stayed at home seem fossilised, their plans and dreams choked by the undergrowth of their lives.

Then another baby boy arrives. We call him Charlie. And our family becomes even stronger and more rounded.

We might not live here forever. But we content ourselves with the knowledge that the Islands of the Winds will be there for us again if we want them.

They're waiting. As islands always do.

Sources

Aesop — From *Aesop's Fables*, translated by George Fyler Townsend

Blake, William — *The Marriage of Heaven and Hell* Facsimile edition. Oxford University Press, USA, 1975

Chesterton, GK — *Autobiography*, Sheed & Ward, NY, USA, 1936

Goethe, J W von — 'Mignon' from *Wilhelm Meister's Apprenticeship*, Vol XIV, Harvard Classics Shelf of Fiction, PF Collier & Son, New York, USA, 1917

Homer — *The Odyssey*, translated by Samuel Butler The Internet Classics Archive

Horace — *Odes*: Book II, 16 and Book I, 11

Lear, Edward — 'The Jumblies'

Miller, Henry — *Big Sur and the Oranges of Hieronymus Bosch*, New Directions Publishing Corporation, USA, 1957

Montaigne, Michel de — *The Essays*, edited and translated by George B Ives, The Heritage Press, New York, USA, 1946

Moore, George — *The Brook Kerith*, 1916

Pindar — *The Odes of Pindar*

Seneca   *On the Shortness of Life*, translated by
                      John W Basore, Loeb Classical Library,
                      William Heinemann, London, UK, 1932
                      On Tranquillity of Mind, translated by
                      John W Basore, Loeb Classical Library.
                      William Heinemann, London, UK,
                      1928–1935

Thoreau, Henry David *Walden*, 1854
                      (and on page 205, a remark attributed to
                      Thoreau by Ralph Waldo Emerson in his
                      eulogy 'Thoreau' in the *Atlantic Monthly*,
                      August 1862)